To Elaine,
        With love & best wishes
on your birthday,
        Edythe & David
May 1981.

The Best of
BAKING

The Best of
BAKING

Annette Wolter and Christian Teubner

Photography by Christian Teubner

Hamlyn
London · New York · Sydney · Toronto

Useful Facts and Figures

English edition published by
The Hamlyn Publishing Group Limited
London · New York · Sydney · Toronto
Astronaut House, Feltham, Middlesex, England
© Copyright The Hamlyn Publishing Group Limited 1979

First published under the title
Back vergnügen wie noch nie
© Copyright by Gräfe und Unzer GmbH, München, 1978

ISBN 0 600 31532 0

The Publisher would like to thank Greens of Brighton for their help
and advice on the use of packet mixes in some of the recipes.

Phototypeset by Tradespools Ltd, Frome, Somerset
Printed in Spain

Phototypeset by Tradespools Ltd, Frome, Somerset
Printed in Spain by Printer industria gráfica sa
Sant Vicenç dels Horts   Barcelona   1979
Depósito legal B. 23099-1979

Notes on metrication

In this book quantities are given in metric and Imperial measures.
Because of the necessity for exact proportions in baking recipes, we
have not followed a standard conversion throughout but have carefully worked out and tested each recipe to the correct proportions
for that recipe. It is therefore especially important to follow *either*
the metric measures *or* the Imperial measures, never both.

Spoon measures All spoon measures given in this book are level
unless otherwise stated.
Can sizes At present, cans are marked with the exact (usually to the
nearest whole number) metric equivalent of the Imperial weight of
the contents, so we have followed this practice when giving can sizes.
Flours Unless specified otherwise, plain flour has been used for all
the recipes in this book. Some of the more unusual flours e.g. maize
or rye flour, can be bought at health food or specialist food shops.
Vanilla sugar This is easily made (see page 234) or can be bought in
sachets.
Eggs Unless specified otherwise, the recipes in this book have been
tested using a size 3 egg; if you use smaller or larger eggs you may
need to adjust the recipe accordingly.
Yeast Fresh yeast has been used in almost all the recipes. If substi-
tuting dried yeast, use only half the specified amount and follow the
directions given on the package.
Quantities Many of the recipes in this book make very generous
quantities, as most cooks find it invaluable to make a large amount
and then freeze at least part of it.

Oven temperatures

The table below gives recommended equivalents.

	°C	°F	Gas Mark
Very cool	110	225	$\frac{1}{4}$
	120	250	$\frac{1}{2}$
Cool	140	275	1
	150	300	2
Moderate	160	325	3
	180	350	4
Moderately hot	190	375	5
	200	400	6
Hot	220	425	7
	230	450	8
Very hot	240	475	9

An Imperial / American guide to solid and liquid measures

Solid measures

IMPERIAL / *AMERICAN*
1 lb butter or margarine / *2 cups*
1 lb flour / *4 cups*
1 lb granulated or
  castor sugar / *2 cups*
1 lb icing sugar / *3 cups*

Liquid measures

IMPERIAL / *AMERICAN*
$\frac{1}{4}$ pint liquid / *$\frac{2}{3}$ cup liquid*
$\frac{1}{2}$ pint / *1$\frac{1}{4}$ cups*
$\frac{3}{4}$ pint / *2 cups*
1 pint / *2$\frac{1}{2}$ cups*
1$\frac{1}{2}$ pints / *3$\frac{3}{4}$ cups*
2 pints / *5 cups (2$\frac{1}{2}$ pints)*

NOTE: WHEN MAKING ANY OF THE RECIPES IN THIS BOOK, ONLY FOLLOW ONE SET OF MEASURES AS THEY ARE NOT INTERCHANGEABLE.

American terms

The list below gives some American equivalents or substitutes for terms and ingredients used in this book

Ingredients

BRITISH / *AMERICAN*
apple, cooking / *apple, baking*
apple purée / *applesauce*
bicarbonate of soda / *baking soda*
biscuits / *crackers or cookies*
biscuit mixture / *cookie dough*
black cherries / *bing cherries*
black treacle / *molasses*
cake mixture / *cake batter*
chocolate caraque / *chocolate curls*
chocolate, plain / *chocolate, semi-sweet*
chocolate vermicelli / *chocolate sprinkles*
cocoa powder / *unsweetened cocoa*
coconut, desiccated / *coconut, shredded*
cornflour / *cornstarch*
cream, single / *cream, light*
cream, double / *cream, heavy*
digestive biscuits / *Graham crackers*
essence / *extract*
flour, plain / *flour, all-purpose*
flour, self-raising / *flour, all-purpose sifted with baking powder*
gelatine / *gelatin*
glacé cherries / *candied cherries*
grapes, black / *grapes, purple*
grapes, green / *grapes, white*
icing / *frosting*
raisins, seedless / *raisins, seeded*
scones / *biscuits*
semolina / *semolina flour*
shortcrust pastry / *basic pie dough*
soured cream / *sour cream*
sponge finger biscuits / *lady-fingers*
sugar, icing / *sugar, confectioners'*
sultanas / *seedless white raisins*
vanilla pod / *vanilla bean*
yeast, fresh (25 g/1 oz) / *yeast, compressed (1 cake)*

Equipment and terms

BRITISH / *AMERICAN*
baking tray / *baking sheet*
base / *bottom*
cake board / *cake plate*
cling film / *saran wrap*
cocktail stick / *toothpick*
deep cake tin / *spring form pan*
double saucepan / *double boiler*
dough or mixture / *batter*
flan tin / *pie pan*
greaseproof paper / *wax paper*
knock back dough / *punch down dough*
liquidiser / *blender*
loaf tin / *loaf pan*
muslin / *cheesecloth*
palette knife / *spatula*
pastry or biscuit cutter / *cookie cutter*
pastry case / *pie shell*
patty or bun tins / *muffin pans or cups*
piping bag / *pastry bag*
polythene / *plastic*
prove dough / *rise dough*
pudding basin / *ovenproof bowl or pudding mold*
roasting tin / *roasting pan*
sandwich tin / *layer cake pan*
stoned / *pitted*
sugar thermometer / *candy thermometer*
Swiss roll tin / *jelly roll pan*
top and tail fruit / *stem fruit*
whisk eggs / *beat eggs*

Notes for American and Australian users

In America the 8-oz measuring cup is used. In Australia metric measures are now used in conjunction with the standard 250-ml measuring cup. The Imperial pint, used in Britain and Australia, is 20 fl oz, while the American pint is 16 fl oz. It is important to remember that the Australian tablespoon differs from both the British and American tablespoons; the table below gives a comparison. The British standard tablespoon, which has been used throughout this book, holds 17.7 ml, the American 14.2 ml, and the Australian 20 ml. A teaspoon holds approximately 5 ml in all three countries.

British	American	Australian
1 teaspoon	1 teaspoon	1 teaspoon
1 tablespoon	1 tablespoon	1 tablespoon
2 tablespoons	3 tablespoons	2 tablespoons
3$\frac{1}{2}$ tablespoons	4 tablespoons	3 tablespoons
4 tablespoons	5 tablespoons	3$\frac{1}{2}$ tablespoons

Contents

Introduction

The Best of Baking introduces you to over 350 of the best ever baking recipes. Each recipe has been fully tested and is illustrated with a beautiful colour photograph, enabling you to see how the finished cake, pastry or biscuit will look. This in itself is an encouragement as well as a tremendous time-saver, as you can appreciate at a glance all the finer details of decoration and garnish.

While choosing the recipes for this book, the following question came up: when do people bake and which recipes do they enjoy making most? The best known recipes have therefore been selected from the widest range available: old-time favourites, speciality recipes, as well as both traditional and modern ones, some for everyday and some for more special times. Such occasions as Christmas, New Year, Easter, family celebrations, parties and entertaining have been covered, giving you many new and unusual ideas. There is a section on cakes and gâteaux made with fruit, and for the health-conscious the chapter on wholemeal baking will prove more than satisfying. If you think a cake or gâteau looks too complicated, do not lose heart; start with the simpler recipes, progressing until you have successfully made even the most elaborate ones – do not set an upper limit for yourself. Practice will make you experienced and more confident, and help you to develop

different ideas. For years to come you will be baking all sorts of delights for friends and family – cakes, gâteaux, tartlets, pastries, biscuits and flans – and you will be surprised how quickly you develop your own ideas and slight variations that can make all the difference.

The section at the end of the book on the Art of Baking gives you much invaluable information on baking techniques and methods. It takes you through the basic recipes in clear and simple stages, so you can master these with confidence before moving on to the more elaborate cakes and gâteaux. Details of icing and decorating techniques are fully explained, so your finished cake will look every bit as professional as the illustration, and often with very little effort. There follows a glossary of baking ingredients, including several more unusual ingredients as well as everything needed to stock a basic store cupboard. Finally comes a section on baking for the freezer and a comprehensive freezing chart. This will prove invaluable to those of you who like to bake extra quantities and freeze the surplus.

So may we wish you much success in baking, pleasure in discovering your own favourite recipes and hope that you will enjoy baking, as well as the fruits of your labour, as never before.

Annette Wolter and Christian Teubner

Blackberry Meringue Pie

PASTRY
200 g/7 oz plain flour
pinch of salt
*100 g/3½ oz butter, cut into
  flakes*
1 egg
2 tablespoons water
25 g/1 oz castor sugar
FILLING
350 g/12 oz blackberries
75 g/3 oz castor sugar
2 teaspoons cornflour
3 tablespoons gooseberry jam
MERINGUE
3 egg whites
100 g/4 oz icing sugar

Sift the flour and salt into a
bowl. Rub in the butter then
stir in the egg, water and sugar.
Form into a pastry dough,
wrap in foil or cling film and
leave for 2 hours in the
refrigerator.

Sprinkle the blackberries
with the sugar and leave to
drain in a sieve over a saucepan. Warm the berry juice.
Blend the cornflour with 1
tablespoon water, stir into the
berry juice, bring to the boil,
stirring, and simmer until
thickened. Add the blackberries
and allow to cool.
  Preheat the oven to moderate
(160°C, 325°F, Gas Mark 3).
Roll out the pastry to line a
20-cm/8-inch loose-bottomed
flan tin. Bake blind for 15–20
minutes then allow to cool.
Spread the jam over the pastry
base and cover with the blackberry mixture.
  Whisk the egg whites until
stiff then whisk in the sifted
icing sugar. Pipe a lattice work
over the blackberry filling and
bake in a moderate oven
(180°C, 350°F, Gas Mark 4)
for 15 minutes. Cool before
serving.

Fresh Plum Tart

PASTRY
300 g/10 oz plain flour
200 g/7 oz butter, cut into flakes
100 g/3½ oz castor sugar
1 egg
FILLING
1·5 kg/3 lb plums
2 tablespoons sugar crystals

Sift the flour into a mixing
bowl. Add the butter, sugar
and egg and mix well until a
dough is formed. Wrap in foil
or cling film and leave for
2 hours in the refrigerator.
  Wash the plums, halve and
remove the stones and cut the
fruit into quarters. Preheat the
oven to moderately hot (200°C,
400°F, Gas Mark 6).
  Roll out the pastry on a
floured surface and use to line a
25-cm/10-inch flan tin. Prick
the base of the flan all over
with a fork. Arrange the plums
in a rosette shape to fill the flan
and sprinkle sugar crystals over
the top. Bake the tart for 30–
35 minutes; cover with foil if
becoming too brown. Leave the
tart to cool on a wire rack,
sprinkle with extra sugar
crystals and serve with whipped
cream.

Favourites Baked with Fruit

Farmhouse Plum Flan

PASTRY
300 g/10 oz plain flour
200 g/7 oz butter, cut into flakes
100 g/3½ oz castor sugar
1 egg
FILLING AND DECORATION
1 kg/2 lb plums
100 g/4 oz sugar
20 g/¾ oz powdered gelatine
25 g/1 oz cornflour
2 tablespoons coarsely ground walnuts
150 ml/¼ pint double cream
12 walnut halves

Sift the flour into a mixing bowl. Add the butter, sugar and egg and mix well until a dough is formed. Wrap in foil or cling film and leave in the refrigerator for 2 hours.

Preheat the oven to moderately hot (200°C, 400°F, Gas Mark 6). Roll out the pastry on a floured surface to line a 25-cm/10-inch flan tin. Prick the base of the pastry case all over and bake blind for 20–25 minutes, until cooked. Leave to cool.

Wash and stone the plums and cook with 2 tablespoons water and the sugar for 10 minutes. Dissolve the gelatine in 3 tablespoons water over a gentle heat. Mix the cornflour with a little cold water, pour on to the plums and bring to the boil, stirring all the time. Stir in the walnuts. Mix the dissolved gelatine with the plum mixture and pour into the flan case. Leave to set in the refrigerator.

Whip the cream until stiff. Mark the flan into 12 portions and decorate with piped whipped cream and walnut halves.

Apricot Slice

YEAST DOUGH
225 g/8 oz plain flour
15 g/½ oz fresh yeast
5 tablespoons lukewarm milk
40 g/1½ oz butter
½ beaten egg
pinch of salt
1 tablespoon castor sugar
TOPPING
675 g/1½ lb apricots or 2 (411-g/ 14½-oz) cans apricot halves
350 g/12 oz curd or cottage cheese
2 eggs
15 g/½ oz cornflour
grated rind and juice of ½ lemon
40 g/1½ oz castor sugar
15 g/½ oz flaked almonds

Sift the flour into a mixing bowl. Cream the yeast with a little of the milk, then add the remaining milk. Make a well in the centre of the flour and pour in the yeast liquid. Sprinkle with a little flour from the edge of the bowl, cover and leave for 15 minutes, until frothy. Melt the butter and mix with the egg, salt and sugar. Pour into the flour, mixing well to form a dough. Knead the dough on a lightly floured board for 5 minutes, then cover and leave to rise for 30 minutes.

Wash, halve and stone the apricots, or drain if using canned fruit. Mix together the curd cheese or sieved cottage cheese, eggs, cornflour, lemon rind and juice and the sugar.

Grease a 33 × 23-cm/ 13 × 9-inch Swiss roll tin and roll out the yeast dough to fit it. Preheat the oven to hot (220°C, 425°F, Gas Mark 7).

Spread the cheese mixture over the dough base and arrange the apricots on top, cut side down. Sprinkle with the almonds and bake towards the top of the oven for 25–30 minutes. Leave to cool a little, cut into slices and remove from the tin.

Favourites Baked with Fruit

Blackcurrant Flan

PASTRY
200 g / 7 oz plain flour
100 g / 3½ oz butter, cut into flakes
50 g / 2 oz castor sugar
1 egg
2 tablespoons water
FILLING
500 g / 1 lb blackcurrants
3 eggs, separated
125 g / 4 oz castor sugar
125 g / 4 oz ground almonds
icing sugar to sprinkle

Sift the flour into a mixing bowl. Add the butter, sugar, egg and water and mix until a dough is formed. Wrap the pastry in foil or cling film and leave in the refrigerator for 2 hours.

Remove the stalks from the blackcurrants, wash and dry on absorbent paper. Beat the egg yolks with half the sugar until frothy, then mix in the ground almonds. Whisk the egg whites until stiff, whisk in the remaining sugar then fold into the egg yolk mixture. Mix in the blackcurrants.

Preheat the oven to moderately hot (190°C, 375°F, Gas Mark 5). Roll out the pastry on a floured surface and use to line a 20-cm/8-inch flan tin. Prick the base lightly with a fork and spread the filling evenly over the pastry. Bake for 40 minutes. Leave to cool for 5 minutes in the tin, then transfer to a wire rack. Sift icing sugar over the top when it is completely cooled.

Cherry Cake

225 g / 8 oz cherries
5 eggs, separated
180 g / 7 oz castor sugar
80 g / 3 oz butter or margarine, melted
180 g / 7 oz plain flour
½ teaspoon baking powder
icing sugar to sprinkle

Remove the stalks from the cherries, wash and stone the fruit and pat dry. Grease and flour a 23-cm/9-inch cake tin. Preheat the oven to moderately hot (190°C, 375°F, Gas Mark 5).

Beat the egg yolks with half the sugar until creamy, then whisk in the melted butter or margarine. Sift together the flour and baking powder and fold into the egg yolk mixture. Whisk the egg whites until stiff and add the rest of the sugar. Whisk again until stiff and fold into the yolk mixture. Turn into the cake tin and scatter the cherries over the top, pressing each one into the mixture with the handle of a wooden spoon. Bake for 50–60 minutes; during this time the cherries will sink into the mixture.

Turn the cake out of the tin, leave to cool on a wire rack and dust with sifted icing sugar.

Cook's Tip

Substitute 100 g / 4 oz glacé cherries for the fresh cherries. Halve and toss in flour before adding to the cake.

Rhubarb Meringue Tart

PASTRY
300 g/10 oz plain flour
200 g/7 oz butter or margarine,
cut into flakes
100 g/3½ oz castor sugar
1 egg
TOPPING
1 kg/2 lb rhubarb
sugar to sprinkle
3 egg whites
150 g/5 oz castor sugar

Sift the flour into a mixing bowl. Add the butter, sugar and egg and mix until a dough is formed. Wrap the pastry in foil or cling film and leave for 2 hours in the refrigerator.

Wash the rhubarb, dry on absorbent paper and pull away the thin outer skin from the top downwards. Cut the sticks of rhubarb into 7·5-cm/3-inch lengths. Preheat the oven to moderately hot (200°C, 400°F, Gas Mark 6).

Roll out the pastry on a floured surface into a rectangle approximately 25 × 20 cm/ 10 × 8 inches. Carefully lift the pastry on to a baking tray and prick all over with a fork. Arrange the lengths of rhubarb next to one another on the pastry base and sprinkle with a little sugar to taste. Bake for 30 minutes then allow to cool slightly.

Whisk the egg whites until stiff, whisk in a little of the sugar then fold in the rest.

Put the meringue mixture into a piping bag fitted with a star nozzle and pipe an even, diagonal trellis over the top of the tart. Return to the oven and cook for a further 10 minutes, until the meringue is lightly browned.

Allow the tart to cool a little, cut into even slices and leave to cool on a wire rack.

Cook's Tip

If piping is too time-consuming, spread the meringue over the rhubarb with a palette knife. The tart won't look quite as distinguished, but it will taste just as good. You can also use blackberries, gooseberries or bilberries to make the flan.

Dutch Apple Cake

PASTRY
300 g/11 oz plain flour
150 g/5½ oz butter, cut into flakes
150 g/5½ oz castor sugar
2 egg yolks
pinch of salt
FILLING
500 g/1 lb cooking apples
75 g/3 oz castor sugar
juice of 1 lemon
pinch of ground cinnamon
50 g/2 oz raisins
50 g/2 oz ground almonds
50 g/2 oz ground hazelnuts
ICING
2 tablespoons apricot jam
50 g/2 oz icing sugar
2 tablespoons Kirsch or cherry brandy

Sift the flour into a bowl. Rub in the butter then stir in the sugar, egg yolks and salt and

mix quickly to a dough. Wrap in foil or cling film and leave for 2 hours in the refrigerator.

Preheat the oven to moderately hot (200°C, 400°F, Gas Mark 6). Roll out just over half the pastry to line a 25-cm/10-inch loose-bottomed flan tin and bake blind for 15 minutes.

Peel, core and slice the apples. Mix with the sugar, lemon juice, cinnamon, raisins and ground nuts. Moisten with a little water to blend. Spoon into the pastry case and smooth over. Roll out the remaining pastry to cover the filling and seal the edges together well. Bake for a further 30 minutes then cool in the tin overnight.

Warm the jam and spread over the top of the cake. Blend the sifted icing sugar with the Kirsch, spread over the jam and leave to set.

Trellised Apple Flan

PASTRY
300 g/10 oz plain flour
200 g/7 oz butter, cut into flakes
100 g/3½ oz castor sugar
1 egg
grated rind of 1 lemon
FILLING
1 kg/2 lb cooking apples
juice of 1 lemon
50 g/2 oz raisins
50 g/2 oz castor sugar
¼ teaspoon ground cinnamon
2 eggs
3 tablespoons milk
1 tablespoon sugar
1 tablespoon custard powder

Sift the flour into a mixing bowl. Add the butter, sugar, egg and lemon rind and mix until a dough is formed. Wrap the pastry in foil or cling film and leave for 2 hours in the refrigerator.

Peel, core and slice the apples and mix with the lemon juice, raisins, castor sugar and cinnamon. Preheat the oven to moderately hot (200°C, 400°F, Gas Mark 6).

Roll out the pastry and use to line a 23-cm/9-inch loose-bottomed flan tin. Keep back some of the pastry for the trellis and cut it into thin strips. Prick the base of the flan all over with a fork and arrange the apple mixture on top. Whisk together the eggs, milk, sugar and custard powder and pour over the apples. Arrange the pastry strips on top in a trellis pattern. Bake the flan for 50–60 minutes, covering with foil if it becomes too brown.

Allow the flan to cool a little in the tin then transfer to a wire rack to cool completely.

Favourites Baked with Fruit

Alsace Apple Tart

PASTRY
200 g/7 oz plain flour
100 g/3½ oz butter or margarine,
  cut into flakes
1 egg yolk
30 g/1 oz castor sugar
pinch of salt
2 tablespoons cold water
FILLING
1 kg/2 lb cooking apples
2 tablespoons lemon juice
100 g/4 oz castor sugar
3 eggs
125 ml/4 fl oz double cream
few drops of vanilla essence

Sift the flour into a mixing
bowl. Add the butter, egg yolk,
sugar, salt and water and mix
until a dough is formed. Wrap
in foil or cling film and leave
for 2 hours in the refrigerator.
    Peel the apples, quarter and
remove the cores. Slice each

apple quarter very thinly,
keeping the quarter in shape,
and sprinkle with the lemon
juice. Preheat the oven to
moderately hot (200°C, 400°F,
Gas Mark 6).
    Roll out the pastry to 5 mm/
¼ inch thick and use to line a
23-cm/9-inch flan tin. Prick the
base all over with a fork and
arrange the sliced apple
quarters on it. Bake for 20–25
minutes.
    Meanwhile, beat the sugar
with the eggs until frothy and
add the cream and vanilla
essence. Pour the egg mixture
into the half-cooked flan and
bake for a further 20–30
minutes.
    Allow the flan to cool for a
while in the tin then transfer to
a wire rack to cool completely.

Apple Lattice Flan

PASTRY
450 g/1 lb plain flour
150 g/5 oz margarine, cut into
  flakes
25 g/1 oz castor sugar
½ teaspoon salt
150 ml/¼ pint water
FILLING
1 kg/2 lb cooking apples
grated rind and juice of 1 lemon
125 g/4½ oz sugar
1 teaspoon ground cinnamon
100 g/4 oz raisins
100 g/4 oz hazelnuts, chopped
GLAZE
1 egg yolk, beaten
4 tablespoons apricot jam
100 g/4 oz icing sugar
1½ tablespoons lemon juice

Sift the flour into a bowl and
rub in the margarine. Add the
sugar, salt and water and mix
to a dough. Wrap in foil or

cling film and leave for 1 hour
in the refrigerator.
    Peel the apples, chop roughly
and mix with the lemon rind
and juice, sugar, cinnamon,
raisins and hazelnuts. Preheat
the oven to moderately hot
(200°C, 400°F, Gas Mark 6).
    Roll out three-quarters of
the pastry to line the base and
sides of a 33 × 23-cm/13 × 9-
inch Swiss roll tin. Spread the
apple mixture over the pastry.
Roll out the remaining pastry,
cut into thin strips and arrange
over the flan in a lattice
pattern. Brush with beaten egg
yolk and bake the flan for 30–
40 minutes. Leave to cool.
    Brush the pastry with the
warmed apricot jam. Mix the
sifted icing sugar and lemon
juice together and use to glaze
the trellis.

Favourites Baked with Fruit

Strawberry Ring

CHOUX PASTE
60 g/2 oz butter
pinch of salt
grated rind of ½ lemon
250 ml/8 fl oz water
200 g/7 oz plain flour
4 eggs, beaten
FILLING
500 g/1 lb strawberries
2 teaspoons vanilla sugar
450 ml/¾ pint double cream

First wash and hull the strawberries. Reserve three large strawberries and mix the rest with the vanilla sugar; leave for a while for the sugar to be absorbed. Lightly grease a baking tray and dust with flour. Preheat the oven to hot (220°C, 425°F, Gas Mark 7).

Melt the butter with the salt, lemon rind and water over a low heat, then bring quickly to the boil. Remove from the heat, add the sifted flour, and beat with a wooden spoon until it comes away from the sides of the pan. Return to the heat for 1 minute, stirring continuously. Allow to cool slightly then add the eggs a little at a time, beating in well.

Fill a piping bag fitted with a large star nozzle with the mixture and pipe 11 rosette shapes in a 25-cm/10-inch ring on the baking tray. When risen they will join together to form a circle. Bake just below the centre for 20–25 minutes.

Purée the strawberries through a nylon sieve. Whip the cream until stiff and put 2 tablespoons of the cream into a clean piping bag fitted with a large star nozzle. Mix the remaining cream with the strawberry purée.

While still warm, split the choux ring to allow it to cool more quickly, then fill with the strawberry cream mixture. Decorate with rosettes of cream and segments of strawberry.

Strawberry Curd Cake

PASTRY
250 g/9 oz plain flour
125 g/4½ oz butter, cut into flakes
100 g/4 oz castor sugar
2 egg yolks
FILLING
225 g/8 oz curd cheese
100 g/4 oz castor sugar
1 tablespoon cornflour
grated rind of 1 lemon
4 eggs
450 ml/¾ pint double cream
225 g/8 oz strawberries
1 small packet quick-setting jel mix (red colour)

Knead together the sifted flour, butter, sugar and egg yolks. Wrap the pastry in foil or cling film and leave in the refrigerator for 2 hours.

Preheat the oven to moderately hot (200°C, 400°F, Gas Mark 6). Roll out the pastry on a lightly floured surface and use to line the base and sides of a 28-cm/11-inch springform cake tin. Prick thoroughly all over with a fork and bake blind for 10 minutes. Reduce the oven temperature to moderate (180°C, 350°F, Gas Mark 4).

Beat the curd cheese, sugar, cornflour, lemon rind and eggs together. Whip the cream until stiff and fold into the cheese mixture. Turn into the pastry case and bake for a further 50–60 minutes. Leave to cool slightly.

Wash and hull the strawberries and dry on absorbent paper. Cut each strawberry in half and arrange over the curd cake. Prepare the jel mix according to the instructions on the packet and pour over the strawberries.

Favourites Baked with Fruit

Gooseberry Meringue Pie

PASTRY
250 g/9 oz plain flour
125 g/4½ oz butter, cut into flakes
25 g/1 oz castor sugar
1 egg
FILLING
500 g/1 lb gooseberries
450 ml/¾ pint water
25 g/1 oz granulated sugar
25 g/1 oz castor sugar
450 ml/¾ pint milk
2 egg yolks
20 g/¾ oz cornflour
MERINGUE
3 egg whites
150 g/5 oz icing sugar

Sift the flour into a bowl. Add the butter, sugar and egg and mix to a dough. Wrap in foil or cling film and chill for 2 hours.

Wash the gooseberries and top and tail them. Cook in the water with the granulated sugar for 15 minutes and allow to cool in a sieve over a basin. Preheat the oven to moderately hot (200°C, 400°F, Gas Mark 6).

Roll out the pastry to line the base and sides of a 23-cm/9-inch sandwich cake tin. Prick all over with a fork and bake blind for 20 minutes.

Meanwhile, whisk the castor sugar with 3 tablespoons milk, the egg yolks and cornflour. Bring the rest of the milk to the boil, pour on to the cornflour mixture then return to the saucepan. Bring to the boil, stirring until thickened. Pour into the pastry case and arrange the gooseberries on top.

Whisk the egg whites until very stiff then add the sifted icing sugar and whisk again. Spread this meringue over the gooseberries and cook for 5–10 minutes in a hot oven (220°C, 425°F, Gas Mark 7).

Raspberry Meringue Nest

MERINGUE
6 egg whites
175 g/6 oz castor sugar
150 g/5 oz icing sugar
30 g/1 oz cornflour
FILLING
250 ml/8 fl oz double cream
1 tablespoon brandy
350 g/12 oz raspberries

Line a baking tray with non-stick baking parchment. Preheat the oven to very cool (110°C, 225°F, Gas Mark ¼).

Whisk the egg whites until stiff then gradually whisk in the castor sugar. Fold in the sifted icing sugar and cornflour. Fill a piping bag fitted with a large plain nozzle with the mixture, and pipe in a spiral on to the baking tray to make a 20–23-cm/8–9-inch round base. Form the sides of the meringue nest by piping individual rosettes over the edge. Allow to dry out in the oven for 12 hours, leaving the oven door slightly ajar.

Remove from the oven and leave to cool. Whip the cream with the brandy until thick. Spread this cream into the meringue nest and cover with the raspberries.

Cook's Tip

To make Gooseberry Meringue Nests, as illustrated on the jacket, pipe 7·5-cm/3-inch nests using a small star nozzle. Fill with whipped cream and drained canned gooseberries.

Exotic Fruit Gâteaux

French Orange Flan

PASTRY
100 g/4 oz butter
50 g/2 oz icing sugar
1 egg yolk
150 g/6 oz plain flour
FILLING
4 tablespoons orange jelly
    marmalade
250 ml/8 fl oz double cream
100 g/4 oz castor sugar
6 eggs
grated rind of 3 lemons
DECORATION
1 orange
50 g/2 oz sugar
2 tablespoons water
4 cherries

Knead together the butter, sifted icing sugar and egg yolk. Sift the flour on to this mixture and work in quickly with the fingertips. Cover the dough and leave for 2 hours in the refrigerator.

Preheat the oven to moderately hot (200°C, 400°F, Gas Mark 6). Roll out the pastry to a thickness of about 3 mm/ ⅛ inch and carefully line two 15-cm/6-inch flan dishes. Spread the base of the flans with the orange marmalade. Beat the cream, sugar, eggs and lemon rind together until frothy and pour into the flan cases. Cook for 45–50 minutes.

Peel the orange carefully, removing all the pith, and slice thinly. Dissolve the sugar in the water over a low heat, stirring continuously until the sugar has completely dissolved. Place the orange slices in the hot sugar syrup, leave for 3 minutes and then drain. Arrange over the flans and top with the cherries, also glazed in the sugar syrup.

Chinese Gooseberry Cream Tart

1 (368-g/13-oz) packet frozen
    puff pastry, thawed
1 egg yolk, beaten to glaze
FILLING
250 ml/8 fl oz double cream
2 tablespoons castor sugar
1½ teaspoons powdered gelatine
1 tablespoon rum
6 Chinese gooseberries
1½ teaspoons arrowroot

Roll out the pastry quite thinly and cut out a 20-cm/8-inch round from the centre. Using a 5-cm/2-inch round cutter, cut out 12 half-moon shapes from the surrounding pastry. Sprinkle a baking tray with cold water, place the pastry round on it and brush with beaten egg yolk. Prick the pastry all over with a fork.

Place the half-moon shapes around the edge of the pastry and brush these with egg yolk. Leave in the refrigerator for 15 minutes. Preheat the oven to hot (220°C, 425°F, Gas Mark 7) and bake towards the top of the oven for 15 minutes. Cool on a wire rack.

Whip the cream and sugar together until stiff. Dissolve the gelatine in 3 tablespoons hot water over a gentle heat. Allow to cool then stir into the cream with the rum. When half-set, spread the cream over the pastry base, mounding it up in the centre, and leave in the refrigerator until firm.

Peel the Chinese gooseberries, cut into slices and arrange overlapping on the cream. Blend the arrowroot in a pan with a little water. Add 150 ml/¼ pint cold water and bring to the boil, stirring continuously. Leave until just warm then pour over the fruit to glaze.

Exotic Fruit Gâteaux

Coconut Mango Cake

SPONGE MIXTURE
2 eggs, separated, plus 2 egg
   yolks
50 g/2 oz castor sugar
40 g/1½ oz plain flour
15 g/½ oz cornflour
20 g/¾ oz cocoa powder
FILLING AND TOPPING
2 mangoes or 2 (415-g/15-oz)
   cans
3 tablespoons white wine
2 egg yolks
100 g/4 oz castor sugar
15 g/½ oz powdered gelatine
450 ml/¾ pint double cream
1 tablespoon icing sugar
50 g/2 oz long-thread coconut

Grease and flour a 23-cm/9-inch cake tin. Preheat the oven to hot (220°C, 425°F, Gas Mark 7).

Beat all the egg yolks with half the sugar until pale and creamy. Whisk the egg whites until stiff and fold in the remaining sugar. Carefully fold into the egg yolk mixture. Sift the flour, cornflour and cocoa powder together then carefully fold into the eggs. Pour into the cake tin and bake for about 15 minutes. Cool on a wire rack then slice into two layers.

Peel or drain the mangoes and dice. Mix the wine, egg yolks and castor sugar in a basin over hot water. Cook until thick, stirring, but do not boil. Remove from the heat. Dissolve the gelatine in 3 tablespoons water over a gentle heat. Stir into the wine mixture with most of the diced mango and allow to cool. Whip the cream. Fold half into the wine mixture and use to sandwich the cake layers together. Leave until set. Mix the remaining cream with the icing sugar and spread over the top and sides. Sprinkle with the coconut and decorate as illustrated.

Tropical Fruit Gâteau

PASTRY
125 g/4 oz plain flour
60 g/2 oz butter
45 g/1½ oz icing sugar
pinch of salt
1 egg yolk
FILLING
2 tablespoons apricot jam
1 (20-cm/8-inch) sandwich cake
   (see page 228)
1 (44-g/1½-oz) packet dessert
   topping mix
150 ml/¼ pint milk
TOPPING
4 pineapple rings
2 Chinese gooseberries
1 mango
5 cocktail cherries
2 tablespoons pineapple juice
50 g/2 oz toasted flaked almonds

Sift the flour into a bowl and knead in the butter, sifted icing sugar, salt and egg yolk. Cover the pastry dough and leave for 2 hours in the refrigerator.

Preheat the oven to hot (220°C, 425°F, Gas Mark 7). Roll out the pastry to line the base of a 20-cm/8-inch loose-bottomed flan tin and bake for 20–30 minutes.

Leave to cool then remove from the tin and brush with the warmed jam. Place the cake on top of the pastry base. Make up the dessert topping with the milk, according to the instructions on the packet, and spread over the top and sides of the gâteau.

Cut the pineapple rings into pieces. Peel the Chinese gooseberries and mango and slice. Halve the cherries. Arrange the fruit over the gâteau and sprinkle with the pineapple juice. Press toasted flaked almonds on to the sides of the gâteau.

Sweet Pecan Nut Pie

PASTRY
180 g/6 oz butter, cut into flakes
pinch of salt
4 tablespoons iced water
250 g/9 oz plain flour
FILLING
3 eggs
100 g/4 oz black treacle
50 g/2 oz golden syrup
40 g/1¼ oz plain flour
60 g/2 oz butter
¼ teaspoon vanilla essence
pinch of salt
250 g/9 oz pecan nuts, halved

Knead the butter, salt and iced water into the sifted flour. Wrap the pastry in foil or cling film and leave for 2 hours in the refrigerator.

Preheat the oven to moderately hot (200°C, 400°F, Gas Mark 6). Roll out the pastry to line the base and sides of a 25-cm/10-inch loose-bottomed flan tin. Do not prick the base with a fork. Bake blind for 10–12 minutes.

Meanwhile, beat the eggs lightly, add the treacle and syrup and beat in well to mix. Stir in the flour and melted, slightly cooled butter. Lastly fold in the vanilla, salt and nuts. Pour this filling into the pastry case and bake the pie for a further 25–30 minutes.

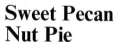

Cook's Tip
Instead of pecan nuts, try making this pie with walnuts or brazil nuts.

Chocolate Almond Roll

5 eggs, separated
180 g/6 oz castor sugar
pinch of salt
pinch of ground cinnamon
¼ teaspoon vanilla essence
grated rind of ½ lemon
50 g/2 oz butter
90 g/3½ oz plain chocolate, grated
100 g/4 oz plain flour
100 g/4 oz ground almonds
ICING
100 g/4 oz plain chocolate
50 g/2 oz toasted flaked almonds

Grease a Balmoral tin or 1-kg/2-lb loaf tin and sprinkle with fine breadcrumbs. Preheat the oven to moderately hot (190°C, 375°F, Gas Mark 5).

Whisk the egg yolks with half the sugar, the salt, cinnamon, vanilla essence and lemon rind, until pale and creamy.

Melt the butter and leave to cool slightly. Whisk the egg whites until stiff and fold in the remaining sugar. Fold a quarter of these egg whites into the egg yolk mixture, then fold in the grated chocolate, sifted flour, ground almonds and remaining egg white. Lastly fold in the melted butter. Turn into the prepared tin, smooth the surface and bake for 40–50 minutes.

Allow the cake to cool on a wire rack. Melt the chocolate in a basin over hot water and spread over the roll. Sprinkle with flaked almonds and leave to set.

Daisy Cake

300 g/12 oz butter
100 g/4 oz ground almonds
6 eggs, separated
grated rind of 1 lemon
few drops of vanilla essence
140 g/5 oz castor sugar
120 g/4½ oz plain flour
80 g/3 oz cornflour
ICING
150 g/5 oz apricot jam
200 g/7 oz icing sugar
1 tablespoon lemon juice
1 tablespoon water

Grease a 23-cm/9-inch round fluted cake tin and sprinkle with fine breadcrumbs. Preheat the oven to moderately hot (190°C, 375°F, Gas Mark 5).

Cream the softened butter with the ground almonds. Stir in the egg yolks, lemon rind and vanilla essence. Whisk the egg whites until stiff then carefully fold in the sugar. Fold the egg whites into the butter mixture. Sift the flour and cornflour together and fold into the mixture. Turn into the prepared cake tin, smooth the surface and bake for 50–60 minutes.

Leave to cool slightly on a wire rack, then spread with the warmed apricot jam. Leave to cool and set for 30 minutes. Mix the sifted icing sugar with the lemon juice and water and spread over the cake.

Cakes for Morning Coffee

Hazelnut Loaf Cake

250 g/9 oz soft margarine
200 g/7 oz castor sugar
25 g/1 oz vanilla sugar
4 eggs
250 g/9 oz ground hazelnuts
250 g/9 oz self-raising flour
1 teaspoon baking powder
1 tablespoon brandy
icing sugar to sprinkle

Grease a 1-kg/2-lb loaf tin.
Preheat the oven to moderate
(180°C, 350°F, Gas Mark 4).
  Cream the margarine, sugar
and vanilla sugar until light
and fluffy. Stir in the eggs, one
at a time, then the hazelnuts.
Sift the flour and baking
powder together and fold into
the mixture, making sure all is
thoroughly mixed. Finally stir
in the brandy. Turn into the
tin and bake for 1–1¼ hours.
  Allow the cake to cool on a
wire rack, then sprinkle with
sifted icing sugar.

Cook's Tip
For deeper cakes, test the
cooking with a warmed
metal skewer. Towards
the end of cooking time,
insert the warmed skewer
into the middle of the
cake and then withdraw;
if it comes out clean then
the cake is cooked.

Crumble Cake

200 g/7 oz soft margarine
200 g/7 oz castor sugar
1 egg
grated rind of 1 lemon
500 g/1 lb 2 oz plain flour
1 teaspoon baking powder
1 (454-g/1-lb) jar cherry jam
50 g/2 oz ground almonds
icing sugar to sprinkle

Grease a 25-cm/10-inch springform cake tin with margarine.
Preheat the oven to hot (220°C,
425°F, Gas Mark 7).
  Beat the margarine and sugar
together until creamy. Stir in
the egg and lemon rind. Sift the
flour and baking powder and
fold a few tablespoons into the
creamed mixture. Tip the
remaining flour on to the mixture and, with the fingertips,
work quickly into crumbs.
Place half this crumb mixture
in the prepared cake tin and
spread with the jam. Mix the
rest with the almonds and
crumble over the jam. Bake the
cake for 50–60 minutes.
  Leave to cool on a wire rack
and dust with sifted icing sugar.

Cakes for Morning Coffee

Iced Orange Loaf Cake

250 g/9 oz soft margarine
250 g/9 oz castor sugar
3 eggs plus 4 egg yolks
100 g/4 oz self-raising flour
pinch of salt
1 tablespoon orange liqueur
grated rind of 2 oranges
grated rind of 1 lemon
2 tablespoons orange juice
1 tablespoon lemon juice
100 g/4 oz cornflour
100 g/4 oz ground almonds
75 g/3 oz candied orange peel,
    finely chopped
ICING
50 g/2 oz orange jelly
    marmalade
200 g/7 oz icing sugar
2 tablespoons orange juice
25 g/1 oz candied orange peel,
    finely chopped

Grease a 1-kg/2-lb loaf tin and sprinkle with fine breadcrumbs.

Preheat the oven to moderate (180°C, 350°F, Gas Mark 4).

Cream the margarine and sugar together until light and fluffy. Stir in the eggs and egg yolks, one by one, along with a few tablespoons of the flour. Mix in the salt, liqueur, fruit rinds and juice. Sift the remaining flour with the cornflour and fold into the cake mixture with the ground almonds and candied peel. Turn into the tin and bake for about 1¼ hours.

Cool on a wire rack then spread the top of the cake with the warmed orange jelly. Mix together the sifted icing sugar and orange juice and spread over the cake. Sprinkle with the candied peel to decorate.

Marzipan Cake

MARZIPAN
120 g/4½ oz almond paste
100 g/4 oz pistachio nuts or
    blanched almonds, grated
1 tablespoon arrack or ouzo
CAKE MIXTURE
250 g/9 oz soft margarine
240 g/8½ oz castor sugar
5 eggs, separated
pinch of salt
1 tablespoon arrack or ouzo
few drops of vanilla essence
230 g/8 oz plain flour
85 g/3 oz cornflour
1 teaspoon baking powder
ICING
175 g/6 oz plain chocolate
25 g/1 oz pistachio nuts, chopped

Grease a 20–23-cm/8–9-inch round fluted cake tin and sprinkle with fine breadcrumbs. Preheat the oven to moderately hot (190°C, 375°F, Gas Mark 5).

Knead the almond paste with the pistachios and arrack, roll out to a thickness of 1 cm/ ½ inch and cut into 1-cm/½-inch cubes.

Beat the margarine with half the sugar, the egg yolks, salt, arrack and vanilla essence until well mixed. Whisk the egg whites until stiff and whisk in the remaining sugar. Fold into the egg yolk mixture. Sift together the flour, cornflour and baking powder and mix in the marzipan cubes. Fold all this thoroughly into the egg mixture. Turn into the cake tin and bake for 1¼–1½ hours. Turn out and cool on a wire rack.

Melt the chocolate in a basin over hot water and spread over the cake. Decorate with the chopped pistachios while still soft and leave the icing to set.

Fresh Strawberry Savarin

SAVARIN DOUGH
20 g/¾ oz fresh yeast
250 ml/8 fl oz lukewarm milk
350 g/12 oz plain flour
4 eggs
40 g/1½ oz castor sugar
1 tablespoon vanilla sugar
½ teaspoon salt
150 g/5 oz butter or margarine
SYRUP
4 tablespoons rum
6 tablespoons white wine
250 ml/8 fl oz water
150 g/5 oz sugar
FILLING
225 g/8 oz strawberries
150 ml/¼ pint double cream
50 g/2 oz castor sugar
1 teaspoon chopped pistachio
  nuts

Grease a 23-cm/9-inch savarin tin and dust with flour.

Cream the yeast with a little of the milk, then add the remaining milk. Sift the flour into a bowl, make a well in the centre and pour in the yeast liquid. Sprinkle with a little of the flour, cover and leave for 15 minutes, until frothy.

Beat the eggs with the sugar until frothy, then mix in the vanilla sugar, salt and melted butter. Add this to the yeast mixture, beating well to an almost pouring consistency. Cover and leave to rise for 10 minutes. Beat the mixture with a wooden spoon and pour into the savarin tin. Cover and leave until the mixture almost reaches the top of the tin.

Preheat the oven to hot (220°C, 425°F, Gas Mark 7). Bake the savarin for 40 minutes then turn out on to a wire rack.

Heat the rum, white wine, water and sugar until the sugar has dissolved. Simmer for 5 minutes. Place a container underneath the wire rack to catch the syrup then pour it over the savarin until completely absorbed. Place on to a serving plate.

Wash, hull and halve the strawberries. Whip the cream with the sugar until stiff. Place most of the strawberries in the centre of the savarin and pipe the cream over them. Use the remaining strawberries and pistachios to decorate.

Cook's Tip

This well known French sweet can also be served in the following classic ways.

Savarin Chantilly The savarin is steeped in sugar syrup and Kirsch, brushed with an apricot glaze and filled with whipped cream.

Savarin with Raspberries (aux Framboises). The savarin is steeped in sugar syrup and raspberry liqueur then filled with whipped cream and raspberries.

Marzipan Twist

YEAST DOUGH
20 g/¾ oz fresh yeast
6 tablespoons lukewarm milk
350 g/12 oz plain flour
50 g/2 oz butter
50 g/2 oz castor sugar
pinch of salt
grated rind of ½ lemon
FILLING
225 g/8 oz ground almonds
2 egg whites
50 g/2 oz castor sugar
2 tablespoons rum
GLAZE
3 tablespoons icing sugar
1 tablespoon lemon juice
2 tablespoons water

Cream the yeast with a little of the milk, then mix in the remaining milk. Sift the flour into a bowl, make a well in the centre and pour in the yeast liquid. Sprinkle a little flour over the yeast, cover and leave for 15 minutes, until frothy.

Melt the butter and mix with the sugar, salt and lemon rind. Stir into the yeast mixture and mix all together to a dough. Knead on a lightly floured board until smooth. Cover and leave to rise for 30–40 minutes.

Mix the ground almonds with the egg whites, sugar and rum. Roll out the yeast dough to an oblong 45 × 30 cm/ 18 × 12 inches, spread with the almond filling, and roll up lengthways. Cut the roll into two equal lengths and twist the two pieces around each other to make a single plait. Place on a greased baking tray and leave to rise for 15 minutes.

Preheat the oven to moderately hot (200°C, 400°F, Gas Mark 6) and bake for 35 minutes. Mix the sifted icing sugar with the lemon juice and water and use to glaze the twist while still warm.

Surprise Almond Plait

YEAST DOUGH
350 g/12 oz plain flour
20 g/¾ oz fresh yeast
6 tablespoons lukewarm milk
50 g/2 oz butter, melted
2 eggs
50 g/2 oz castor sugar
¼ teaspoon salt
FILLING
50 g/2 oz ground almonds
4 tablespoons apricot jam
50 g/2 oz raisins
50 g/2 oz almonds, chopped
GLAZE
1 egg yolk, beaten
1 tablespoon sugar
1 tablespoon water

Sift the flour into a bowl and make a well. Cream the yeast with the milk and pour into the flour well. Cover and leave for 15 minutes, until frothy. Mix the butter with the eggs, sugar

and salt. Pour into the yeast liquid and work with the flour to form a dough. Knead for 5 minutes, cover and leave to rise for 30–40 minutes. Roll out to a 45 × 30-cm/18 × 12-inch rectangle, and mark into three equal strips lengthways.

Mix the ground almonds with the jam and spread over the middle strip. Sprinkle with the raisins and almonds. Cut the two outside strips into 1·5-cm/¾-inch wide slanting strips and plait together over the filling. Place on a greased baking tray, cover and leave to rise for 15 minutes.

Preheat the oven to hot (220°C, 425°F, Gas Mark 7). Brush the plait with beaten egg yolk and bake for 10 minutes. Reduce to 190°C, 375°F, Gas Mark 5 and bake for a further 10–12 minutes. Brush with a sugar and water glaze.

Berlin Speciality Cake

300 g/11 oz plain flour
15 g/½ oz fresh yeast
5 tablespoons lukewarm milk
100 g/4 oz castor sugar
175 g/6 oz butter
pinch of salt
3 eggs
grated rind of 1 lemon
200 g/7 oz currants
ICING
100–150 g/4–6 oz plain
  chocolate
1 tablespoon pine nuts

Grease a 20–23-cm/8–9-inch kugelhopf tin and sprinkle with fine breadcrumbs.

Sift the flour into a bowl and make a well in the centre. Cream the yeast with the milk and a little of the sugar. Pour into the well and sprinkle over a little flour. Cover and leave for 15 minutes, until frothy.

Melt the butter and combine with the remaining sugar, the salt, eggs and lemon rind. Pour into the well in the flour, mix all together and beat the dough until it bubbles. Cover and leave to rise for 30–40 minutes.

Preheat the oven to moderate (180°C, 350°F, Gas Mark 4). Wash and dry the currants and knead into the dough. Turn into the prepared tin and bake for 50–60 minutes.

Turn the cake out on to a wire rack and leave to cool. Melt the chocolate in a basin over hot water and pour over the cake to cover it completely. Sprinkle with the pine nuts while the icing is still soft.

Viennese Kugelhopf

500 g/1 lb 2 oz plain flour
25 g/1 oz fresh yeast
7 tablespoons lukewarm milk
150 g/5 oz castor sugar
150 g/5 oz butter
5 eggs, separated
pinch of salt
6 tablespoons single cream
75 g/3 oz sultanas
2 tablespoons rum
grated rind of 1 lemon
icing sugar to sprinkle

The Viennese kugelhopf is particularly small; if possible bake the given quantity of dough in three 16-cm/6½-inch kugelhopf tins. To bake the slightly larger kugelhopfs, illustrated on the jacket, use two 20-cm/8-inch tins. Grease the tins.

Sift the flour into a mixing bowl and make a well in the centre. Cream the yeast with the milk and a little of the sugar. Pour into the well and sprinkle over a little flour. Cover and leave for 15 minutes, until frothy.

Melt the butter and whisk with the remaining sugar, the egg yolks, salt and cream until frothy. Stir into the yeast mixture with the sultanas, rum and lemon rind and work in the rest of the flour. Whisk the egg whites until stiff, fold them into the dough and beat the mixture until it bubbles. Turn into the prepared tins, filling each one two-thirds full. Leave to rise for 15 minutes.

Preheat the oven to moderately hot (200°C, 400°F, Gas Mark 6) and bake for 40–60 minutes. Turn out on to a wire rack and sift with icing sugar when cool.

Cakes for Morning Coffee

Poppy Seed Garland

YEAST DOUGH
500 g/1 lb 2 oz plain flour
40 g/1½ oz fresh yeast
100 g/4 oz castor sugar
250 ml/8 fl oz lukewarm milk
125 g/4½ oz butter
2 eggs
grated rind and juice of 1 lemon
pinch of salt
1 egg yolk, beaten
FILLING
2 teaspoons poppy seeds
1 tablespoon hot water
175 g/6 oz raisins
pinch of salt
pinch of ground cinnamon
ICING
3 tablespoons icing sugar
1 teaspoon lemon juice
1 tablespoon water
4 glacé cherries

Grease a 23-cm/9-inch ring tin with butter or margarine.

Sift the flour into a bowl and form a well in the centre. Cream the yeast with 1 teaspoon of the sugar, the milk and a little of the flour. Pour into the well and leave for 15 minutes, until frothy.

Melt the butter and add to the yeast mixture with the remaining sugar, the eggs, lemon rind and juice, and salt. Mix to a smooth dough with the rest of the flour and beat until the mixture comes away from the sides of the bowl. Cover the dough and leave to rise for 20 minutes.

Put the poppy seeds in a bowl, cover with the hot water and leave to soak for 5 minutes. Wash the raisins in hot water, dry well on absorbent paper and chop finely. Carefully drain the poppy seeds and mix in the chopped raisins, salt and cinnamon.

Preheat the oven to moder-ately hot (200°C, 400°F, Gas Mark 6). Roll the dough out to a 50 × 25-cm/20 × 10-inch rectangle on a floured surface. Sprinkle the poppy seed mixture over the top and roll up the dough from the longest edge, making sure the ends are as thick as the centre. Brush the edges and ends with beaten egg yolk and press to seal. Place the roll in the ring tin with the seam on top and press the ends together firmly so the filling does not escape. Bake for 50–60 minutes.

Turn the cake out on to a wire rack to cool. Mix together the sifted icing sugar, lemon juice and water and use to ice the cake, then decorate with halved glacé cherries.

Cook's Tip

Yeast mixtures rise more quickly in a warm room temperature. However, if more convenient the dough may be covered and left overnight in the refrigerator to rise. The following day the dough should be returned to room temperature for about 1 hour before proceeding.

Pear Cheesecake

PASTRY
125 g/4 oz plain flour
60 g/2 oz butter, cut into flakes
45 g/1½ oz icing sugar
½ teaspoon vanilla sugar
pinch of salt
1 egg yolk
FILLING
1 (410-g/14½-oz) can pear
   halves
3 tablespoons Kirsch
250 g/9 oz curd or cream cheese
125 g/4½ oz castor sugar
juice of 1 lemon
20 g/¾ oz powdered gelatine
TOPPING
250 ml/8 fl oz double cream
25 g/1 oz castor sugar
3 tablespoons crushed praline
   (see page 231)
4 tablespoons redcurrant jelly

Sift the flour into a bowl. Add
the butter, icing sugar, vanilla
sugar, salt and egg yolk and
mix to a dough. Cover and

chill in the refrigerator for
2 hours.
   Preheat the oven to moderately hot (200°C, 400°F, Gas
Mark 6). Roll out the pastry to
line a 20-cm/8-inch loose-
bottomed flan tin and bake
blind for 30 minutes. Cool.
   Drain the pears and reserve
the juice. Moisten the pears
with a little Kirsch. Beat the
cheese, sugar, lemon juice and
remaining Kirsch together.
Dissolve the gelatine in 3 tablespoons of the oear juice over a
gentle heat. Stir into the cheese
mixture. Arrange the pears in
the pastry case, spread over the
cheese mixture and leave to set.
   Whip the cream with the
sugar until stiff. Mix two-thirds
of the cream with 2 tablespoons
of the crushed praline and half
the redcurrant jelly. Spread
over the cheesecake. Decorate
with rosettes of the remaining
cream, redcurrant jelly and
crushed praline.

Grape Cheesecake

SPONGE MIXTURE
4 eggs, separated
2 tablespoons lukewarm water
140 g/5 oz castor sugar
120 g/4 oz plain flour
60 g/2 oz cornflour
1 teaspoon baking powder
FILLING
450 g/1 lb curd or cream cheese
2 egg yolks
150 g/5 oz castor sugar
juice of 1 lemon
20 g/¾ oz powdered gelatine
250 ml/8 fl oz double cream
TOPPING
100 g/4 oz green grapes
225 g/8 oz black grapes
1 small packet quick-setting jel
   mix
100 g/4 oz toasted flaked
   almonds

Grease the base of a 23-cm/9-
inch springform cake tin.

Preheat the oven to moderately hot (190°C, 375°F, Gas
Mark 5).
   Whisk the egg yolks with the
water and half the sugar until
frothy. Whisk the whites until
stiff then fold in the remaining
sugar. Fold into the egg yolks.
Sift the flour with the cornflour
and baking powder and fold in.
Turn into the cake tin and
bake for 40 minutes. Cool on a
wire rack for 2 hours.
   Beat the cheese with the egg
yolks, sugar and lemon juice.
Dissolve the gelatine in 3 tablespoons water over a gentle
heat. Whip the cream until
thick and fold into the cheese
mixture with the cooled
gelatine. Cut the sponge into
two layers, sandwich thickly
together with the cheese mixture, spreading the rest over the
top and sides of the cake.
Arrange the grapes on top, as
illustrated. Glaze with the jel
mix and finally press the flaked
almonds on to the sides.

Rich Cream Cheesecake

SHORTBREAD
200 g/7 oz plain flour
120 g/4 oz butter, cut into flakes
70 g/2½ oz castor sugar
1 egg yolk
pinch of salt
grated rind of ¼ lemon
FILLING
250 ml/8 fl oz milk
200 g/7 oz castor sugar
pinch of salt
grated rind of 1 lemon
4 egg yolks
25 g/1 oz powdered gelatine
450 ml/¾ pint double cream
450 g/1 lb curd or cream cheese
icing sugar to sprinkle

Sift the flour on to a large board and dot with the flaked butter. Make a well in the centre, add the sugar, egg yolk, salt and lemon rind. Working from the centre outwards, quickly knead all the ingredients to a smooth dough. Shape into a ball, wrap in foil or cling film and leave for 2 hours in the refrigerator.

Preheat the oven to moderately hot (190°C, 375°F, Gas Mark 5). Roll the shortbread out thinly on a floured surface to make two 25-cm/10-inch rounds. Place on greased baking trays and bake for 8–10 minutes, until golden brown. While still warm, cut one round into 12 equal portions and cool on wire rack with the other round.

Place the milk, sugar, salt, lemon rind and egg yolks in the top of a double saucepan or in a basin over a pan of hot water. Heat gently, stirring continuously until smooth and thickened. Remove from the heat. Dissolve the gelatine in 3 tablespoons water over a gentle heat. Stir into the custard and leave to cool. Whip the cream until thick. When the custard begins to set, stir in the beaten cream cheese then carefully fold in the whipped cream.

Line the sides of a 25-cm/10-inch springform cake tin with a strip of greaseproof paper. Place the uncut shortbread round in the base of the tin, spoon over the cheese filling and smooth the surface. Arrange the cut shortbread on top to form a complete round then allow to set in the refrigerator.

Remove the cheesecake from the tin and carefully peel away the greaseproof paper. Finally sprinkle with sifted icing sugar.

Cook's Tip

If wished, fresh or frozen strawberries, raspberries, redcurrants or blackcurrants can be added to the cheese mixture. Make sure the frozen fruit has thawed sufficiently and is drained and sweetened to taste. If fresh fruit is used, wash, pat dry and sprinkle with sugar. Leave for a few minutes before adding to the mixture.

Pineapple Cream Gâteau

SPONGE MIXTURE
6 eggs, separated
150 g/5 oz castor sugar
100 g/4 oz plain flour
50 g/2 oz cornflour
50 g/2 oz cocoa powder
50 g/2 oz ground almonds
50 g/2 oz butter
FILLING AND TOPPING
25 g/1 oz cornflour
160 g/5½ oz castor sugar
500 ml/17 fl oz milk
250 g/9 oz butter
1 tablespoon rum
7 slices canned pineapple
80 g/3 oz toasted flaked almonds
7 glacé cherries

Grease the base and sides of a 25-cm/10-inch springform cake tin. Preheat the oven to moderately hot (190°C, 375°F, Gas Mark 5).

Whisk the egg yolks with a third of the sugar until thick and creamy. Whisk the egg whites until stiff, gradually add the remaining sugar and fold in well. Sift the flour with the cornflour and cocoa powder and mix in the ground almonds. Fold the egg whites into the egg yolks and then carefully fold in the flour mixture. Melt the butter, cool slightly and stir into the mixture. Turn into the prepared tin and bake for 35–45 minutes. Cool for a few minutes in the tin then remove to a wire rack for at least 2 hours.

Blend the cornflour and sugar with a little of the milk. Heat the remaining milk and pour on to the blended cornflour. Return to the saucepan and bring to the boil, stirring

continuously. Cook for a few minutes to thicken then allow to cool, stirring frequently. Beat the butter until pale and creamy then beat in the rum. When the sauce is sufficiently cooled, add it gradually to the butter, beating each addition in well.

Cut the cake through twice, to make three layers. Cut the pineapple slices into small cubes and reserve 14 for decoration. Spread the bottom cake layer with butter cream, arrange the pineapple cubes on top and cover with a little more of the cream. Place the second cake layer over this, spread with butter cream and top with the last cake layer. Spread the top and sides of the cake thinly with the cream and put the remainder into a piping bag. Cover the gâteau with toasted flaked almonds, pipe 14 rosettes of cream around the top and place a pineapple cube and halved glacé cherry on each.

Cook's Tip

When whisking egg yolks and sugar together for a sponge it is quicker to use an electric mixer. If you do not have an electric mixer, stand the bowl over a pan of hot water and use a rotary or balloon whisk. The mixture is ready when the whisk leaves a trail.

Gooseberry Meringue Gâteau

SPONGE MIXTURE
6 eggs, separated
150 g/5 oz castor sugar
120 g/4 oz plain flour
60 g/2 oz cornflour
50 g/2 oz ground almonds
50 g/2 oz butter
FILLING
150 g/5 oz ground almonds
3 tablespoons rum
2 tablespoons icing sugar
3 tablespoons water
TOPPING
500 g/1 lb gooseberries
3 tablespoons granulated sugar
6 tablespoons water
4 egg whites
170 g/6 oz castor sugar
few drops of vanilla essence
*100 g/4 oz toasted flaked
   almonds*

Grease the base and sides of a 25-cm/10-inch springform cake tin. Preheat the oven to moderately hot (190°C, 375°F, Gas Mark 5).

Whisk the egg yolks with a third of the sugar until creamy. Whisk the egg whites until stiff, then gradually fold in the rest of the sugar. Sift the flour with the cornflour and mix with the ground almonds. Fold the egg whites into the egg yolks then fold in the flour mixture. Melt the butter, cool slightly and stir into the mixture. Turn into the prepared tin and bake for 35–40 minutes. Cool on a wire rack for at least 2 hours then slice through into two layers.

Mix the ground almonds with the rum, icing sugar and water to form a smooth paste. Use to sandwich the cake layers together.

Top, tail and wash the gooseberries. Mix the granulated sugar with the water, bring to the boil, add the gooseberries

and simmer over a gentle heat for 10 minutes. Drain thoroughly in a sieve over a basin.

Preheat the oven to hot (230°C, 450°F, Gas Mark 8). Whisk the egg whites until stiff, then whisk in the sugar and fold in the vanilla essence. Arrange the gooseberries over the cake, reserving 14 whole gooseberries for decoration. Spread the meringue mixture thickly over the top and sides. Pipe 14 meringue garlands on top, working from the centre outwards and ending each in a rosette. Bake the cake for 1 minute only until the meringue is light golden brown on top. Decorate the centre and sides of the gâteau with toasted flaked almonds and top each meringue rosette with a gooseberry.

Cook's Tip

In order to achieve a light sponge, when folding in the ingredients use a metal tablespoon and work quickly and lightly. An uncooked sponge mixture must be put into the preheated oven without delay.

Caribbean Coconut Cake

SPONGE MIXTURE
4 eggs, separated
2 tablespoons lukewarm water
140 g/4½ oz castor sugar
grated rind of ½ lemon
120 g/4 oz plain flour
60 g/2 oz cornflour
1 teaspoon baking powder
FILLING AND TOPPING
1 coconut or 225 g/8 oz
    desiccated coconut
2 tablespoons coconut milk
40 g/1½ oz sugar
1 tablespoon dark rum
25 g/1 oz cornflour
500 ml/17 fl oz milk
3 eggs, separated
180 g/6 oz castor sugar
¼ teaspoon vanilla essence
16 glacé cherries

Grease the base of a 20-cm/
8-inch springform cake tin.
Preheat the oven to moderately
hot (190°C, 375°F, Gas Mark
5).
    Whisk the egg yolks with the
water, half the sugar and the
lemon rind until creamy. Whisk
the egg whites until stiff, fold in
the remaining sugar and carefully fold into the egg yolk mixture. Sift the flour with the
cornflour and baking powder
and fold into the egg mixture.
Turn into the prepared tin,
smooth the surface and bake
for 35–40 minutes. Allow to
cool slightly in the tin then turn
on to a wire rack to cool completely. Leave overnight if
possible, then cut into three
layers.
    Pierce the coconut twice at
the thinnest part of the shell,
pour off the milk and reserve.
Cut the coconut in half, scoop
out the flesh, cover and reserve.
Boil 2 tablespoons of the coconut milk with the 40 g/1½ oz

sugar until the sugar dissolves
completely. Add the rum and
leave to cool. (If using desiccated coconut, 100 g/4 oz of
this should be infused in
300 ml/½ pint boiling water
overnight, then strained. This
liquid may be used instead of
the fresh coconut milk.)
    Blend the cornflour with 3
tablespoons fresh milk and
the egg yolks. Heat the remaining fresh milk with half the
castor sugar until almost boiling. Whisk the egg whites until
stiff then carefully fold in the
rest of the castor sugar. Pour
the hot milk on to the cornflour
mixture. Return to the heat and
bring to the boil, stirring continuously. Remove from the
heat, stir in the vanilla essence,
cool slightly and carefully fold
in the whisked egg whites.
    Allow this vanilla cream to
cool slightly then spread thickly
over the bottom cake layer.
Place the second cake layer on
top, sprinkle over half the

coconut milk mixture and
allow it to soak in. Spread over
a layer of the cream then top
with the last cake layer.
Sprinkle over the rest of the
coconut milk, allowing it to
soak in, and then spread the
top and sides of the cake with
the remaining vanilla cream.
    Grate the coconut flesh finely
and use to cover the cake
thickly all over. Alternatively,
use the remaining desiccated
coconut. Arrange the glacé
cherries around the edge of the
cake.

Austrian Hazelnut Cake

100 g/4 oz butter
100 g/4 oz castor sugar
4 eggs, separated
100 g/4 oz ground hazelnuts
30 g/1 oz candied lemon peel,
*   finely chopped*
icing sugar to sprinkle

Line the base of a 25-cm/10-inch greased sandwich tin with greaseproof paper. Grease the paper and sprinkle with fine breadcrumbs. Preheat the oven to moderate (180°C, 350°F, Gas Mark 4).

Cream the butter and sugar until light and fluffy. Add the egg yolks, one at a time, then the hazelnuts and chopped peel. Whisk the egg whites until very stiff and fold into the mixture. Turn into the pre-pared tin and smooth the surface. Bake for 40 minutes.

Turn on to a wire rack to cool. Place a paper doily on the cake as a stencil and then sift icing sugar over. Remove the doily carefully to leave a pretty pattern.

Walnut Cream Pie

PASTRY
160 g/5½ oz butter
150 g/5 oz castor sugar
pinch of salt
1 egg
300 g/11 oz plain flour
1 egg yolk, beaten to glaze
FILLING
20 g/¾ oz butter
300 g/11 oz granulated sugar
250 g/9 oz walnuts, roughly
*   chopped*
250 ml/8 fl oz double cream

Cream the softened butter with the sugar, salt and egg. Sift the flour over the top and knead all the ingredients together to make a pastry dough. Cover and leave for 2 hours in the refrigerator.

Roll out two-thirds of the pastry to line the base and sides of a 23-cm/9-inch flan tin, allowing the pastry to overlap the top all the way round. Pre-heat the oven to moderately hot (200°C, 400°F, Gas Mark 6).

Melt the butter in a pan, add the sugar and cook, stirring continuously, until it caramel-ises to a light golden brown. Add the walnuts and cream and bring to just below boiling point. Allow to cool then spread into the pastry case. Roll out the remaining pastry to make a lid, brush the over-lapping sides with egg yolk and press on to the pastry lid to seal. Brush the top of the pie with egg yolk and prick several times with a fork. Bake for 30–40 minutes then cool on a wire rack.

Swedish Almond Flan

PASTRY
150 g/5 oz butter or margarine
40 g/1½ oz castor sugar
¼ teaspoon vanilla essence
pinch of salt
2 egg yolks
200 g/7 oz plain flour
FILLING
125 g/4½ oz butter
125 g/4½ oz icing sugar
2 eggs
125 g/4½ oz ground almonds
grated rind of 1 lemon
20 g/¾ oz plain flour

Cream the softened butter with the sugar, vanilla essence, salt and egg yolks. Sift the flour on to this and knead all the ingredients to a pastry dough. Wrap in foil or cling film and leave for 2 hours in the refrigerator.

Preheat the oven to moderate (180°C, 350°F, Gas Mark 4). Cream the butter with the sifted icing sugar and eggs until creamy. Stir in the almonds, lemon rind and flour. Roll out the pastry to line the base and sides of a 20-cm/8-inch flan tin. Spread the filling into this and bake for 45 minutes. Allow to cool in the tin.

Spanish Vanilla Cake

250 g/9 oz ground almonds
150 g/5 oz castor sugar
¼ teaspoon vanilla essence
pinch of salt
1 whole egg plus 6 eggs, separated
100 g/4 oz plain flour
50 g/2 oz cornflour
60 g/2 oz cooking chocolate, chopped
ICING
200 g/7 oz plain chocolate
1–2 tablespoons chopped pistachio nuts

Grease a 23-cm/9-inch petal-patterned cake tin. Preheat the oven to moderately hot (190°C, 375°F, Gas Mark 5).

Mix the ground almonds with half the sugar, the vanilla essence, salt, egg and egg yolks, and beat until creamy. Whisk the egg whites until stiff and fold in the remaining sugar. Fold into the egg yolk mixture. Sift the flour and cornflour over this and fold in carefully. Finally fold in the chopped chocolate. Turn into the prepared cake tin, smooth the surface and bake for 45–50 minutes. Allow the cake to cool a little in the tin then turn on to a wire rack to cool completely.

Melt the chocolate in a basin over hot water, spread over the top and sides of the cake and sprinkle with pistachio nuts while still soft.

Viennese Cherry Cake

PASTRY
100 g/4 oz butter
60 g/2 oz castor sugar
150 g/6 oz plain flour
1–2 tablespoons water
CAKE MIXTURE
300 g/11 oz butter
300 g/11 oz castor sugar
6 eggs, separated
grated rind of 1 lemon
pinch of salt
150 g/5¼ oz plain flour
150 g/5¼ oz cornflour
450 g/1 lb fresh or 225 g/8 oz glacé cherries
icing sugar to sprinkle

Cream the butter with the sugar, sift over the flour and knead well with the water to form a pastry dough. Cover and leave for 2 hours in the refrigerator.

Preheat the oven to hot

(220°C, 425°F, Gas Mark 7). Roll out the pastry to line the base of a 23-cm/9-inch cake tin. Prick the base all over with a fork and bake blind for 15 minutes.

For the cake mixture, cream the butter with half the sugar, the egg yolks, lemon rind and salt, until pale and light. Whisk the egg whites until stiff and fold in the remaining sugar. Carefully fold into the creamed mixture. Sift the flour and cornflour on to this and fold in well. Pour the cake mixture over the pastry and scatter the cherries on top. If using glacé cherries, toss lightly in flour first. Bake the cake for a further 1–1¼ hours in a moderately hot oven (190°C, 375°F, Gas Mark 5), covering with foil if the cake becomes too brown. Allow to cool then dust with sifted icing sugar.

Orange Almond Cake

7 eggs, separated
280 g/10 oz castor sugar
grated rind and juice of 2 oranges
30 g/1 oz plain flour
80 g/3 oz cake crumbs
280 g/10 oz ground almonds
TOPPING
200 g/7 oz orange jelly marmalade
100 g/4 oz toasted flaked almonds
14 candied orange segments

Grease a 23-cm/9-inch spring-form cake tin and sprinkle with fine breadcrumbs. Preheat the oven to moderately hot (200°C, 400°F, Gas Mark 6).

Whisk the egg yolks with half the sugar until creamy, then whisk in the orange rind and juice. Whisk the egg whites until stiff and fold in the

remaining sugar. Carefully fold into the egg yolk mixture. Sift the flour over this and fold in with the cake crumbs and ground almonds. Turn into the prepared tin, smooth the surface and bake for 30–40 minutes.

Allow the cake to cool slightly on a wire rack, then spread the top and sides with the warmed orange jelly. Cover with the flaked almonds and finally decorate with the candied orange segments.

Festive Chocolate Gâteau

SPONGE MIXTURE
200 g/7 oz castor sugar
4 eggs, separated
3 tablespoons hot water
pinch of salt
200 g/7 oz plain flour
1 teaspoon baking powder
FILLING AND TOPPING
3 tablespoons orange jelly
   marmalade
1 tablespoon Cointreau
250 g/9 oz butter
225 g/8 oz icing sugar
15 g/½ oz cocoa powder
4 eggs
7 candied orange segments
14 glacé cherries
50 g/2 oz chocolate vermicelli or
   chopped chocolate

Line a 23-cm/9-inch spring-form cake tin with greaseproof paper, then grease this with butter or margarine. Preheat the oven to hot (220°C, 425°F, Gas Mark 7).

Reserve 3 tablespoons sugar and whisk the remainder with the egg yolks and hot water until creamy. Whisk the egg whites with the salt until stiff then fold in the remaining sugar. Drop the egg whites on top of the egg yolk mixture. Sift the flour and baking powder on to the egg whites and fold altogether into the yolk mixture. Turn into the prepared tin, smooth the surface and bake for 30 minutes.

Turn on to a wire rack to cool for about 2 hours and remove the greaseproof paper. Mix the orange marmalade and Cointreau together. Beat the butter until pale and creamy. Sift the icing sugar with the cocoa powder. Whisk the eggs and mix in the icing sugar and

cocoa powder. Add this mixture a little at a time to the butter, beating well to incorporate.

Cut the cooled cake horizontally into four layers. Spread three layers thinly with the orange marmalade and a little of the butter cream. Place one on top of the other and spread the top layer and sides with butter cream. Place the remaining cream in a piping bag fitted with a star nozzle. With a sharp knife mark the cake into 14 equal portions and decorate each with a swirl of butter cream ending in a rosette. Halve the orange segments and place on each rosette, topping with a glacé cherry. Decorate the sides of the gâteau with chocolate vermicelli or chopped chocolate.

Cook's Tip

When freezing elaborate cream gâteaux, interleave the slices with grease-proof paper. This way you can take as many slices from the freezer as you want at one time, and there is no wastage.

Weekend Specialities

Coffee Layer Gâteau

CAKE MIXTURE
130 g/5 oz butter
200 g/7 oz castor sugar
pinch each of salt, ground
  cinnamon and grated lemon
  rind
6 eggs, separated
130 g/5 oz plain chocolate
130 g/5 oz plain flour
FILLING AND TOPPING
300 ml/½ pint milk
25 g/1 oz cornflour
1 tablespoon instant coffee
  powder
150 g/5 oz castor sugar
250 g/9 oz butter
15 candied coffee beans
50 g/2 oz toasted flaked almonds

Grease the base of a 23-cm/ 9-inch springform cake tin. Preheat the oven to moderately hot (190°C, 375°F, Gas Mark 5).

Beat the softened butter with half the sugar, the salt, cinnamon and lemon rind, until light and fluffy. Add the egg yolks to the mixture one by one. Melt the chocolate in a basin over hot water but do not allow to get too hot. Stir into the butter mixture. Whisk the egg whites until stiff then whisk in the remaining sugar and fold into the chocolate mixture. Finally fold in the sifted flour. Turn the mixture into the prepared tin, smooth over and bake in the centre of the oven for 50–60 minutes. Turn on to a wire rack to cool for at least 2 hours, then cut into four layers.

Mix 4 tablespoons milk with the cornflour. Bring the rest of the milk to the boil with the coffee and sugar. Stir into the cornflour mixture then pour

back into the saucepan and bring to the boil, stirring continuously until smooth and thickened. Remove from the heat and cool completely, stirring often. Beat the butter until light and fluffy then gradually add to it the cooled coffee cream, beating well with each addition.

Spread three cake layers with coffee cream and arrange them one on top of the other. Spread the top and sides of the gâteau with the cream and mark into 14 portions with a sharp knife. Put the rest of the coffee cream into a piping bag fitted with a star nozzle and decorate each portion with a swirl ending in a rosette. Pipe a double rosette in the centre of the gâteau. Top each rosette with a candied coffee bean and sprinkle the centre and sides of the gâteau with flaked almonds.

Cook's Tip
To cut a cream gâteau, dip the longest and sharpest knife you possess into warm water before making each cut.

Fruit Layer Gâteau

SPONGE MIXTURE
4 eggs, separated
2 tablespoons lukewarm water
140 g/5 oz castor sugar
grated rind of ½ lemon
120 g/4 oz plain flour
60 g/2 oz cornflour
1 teaspoon baking powder
FILLING
100 g/4 oz nougat
100 g/4 oz ground almonds
1–2 tablespoons Kirsch
2 tablespoons water
1 tablespoon icing sugar
TOPPING
100 g/4 oz apricot jam
75 g/3 oz toasted flaked almonds
675 g/1½ lb mixed fruit or
   1 (825-g/1 lb 13-oz) can
   fruit salad
1 small packet quick-setting jel
   mix

Grease a 25-cm/10-inch spring-form cake tin. Preheat the oven to moderately hot (190°C, 375°F, Gas Mark 5).

Whisk the egg yolks with the water, half the sugar and the lemon rind, until frothy. Whisk the egg whites until stiff, fold in the remaining sugar then fold into the egg yolks. Sift the flour with the cornflour and baking powder and fold evenly into the mixture. Turn into the prepared tin and bake for 40 minutes.

Remove the cake from the tin and cool on a wire rack for at least 2 hours, then cut into three layers.

Melt the nougat in a basin over hot water and spread over one cake layer. Put the next layer on top. Mix the ground almonds with the Kirsch, water and sifted icing sugar and spread over the second layer. Cover with the third cake layer, spread the top and sides with the warmed apricot jam and cover the sides with flaked almonds, pressing in well. Arrange the prepared and drained fruit over the cake and glaze with the jel mix, made up according to the packet instructions.

Fresh Cream Pear Gâteau

SPONGE MIXTURE
6 eggs, separated
150 g/5 oz castor sugar
100 g/3½ oz plain flour
30 g/1 oz cornflour
50 g/2 oz cocoa powder
50 g/2 oz ground almonds
50 g/2 oz butter or margarine
FILLING AND TOPPING
1 kg/2 lb ripe dessert pears
1 litre/1¾ pints water
50 g/2 oz sugar
juice of 1 lemon
225 g/8 oz blackcurrant
  preserve
600 ml/1 pint double cream
60 g/2 oz icing sugar
50 g/2 oz toasted flaked almonds
7 glacé cherries

Grease a 25-cm/10-inch cake tin. Preheat the oven to moderately hot (190°C, 375°F, Gas Mark 5).

Whisk the egg yolks with a third of the sugar until pale and thick. Whisk the egg whites until stiff then add the remaining sugar. Whisk again until stiff and fold into the egg yolks. Sift the flour, cornflour and cocoa powder together, mix with the ground almonds and fold all thoroughly into the egg mixture. Melt the butter or margarine, cool a little and carefully fold into the cake mixture. Turn into the prepared tin, smooth the surface and bake in the centre of the oven for 40–50 minutes.

Cool on a wire rack for at least 2 hours then cut into three layers.

Peel the pears, divide each into eight segments and remove the cores. Bring the water to the boil with the sugar and lemon juice and poach the

pears in this syrup for about 10 minutes, keeping the pan covered. Leave to drain in a sieve over a basin and allow the fruit to cool.

Spread two cake layers with the blackcurrant preserve and arrange the pear segments over, reserving 14 segments for decoration. Whip the cream with the sifted icing sugar until stiff. Spread half the cream over both the cake layers, sandwich them together and finally place the last layer on top. Spread the top and sides thickly with cream, smoothing over carefully. Sprinkle the sides with flaked almonds and mark the top of the gâteau into 14 equal portions. Place the remaining cream in a piping bag fitted with a star nozzle and pipe a rosette on each portion. Finally decorate each with a segment of pear and a halved cherry.

Cook's Tip
Instead of fresh dessert pears, use a large can of pear halves, drained and sliced.

Strawberry Cream Roll

SPONGE MIXTURE
3 large eggs, separated
50 g/2 oz castor sugar
50 g/2 oz icing sugar
60 g/2¼ oz plain flour
40 g/1½ oz cornflour
FILLING
225 g/8 oz strawberries
25 g/1 oz castor sugar
150 ml/¼ pint double cream
50 g/2 oz icing sugar

Line a 23 × 30-cm/9 × 12-inch Swiss roll tin with greased greaseproof paper. Preheat the oven to hot (220°C, 425°F, Gas Mark 7).

Whisk the egg yolks with the castor sugar. Whisk the egg whites until frothy, then add the sifted icing sugar. Whisk until stiff then fold into the yolk mixture. Sift the flours and fold in quickly but thor-oughly. Spread smoothly in the prepared Swiss roll tin and bake towards the top of the oven for 10–12 minutes.

Turn out carefully on to clean greaseproof paper sprinkled with sugar, with a dampened tea towel under-neath. Peel off the lining paper and roll up with the clean paper inside. Cool.

Hull and quarter the straw-berries, sprinkle with the castor sugar and leave for 30 minutes. Drain the strawberry juice and whip with the cream until thick. Fold in the sifted icing sugar and the strawberries. Unroll the cake. Spread over the filling and roll up, using the paper to lift the cake. Sprinkle with extra icing sugar and serve.

Lemon Curd Rolls

SPONGE MIXTURE
4 eggs, separated, plus 2 egg yolks
grated rind of 1 lemon
100 g/4 oz castor sugar
75 g/3 oz plain flour
25 g/1 oz cornflour
FILLING AND TOPPING
6 tablespoons lemon curd
icing sugar to sprinkle
6 glacé cherries

Line a 33 × 23-cm/13 × 9-inch Swiss roll tin with greased greaseproof paper. Preheat the oven to hot (220°C, 425°F, Gas Mark 7).

Whisk all the egg yolks with the lemon rind and half the sugar until pale and thick. Whisk the egg whites until stiff then whisk in the remaining sugar and fold into the egg yolks. Sift the flour and corn-flour over the top and fold into the egg mixture. Spread evenly into the Swiss roll tin and bake in the centre of the oven for 10–12 minutes.

Remove from the oven and leave in the tin covered with a dampened tea towel until cold. Turn out and strip off the greaseproof lining paper. Spread the lemon curd evenly over the cake. Cut into 12 squares and roll each one up with the lemon curd inside. Dust with sifted icing sugar and decorate each roll with a halved glacé cherry.

Raspberry Cream Roll

SPONGE MIXTURE
4 eggs, separated, plus 2 egg yolks
100 g/4 oz castor sugar
80 g/3 oz plain flour
20 g/1 oz cornflour
FILLING
225 g/8 oz fresh or frozen raspberries
300 ml/½ pint double cream
50 g/2 oz icing sugar

Allow the frozen raspberries to defrost at room temperature. Line a 33 × 23-cm/13 × 9-inch Swiss roll tin with grease-proof paper and grease well. Preheat the oven to hot (220°C, 425°F, Gas Mark 7).

Whisk all the egg yolks with half the sugar until creamy and thick. Whisk the egg whites until stiff, then whisk in the remaining sugar and fold into the whisked egg yolks. Sift the flour and cornflour over this mixture and fold in. Spread evenly in the Swiss roll tin and bake towards the top of the oven for 10–12 minutes.

Turn the sponge out on to a clean sheet of greaseproof paper sprinkled with sugar, with a dampened tea towel underneath. Strip off the lining paper, trim the edges of the sponge and roll up with the clean greaseproof inside. Allow to cool.

Crush the raspberries with a wooden spoon, reserving a few for decoration. Whip the cream and sifted icing sugar together until stiff, place about one-quarter in a piping bag and mix the remainder with the crushed raspberries. Carefully unroll the Swiss roll and remove the greaseproof paper. Spread with the raspberry cream and roll up. Pipe cream rosettes on top and decorate with the reserved raspberries.

Chocolate Cream Roll

SPONGE MIXTURE
4 eggs, separated, plus 2 egg yolks
100 g/4 oz castor sugar
80 g/3 oz plain flour
20 g/1 oz cornflour
40 g/1½ oz cocoa powder
FILLING
100 g/4 oz fresh or frozen strawberries
300 ml/½ pint double cream
50 g/2 oz icing sugar
1 tablespoon drinking chocolate powder

Allow the frozen strawberries to defrost at room temperature. Line a 33 × 23-cm/13 × 9-inch Swiss roll tin with greaseproof paper and grease well. Preheat the oven to hot (220°C, 425°F, Gas Mark 7).

Whisk all the egg yolks with half the sugar until creamy and thick. Whisk the egg whites until stiff, then whisk in the remaining sugar and fold into the whisked egg yolks. Sift the flour, cornflour and cocoa powder over the egg mixture and fold in. Spread evenly in the Swiss roll tin and bake towards the top of the oven for 10–12 minutes.

Turn the sponge out on to a clean sheet of greaseproof paper sprinkled with sugar, with a dampened tea towel underneath. Strip off the lining paper, trim the edges and roll up with the greaseproof paper inside. Allow to cool.

Purée the strawberries in a liquidiser or press through a sieve. Whip the cream with the sifted icing sugar until stiff and mix with the puréed strawberries. Carefully unroll the Swiss roll and remove the greaseproof paper. Spread with the strawberry cream and roll up. Dredge the top with sifted chocolate powder.

Gooseberry Meringue Tartlets

PASTRY
160 g/5 oz plain flour
100 g/3 oz butter
60 g/2 oz castor sugar
pinch of salt
1 tablespoon soured cream
2 egg yolks
FILLING
500 g/1 lb gooseberries
60 g/2 oz sugar
4 tablespoons brandy
300 ml/½ pint milk
2 tablespoons cornflour
3 tablespoons double cream
25 g/1 oz icing sugar
MERINGUE
4 egg whites
150 g/5 oz icing sugar

Knead the sifted flour with the butter, sugar, salt, cream and egg yolks, to make a dough.

Cover and chill for 2 hours.

Top and tail the gooseberries, wash them and cook gently in a covered pan with the sugar and brandy, until soft.

Blend 2 tablespoons milk with the cornflour. Bring the remaining milk to the boil with the cream and icing sugar. Stir into the cornflour, return to the pan and bring to the boil, stirring until thickened. Cool.

Preheat the oven to moderately hot (200°C, 400°F, Gas Mark 6). Roll out the pastry to 3 mm/⅛ inch thick and line eight to ten 7·5-cm/3-inch tartlet tins. Bake blind for 10–15 minutes, then cool in their tins.

Fill the cooled tartlet cases with the cooled cream and cover with the gooseberries. Whisk the egg whites until stiff then whisk in the sifted icing sugar. Pipe a meringue lattice over each. Brown the meringue in a hot oven (220°C, 425°F, Gas Mark 7) for a few minutes with the door slightly open.

Raspberry Tartlets

PASTRY
125 g/4 oz plain flour
60 g/2 oz butter
50 g/2 oz icing sugar
few drops of vanilla essence
pinch of salt
1 small egg yolk
FILLING
225 g/8 oz fresh or frozen raspberries
150 g/5 oz butter
150 g/5 oz castor sugar
3 egg yolks
grated rind and juice of 3 lemons
1 tablespoon cornflour
DECORATION
3 tablespoons apricot jam
75 g/3 oz toasted flaked almonds
150 ml/¼ pint double cream
1 tablespoon icing sugar

Knead together the sifted flour, butter, icing sugar, vanilla essence, salt and egg yolk, to make a pastry dough. Cover and leave in the refrigerator for 2 hours. Allow the frozen raspberries to defrost.

Preheat the oven to moderately hot (200°C, 400°F, Gas Mark 6). Roll out the pastry thinly and use to line six to eight 7·5-cm/3-inch tartlet tins. Bake blind for 10–15 minutes then remove from their tins and cool on a wire rack.

Place the butter in a saucepan with the sugar, egg yolks, lemon rind and juice and the cornflour. Bring gently to the boil, stirring continuously until smooth and thickened. Cool.

Spread the warmed apricot jam over the sides of the tartlets and sprinkle with the flaked almonds, pressing them on well. Fill the tartlets with the lemon cream and cover with the raspberries. Whip the cream with the sugar until stiff and pipe on to the centre of the tartlets, decorating with a few flaked almonds.

From the Cake Tray

Cream Horns

1 (368-g/13-oz) packet frozen
 puff pastry
1 egg yolk
1 tablespoon milk
50 g/2 oz flaked almonds
icing sugar to sprinkle
FILLING
150 g/5 oz strawberries
25 g/1 oz icing sugar
150 ml/¼ pint double cream
few drops of vanilla essence

To make these, you will require special cream horn tins. Allow the pastry to thaw for 1 hour at room temperature.

Roll out the pastry on a floured surface to a rectangle 30 × 20 cm/12 × 8 inches. Using a pastry wheel or sharp knife, cut the pastry into eight long strips, each 2·5 cm/1 inch wide. Leave to stand for 15 minutes. Preheat the oven to hot (220°C, 425°F, Gas Mark 7).

Rinse eight cream horn tins in cold water. Beat the egg yolk and milk together. Brush the strips of pastry along one edge with the beaten egg. Starting from the narrow end of the tin, roll the pastry around the tins so that the edge brushed with egg overlaps the unbrushed side by about 5 mm/¼ inch. Press both edges together and brush the pastry horns with the remaining beaten egg. Sprinkle half the horns with flaked almonds. Place them all on a dampened baking tray and bake for 15 minutes, until puffed up and golden brown.

While still hot, carefully loosen the horns from their tins and cool on a wire rack. Sift icing sugar over those not decorated with almonds.

Wash and hull the strawberries, drain and purée in a liquidiser or press through a sieve. Stir the icing sugar into this strawberry purée. Whip the cream with the vanilla essence until stiff. Put just over half the cream into a piping bag fitted with a star nozzle and pipe into the horns sprinkled with icing sugar. Mix the rest of the cream with the strawberry purée and pipe this into the remaining horns.

Cook's Tip

If you want to make cream horns, but do not have the special tins, the shape can be made using cardboard and covering it with foil. Allow 2–3 minutes longer baking time as foil is not such a good conductor of heat. During these last few minutes of baking, cover the horns with grease-proof paper, so they do not turn too brown on the outside before cooking through completely.

Cherry Cream Cones

BISCUIT MIXTURE
50 g/2 oz ground almonds
100 g/4 oz icing sugar
100 g/4 oz plain flour
2 eggs plus 1 egg white
few drops of almond essence
pinch of salt
FILLING
1 tablespoon Kirsch
225 g/8 oz cherry jam
300 ml/½ pint double cream
slivers of grated chocolate to
   decorate

Grease a large baking tray.
Preheat the oven to moderate
(180°C, 350°F, Gas Mark 4).
   Mix together the ground
almonds, sifted icing sugar,
sifted flour, eggs, egg white,
almond essence and salt. Beat
well until smooth. Spread 2 teaspoons of the mixture thinly
into a 12·5-cm/5-inch circle on

the greased baking tray, using
the back of the teaspoon. You
will only be able to bake two at
a time on the baking tray. Bake
in the centre of the oven for
5–7 minutes, or until the edges
just start turning brown.
Repeat this process until all the
mixture is used up.
   As soon as the cones come
out of the oven, quickly remove
them from the baking tray and
shape into cones while warm,
using a cream horn tin to help
you. Allow to cool on a wire
rack.
   Mix the Kirsch with the
cherry jam. Whip the cream
until stiff and reserve a little
for piping. Mix half the cherry
jam with the remaining cream
and half fill the cones with it.
Add a spoonful of the remaining cherry jam to each and
finally pipe a rosette of cream
on top, decorating it with
chocolate slivers.

Chocolate Fruit Boats

25 g/1 oz ground almonds
CAKE MIXTURE
40 g/1½ oz dates
50 g/2 oz candied pineapple
40 g/1½ oz raisins
40 g/1½ oz currants
40 g/1½ oz toasted almonds,
   chopped
2 tablespoons rum
190 g/7 oz plus 2 tablespoons
   plain flour
190 g/7 oz butter
190 g/7 oz castor sugar
grated rind of ½ lemon
3 eggs plus 3 egg yolks
ICING
100 g/4 oz plain chocolate
3 tablespoons coarsely crushed
   biscuit crumbs

Grease 16 boat-shaped patty
tins and sprinkle with the
ground almonds.
   Chop the dates and pine-

apple finely and mix with the
raisins, currants and toasted
almonds. Sprinkle over the
rum, cover and leave for 2
hours. Mix the 2 tablespoons
flour into the fruit. Preheat the
oven to moderate (180°C,
350°F, Gas Mark 4).
   Beat the butter and sugar
with the lemon rind until light
and fluffy. Beat in the eggs and
egg yolks, one by one, then add
the rest of the flour, sifted.
Finally fold in the fruit mixture. Fill the patty tins up to
the top and bake for 15
minutes.
   Turn the boats out on to a
wire rack to cool. Melt the
chocolate in a basin over hot
water and use to ice the top of
the boats. Sprinkle with biscuit
crumbs before the icing sets.

Chocolate Chimneys

BISCUIT MIXTURE
120 g/4 oz ground almonds
100 g/3¼ oz icing sugar
30 g/1 oz plain flour
4 egg whites
¼ teaspoon ground cinnamon
grated rind of ½ lemon
6 tablespoon double cream
ICING AND FILLING
140 g/5 oz plain chocolate
250 ml/8 fl oz double cream

Mix the ground almonds with the sifted icing sugar and flour, the egg whites, cinnamon and lemon rind, and beat well until smooth. Cover the mixture and leave overnight in the refrigerator.

Preheat the oven to moderately hot (190°C, 375°F, Gas Mark 5). Grease two baking trays and dust with flour. Stir the cream into the almond mixture and spread thinly and evenly over the baking trays. Bake, one tray after the other, in the centre of the oven for 5–7 minutes. Remove and cut into 11·5-cm/4½-inch squares with a pastry wheel or sharp knife. Bake the squares for a further 5 minutes, until set but not browned. Remove the squares one at a time from the baking tray, while still warm, and curl quickly round the handle of a wooden spoon, pressing the edges together. Remove from the wooden handle and allow the rolls to cool on a wire rack.

Melt the chocolate in a basin over hot water and coat the rolls all over with it. Whip the cream thickly and use to fill the chocolate chimneys.

Marzipan Wheels

PASTRY
250 g/9 oz butter
150 g/5 oz icing sugar
2 egg yolks
pinch of salt
400 g/14 oz plain flour
1 egg yolk, beaten to glaze
FILLING
200 g/7 oz ground almonds
few drops of almond essence
3 tablespoons Kirsch or sherry
120 g/4 oz chopped mixed peel
DECORATION
small pieces candied lemon peel
blanched almonds

Mix the softened butter with the sifted icing sugar, egg yolks, salt and sifted flour. Knead all together to a pastry dough, wrap in foil or cling film and leave for 2 hours in the refrigerator.

Preheat the oven to moderately hot (200°C, 400°F, Gas Mark 6). Roll out the pastry on a floured surface to a 25 × 40-cm/10 × 16-inch rectangle, 5 mm/¼ inch thick. Mix the ground almonds with the almond essence and Kirsch to a stiff spreading consistency. Spread over the pastry and sprinkle with the finely chopped peel. Roll up from the long side and cut into 2·5-cm/1-inch slices. Stand the slices upright on a baking tray, a good distance apart. Brush the tops with beaten egg yolk and arrange a piece of lemon peel and an almond on each. Bake for 20 minutes then leave to cool on a wire rack.

Swedish Apple Tartlets

PASTRY
100 g/4 oz plain flour
50 g/2 oz butter, cut into flakes
60 g/2 oz icing sugar
1 egg yolk
2 tablespoons water
icing sugar to sprinkle
FILLING
2 tablespoons roasted chopped
*   almonds*
2 cooking apples, cooked,
*   puréed and sweetened to taste*

Grease six to eight fluted tartlet or bun tins.

Sift the flour into a bowl and knead well with the butter, sifted icing sugar, egg yolk and water. Mix to a pastry dough, cover and leave for 2 hours in the refrigerator.

Preheat the oven to moderate (180°C, 350°F, Gas Mark 4). Mix the almonds into the apple purée. Roll out two-thirds of the pastry to a thickness of 5 mm/¼ inch. Cut into six to eight rounds and use to line the tartlet tins. Place a little apple purée in each tartlet case. Roll out the remaining pastry to a thickness of 3 mm/⅛ inch and cut out the lids. Brush the edges with water, lay over the tartlets and seal down well. Using a sharp knife, pierce an air vent in the side of the tartlets. Bake for 35 minutes.

Remove from the oven, allow to cool then sprinkle with sifted icing sugar.

Orange Slices

CAKE MIXTURE
100 g/4 oz butter
25 g/1 oz vanilla sugar
120 g/4½ oz castor sugar
pinch of salt
3 eggs, separated, plus 1 egg
*   yolk*
grated rind of 2 oranges
juice of 1 orange
90 g/3½ oz plain flour
30 g/1 oz cornflour
100 g/4 oz ground almonds
FILLING AND ICING
200 g/7 oz orange jelly
*   marmalade*
200 g/7 oz icing sugar
3 tablespoons orange juice
1 tablespoon Cointreau

Grease a 33 × 23-cm/13 × 9-inch Swiss roll tin and dust with flour. Preheat the oven to moderately hot (200°C, 400°F, Gas Mark 6).

Cream together the butter, vanilla sugar, half the sugar and the salt. Beat in the egg yolks, one at a time, with the orange rind and juice. Whisk the egg whites until stiff then whisk in the remaining sugar. Fold into the creamed mixture. Sift the flour and cornflour, mix with the ground almonds and fold all thoroughly into the egg mixture. Spread evenly over the Swiss roll tin and bake for 10 minutes. Allow to cool slightly in the tin then turn on to a wire rack to cool completely.

After about 2 hours, cut into two layers and sandwich these together with the orange marmalade. Blend the sifted icing sugar with the orange juice and Cointreau and use to ice the cake. Cut into slices to serve.

From the Cake Tray

Cherry Cream Tartlets

PASTRY
125 g/4½ oz butter
90 g/3½ oz icing sugar
1 teaspoon vanilla sugar
pinch of salt
1 egg
250 g/9 oz plain flour
FILLING
1 (425-g/15-oz) can pitted
*   black cherries*
150 ml/¼ pint double cream
6 tablespoons milk
50 g/2 oz butter
1 egg plus 1 egg yolk
20 g/¾ oz cornflour
pinch of salt
2 teaspoons castor sugar

Cream the softened butter with the sifted icing sugar, vanilla sugar, salt and egg. Sift over the flour and knead all the ingredients together to form a pastry dough. Cover and leave for 2 hours in the refrigerator.

Preheat the oven to moderately hot (200°C, 400°F, Gas Mark 6). Roll out the pastry thinly to line ten to twelve 7·5-cm/3-inch flan tins, prick the pastry with a fork and bake blind for 10 minutes. Remove the tartlets from the oven but leave in their tins. Reduce the oven temperature to moderate (180°C, 350°F, Gas Mark 4).

Drain the cherries, pat dry on absorbent paper, and put a few in each of the tartlet cases. Put the cream, milk, butter, egg and egg yolk, cornflour, salt and sugar into a pan and cook gently, stirring constantly until thickened. Pour over the cherries and bake the tartlets for a further 20–25 minutes.

Allow to cool slightly in their tins, then transfer the tartlets to a wire rack to cool completely.

Lemon Puff Slices

2 (368-g/13-oz) packets frozen
*   puff pastry*
1 egg yolk, beaten to glaze
FILLING
100 g/3½ oz castor sugar
200 g/7 oz ground almonds
1 egg yolk
grated rind and juice of 2 lemons
3 tablespoons lemon jelly
*   marmalade*

Allow the pastry to thaw for 1 hour at room temperature. Preheat the oven to hot (220°C, 425°F, Gas Mark 7).

Roll out each piece of pastry on a floured surface to an oblong 58 × 25 cm/23 × 10 inches. Cut each piece in half across the shorter width.

Sprinkle two baking trays with cold water. Place one piece of pastry on each of the dampened baking trays. Mix the sugar, almonds, egg yolk, lemon rind and juice together and spread over the pastry, leaving a small margin around the edge. Brush the edges of the pastry with the beaten egg yolk and lay the remaining pieces of pastry on top. Press the sides together lightly, brush the tops with beaten egg yolk and prick several times with a fork. Bake for 10–15 minutes towards the top of the oven.

Warm the lemon jelly marmalade and, while the pastry is still hot, spread it over the top. Cut into slices when cold.

Greek Doughnuts

YEAST DOUGH
450 g/1 lb plain flour
30 g/1 oz fresh yeast
2 teaspoons castor sugar
250 ml/8 fl oz lukewarm milk
1 egg
375 ml/13 fl oz lukewarm water
½ teaspoon salt
grated rind of 1 lemon
oil or fat to deep fry
SYRUP
225 g/8 oz sugar
100 g/4 oz honey
7 tablespoons water
1 tablespoon lemon juice
DECORATION
25 g/1 oz pistachio nuts, chopped

Sift the flour into a bowl and make a well in the centre. Cream the yeast with the sugar and milk. Pour the yeast liquid into the well, sprinkle over a little flour and leave covered for 15 minutes.

Whisk the egg with the water, salt and lemon rind, and add to the flour and yeast mixture. Beat to a smooth, elastic batter. Cover and leave for a further 20 minutes then beat thoroughly again.

Heat the cooking oil to 180°C/350°F. Using a wet tablespoon, take small spoonfuls of the yeast batter and cook them in the hot oil three or four at a time. Dip the tablespoon in cold water before taking each spoonful. Fry the doughnuts for about 4 minutes, turning once. Drain on absorbent paper and keep warm while cooking the remaining doughnuts.

Place the sugar, honey, water and lemon juice in a pan and heat gently until the sugar has dissolved, stirring continually. Boil for 5 minutes, until the syrup is quite thick. Pour over the warm doughnuts and sprinkle with the chopped pistachios. Arrange on a heated plate to serve.

Cook's Tip

To test whether the cooking oil has reached the correct temperature, do the bread cube test. Drop a cube of day-old bread into the hot oil; if it turns crisp and golden brown within a few seconds then the oil is sufficiently hot.

Danish Scrolls

YEAST PASTRY DOUGH
450 g/1 lb plain flour
30 g/1 oz fresh yeast
250 ml/8 fl oz lukewarm milk
225 g/8 oz butter
1 egg
¼ teaspoon salt
FILLING
2 tablespoons soft brown sugar
¼ teaspoon ground cinnamon
50 g/2 oz raisins

Sift the flour into a bowl and make a well. Cream the yeast with the milk and pour into the flour well. Sprinkle over a little flour, cover and leave for 15 minutes, until frothy. Melt 50 g/2 oz butter and add to the bowl with the egg and salt. Beat all to a smooth dough and knead. Cover and leave to rise for 15 minutes.

Roll out the dough to a 20 × 35-cm/8 × 14-inch oblong and mark into three

sections. Dot half the remaining butter over the top two sections and fold the bottom section over the middle section. Fold the top section down over this. Press the edges firmly together, turn the dough once in an anticlockwise direction and carefully roll out to an oblong 20 × 35 cm/8 × 14 inches. Repeat this process using the remaining butter, then repeat once more without using any butter. Chill for 15 minutes between each rolling.

Preheat the oven to 200°C, 400°F, Gas Mark 6. Roll out the pastry to measure 35 × 50 cm/14 × 20 inches, and brush with water. Spread over the mixed sugar, cinnamon and raisins and from the long sides roll the pastry in to meet at the centre. Cut into 2·5-cm/1-inch slices and place flat on greased baking trays. Bake for 10 minutes then reduce to 180°C, 350°F, Gas Mark 4 for 10–15 minutes.

Hazelnut Combs

1 (212-g/7½-oz) packet frozen puff pastry
1 egg yolk, beaten to glaze
FILLING
150 g/5 oz ground hazelnuts
1 egg, beaten
80 g/3 oz castor sugar
1 tablespoon rum

Allow the pastry to thaw for 1 hour at room temperature.

Roll out the pastry on a floured surface to make a 30-cm/12-inch square. Cut out nine 10-cm/4-inch squares. Mix together the hazelnuts, beaten egg, sugar and rum. Place a strip of this nut filling down the centre of each square. Brush one side of each square with the beaten egg yolk and fold over the opposite side. Make even cuts along this sealed edge and spread a little to form a comb.

Sprinkle a large baking tray

with cold water and place the hazelnut combs on it. Brush the tops with beaten egg yolk and leave to stand in the refrigerator for 15 minutes. Preheat the oven to hot (220°C, 425°F, Gas Mark 7). Bake the hazelnut combs for 15 minutes, then cool on a wire rack.

From the Cake Tray

Hazelnut Pastries

YEAST PASTRY DOUGH
500 g/1 lb 2 oz plain flour
30 g/1 oz fresh yeast
250 ml/8 fl oz lukewarm milk
225 g/8 oz butter
1 egg
½ teaspoon salt
FILLING
100 g/4 oz toasted hazelnuts,
  ground
50 g/2 oz castor sugar
2 tablespoons rum
½ teaspoon almond essence
1 egg white
GLAZE
3 tablespoons icing sugar
1–2 teaspoons rum

Prepare the yeast pastry dough
according to the recipe for
Danish Scrolls (see page 49).
Work the remaining 50 g/2 oz
flour into the remaining 175 g/
6 oz butter; chill, fold and roll
with the yeast dough, as
described in the same recipe.

Roll and fold three times in all,
allowing to rest in the refrigerator in between each rolling.
   Preheat the oven to hot
(220°C, 425°F, Gas Mark 7).
Finally divide the dough in
half and roll out each piece to
measure 23 × 55 cm/9 × 22
inches.
   Mix the hazelnuts, sugar,
rum, almond essence and egg
white together, and spread over
one of the pastry rectangles.
Place the other pastry rectangle
over this and press the edges
firmly together to seal. Cut
widthways into 2·5-cm/1-inch
wide pieces, make a 7·5-cm/
3-inch long slit near one end of
each piece and carefully twist
the other end before pulling it
through this opening (see
illustration). Seal the ends
together well. Place on a baking
tray and bake for 15 minutes.
   Mix the sifted icing sugar
with the rum and use to glaze
the pastries while still warm.

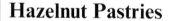

Orange Almond Croissants

YEAST PASTRY DOUGH
450 g/1 lb plain flour
30 g/1 oz fresh yeast
250 ml/8 fl oz lukewarm milk
225 g/8 oz butter
1 egg
½ teaspoon salt
FILLING
175 g/6 oz ground almonds
grated rind and juice of 1 orange
2 tablespoons orange liqueur
30 g/1 oz candied orange peel,
  finely chopped
1 egg white
GLAZE
1 egg yolk, beaten
3 tablespoons icing sugar
1 tablespoon orange juice
50 g/2 oz toasted flaked almonds

Prepare and roll the yeast
dough according to the recipe
for Danish Scrolls (see page
49). Finally roll out the dough

to a 40 × 50-cm/16 × 20-inch
rectangle.
   Mix the ground almonds
with the rest of the filling ingredients. Cut the dough into
four 10 × 50-cm/4 × 20-inch
strips, then cut each strip into
five to give 10-cm/4-inch
squares. Cut each square in
half diagonally to give triangles
with two sides measuring
10 cm/4 inches each. Place a
little of the filling in the centre
of each triangle and roll up
from the long side. Place on
greased baking trays and leave
to rise for 15 minutes in a warm
place. Preheat the oven to hot
(220°C, 425°F, Gas Mark 7).
   Brush the croissants with
beaten egg yolk and bake for
15–20 minutes. While still hot,
glaze with the mixed icing sugar
and orange juice, and sprinkle
with flaked almonds.

From the Cake Tray

Cream-Filled Choux Puffs

CHOUX PASTE
250 ml/8 fl oz water
60 g/2 oz butter or margarine
pinch of salt
grated rind of ½ lemon
200 g/7 oz plain flour
4 eggs, beaten
FILLING
450 ml/¾ pint double cream
60 g/2 oz castor sugar
icing sugar to sprinkle

In a heavy-based pan gently heat the water with the butter or margarine, salt and lemon rind, until the fat is melted. Bring to the boil then tip in the sifted flour all at once, remove from the heat and beat well until the ingredients form a ball and come away from the sides of the pan. Return to the heat and cook for 1 minute, stirring all the time. Turn the mixture into a bowl, allow to cool slightly then add the eggs a little at a time, beating well with each addition.

Preheat the oven to hot (220°C, 425°F, Gas Mark 7). Pipe the choux paste in different shapes on to a baking tray, leaving sufficient space between each to allow for rising during cooking. Bake for 20 minutes. Do not open the oven door during the first 10 minutes' baking time, or the pastry will collapse.

While the choux puffs are still warm, split through to let any steam escape. Allow to cool. Whip the cream stiffly with the sugar and pipe into each puff. Dust the tops with icing sugar.

Cook's Tip
You can pipe long éclair shapes from the choux paste, then fill these with coffee cream and ice with a coffee icing.

Chocolate Slice

CAKE MIXTURE
130 g/5 oz plain chocolate
130 g/5 oz butter
200 g/7 oz castor sugar
pinch each of salt, ground
cinnamon and grated lemon
rind
6 eggs, separated
130 g/5 oz plain flour
ICING
200 g/7 oz plain chocolate
2 eggs
400 g/14 oz icing sugar
120 g/4 oz coconut oil or butter
3 tablespoons rum

Line a 25 × 35-cm/10 × 14-inch Swiss roll tin with greased greaseproof paper. Preheat the oven to moderate (180°C, 350°F, Gas Mark 4).

Melt the chocolate in a basin over hot water. Cream the butter with half the sugar until light and fluffy. Add the salt, cinnamon and lemon rind, then beat in the egg yolks, one at a time, with the melted chocolate. Whisk the egg whites until stiff and fold in the remaining sugar. Fold into the creamed mixture with the sifted flour. Spread evenly into the Swiss roll tin and bake in the centre of the oven for 20 minutes.

Turn the cake out on to greaseproof paper sprinkled with sugar, remove the greaseproof lining paper and leave to cool for 2 hours. Cut the cake lengthways into two strips.

Grate the chocolate finely and mix with the beaten eggs, sifted icing sugar, melted coconut oil or butter, and rum. Heat gently in a basin over a pan of boiling water, stirring until the chocolate melts and all the ingredients are thoroughly combined. Cool. Use to sandwich the strips of cake together and spread thickly over the top. Cut into slices when the icing is firm.

Nougat Slice

SPONGE MIXTURE
4 eggs, separated, plus 2 egg
yolks
100 g/4 oz castor sugar
80 g/3 oz plain flour
20 g/1 oz cornflour
40 g/1½ oz cocoa powder
FILLING AND ICING
25 g/1 oz cornflour
2 egg yolks
50 g/2 oz castor sugar
300 ml/½ pint milk
250 g/9 oz butter
100 g/4 oz nougat
175 g/6 oz plain chocolate
glacé cherries to decorate

Line a 33 × 23-cm/13 × 9-inch Swiss roll tin with greased greaseproof. Preheat the oven to 220°C, 425°F, Gas Mark 7.

Whisk the egg yolks with half the sugar until pale. Whisk the egg whites until stiff and fold in the remaining sugar. Fold into the egg yolks. Sift the flour, cornflour and cocoa powder and fold in. Spread over the Swiss roll tin and bake for 10–12 minutes. Turn out on to clean greaseproof and peel off the lining paper. Cool then cut lengthways into three strips.

Blend the cornflour with the egg yolks, sugar and a little milk. Heat the remaining milk, stir into the cornflour mixture and return to the heat. Bring to the boil, stirring until thickened. Leave to cool. Cream the butter until pale and soft, then gradually beat in the cornflour sauce. Melt the nougat with 50 g/2 oz of the chocolate in a basin over hot water, then beat into the butter cream a tablespoon at a time. Spread this nougat cream over two of the strips of cake, then place the strips on top of each other and spread a thin layer of nougat cream over the top and sides.

Melt the remaining chocolate and ice the cake. Decorate as illustrated.

From the Cake Tray

Hungarian Chocolate Roll

SPONGE MIXTURE
6 eggs, separated
100 g/4 oz castor sugar
¼ teaspoon vanilla essence
100 g/4 oz plain flour
75 g/3 oz cocoa powder
FILLING
100 g/4 oz raspberry jam
15 g/½ oz cornflour
150 ml/¼ pint milk
50 g/2 oz castor sugar
100 g/4 oz butter
1 tablespoon Kirsch
1 tablespoon drinking chocolate
    powder

Line a 33 × 23-cm/13 × 9-inch Swiss roll tin with greased greaseproof. Preheat the oven to 200°C, 400°F, Gas Mark 6.

Whisk the egg yolks with the sugar and vanilla until pale. Whisk the egg whites until stiff and fold into the yolks. Care-fully fold in the sifted flour and cocoa powder. Pipe the mixture in strips across the width of the tin and bake for 10–12 minutes. Turn the cake out on to a tea towel and remove the lining paper. Cover with a clean piece of greaseproof and roll up with the grease-proof inside. Cool on a wire rack.

Unroll the cake and spread with almost all the jam. Blend the cornflour with a little of the milk and the sugar. Bring the remaining milk to the boil, pour on to the cornflour mix-ture, return to the heat and bring to the boil, stirring con-tinuously until thickened. Leave to cool. Beat the butter until light and fluffy then gradually beat in the cornflour sauce and Kirsch. Reserving 3 table-spoons of this cream, spread the cake with the remainder, roll up from the long side and dredge with sifted chocolate powder. Decorate as illustrated.

Coffee Cream Slice

SPONGE MIXTURE
4 eggs, separated, plus 2 egg
    yolks
100 g/4 oz castor sugar
60 g/2 oz plain flour
20 g/¾ oz cornflour
80 g/3 oz ground almonds
FILLING AND ICING
25 g/1 oz cornflour
50 g/2 oz castor sugar
2 tablespoons instant coffee
    powder
300 ml/½ pint milk
250 g/9 oz butter
2 tablespoons icing sugar
50 g/2 oz coarse biscuit crumbs
10 candied coffee beans

Line a 33 × 23-cm/13 × 9-inch Swiss roll tin with greased greaseproof paper. Preheat the oven to hot (220°C, 425°F, Gas Mark 7).

Whisk all the egg yolks with half the sugar until pale and creamy. Whisk the egg whites until stiff then whisk in the remaining sugar. Fold into the egg yolks. Sift the flour and cornflour on to the eggs, add the ground almonds and care-fully fold in. Spread evenly over the Swiss roll tin and bake for 10–12 minutes. Turn the cake out on to greaseproof paper and remove the lining paper. Leave to cool then cut lengthways into three strips.

Blend the cornflour, sugar and coffee with a little milk. Heat the remaining milk, stir into the cornflour and return to the heat. Bring to the boil, stir-ring until thickened. Cool. Cream the butter with the sifted icing sugar then gradually beat in the coffee sauce. Spread this over two of the strips of cake, then sandwich them all to-gether to make three layers. Cover with the coffee cream and sprinkle with biscuit crumbs. Decorate as illustrated.

From the Cake Tray

Petits Fours à la Ritz

PASTRY
190 g/7 oz plain flour
65 g/2¼ oz castor sugar
1 egg
2 tablespoons water
95 g/3¼ oz butter, cut into flakes
FILLING
4 egg yolks
125 g/4¼ oz castor sugar
pinch of salt
15 g/½ oz cornflour
250 ml/8 fl oz milk
¼ teaspoon vanilla essence
200 g/7 oz butter
80 g/3 oz icing sugar
1 tablespoon cocoa powder
2 tablespoons boiling water
2 teaspoons orange liqueur
1 tablespoon instant coffee powder
2 teaspoons coffee liqueur
2 tablespoons brandy

DECORATION
glacé cherries, chocolate vermicelli, crystallised violets, candied coffee beans

Sift the flour into a mixing bowl. Add the sugar, egg, water and butter, and mix until a dough is formed. Wrap the pastry in foil or cling film and leave for 2 hours in the refrigerator.

Preheat the oven to moderately hot (200°C, 400°F, Gas Mark 6). Roll out the pastry to 3 mm/⅛ inch thick and use to line 24 petits fours tins. Arrange on baking trays and bake blind for 8–10 minutes, until golden brown. Remove the pastry cases from their tins, loosening them carefully with a knife. Place on a wire rack and leave to cool.

Blend the egg yolks, sugar, salt and cornflour with a little of the milk. Heat the rest of the milk with the vanilla essence. Stir into the cornflour mixture, return to the heat and bring to the boil, stirring continuously until smooth and thickened. Allow to cool, stirring frequently. Cream the butter with the sifted icing sugar until pale and fluffy and add a spoonful at a time to the cooled vanilla cream, beating in well.

Divide the cream into three portions. Dissolve the cocoa powder in 1 tablespoon boiling water and mix with the orange liqueur into one portion. Dissolve the coffee powder in 1 tablespoon boiling water and mix with the coffee liqueur into another portion. Mix the brandy into the final portion. Pipe each of these creams into one-third of the petits fours cases, then leave in the refrigerator for 2 hours, for the creams to set.

Decorate the petits fours with glacé cherries, chocolate vermicelli, crystallised violets or candied coffee beans, as illustrated.

Cook's Tip

The petits fours will look especially professional if some are dipped in melted chocolate, then decorated with silver balls, chocolate vermicelli or chopped pistachio nuts, as illustrated.

From the Cake Tray

Classical Petits Fours

SPONGE MIXTURE
5 eggs, separated, plus 1 egg yolk
80 g/3 oz ground almonds
grated rind of 1 lemon
120 g/4½ oz castor sugar
120 g/4½ oz plain flour
FILLING
175 g/6 oz apricot jam
225 g/8 oz almond paste
ICING
225 g/8 oz icing sugar
1–2 tablespoons water
1 tablespoon white rum
red and yellow food colouring
DECORATION
glacé cherries, crystallised violets, chopped pistachios, silver balls

Line two 28 × 18-cm/11 × 7-inch Swiss roll tins with greased greaseproof paper. Preheat the oven to hot (220°C, 425°F, Gas Mark 7).

Beat all the egg yolks with the ground almonds, lemon rind and half the sugar, until creamy. Whisk the egg whites until stiff, then fold in the remaining sugar. Fold into the egg yolk mixture and finally fold in the sifted flour. Spread the sponge mixture evenly over both Swiss roll tins and bake for 10–12 minutes. Remove the cakes from the tins while still warm, turning out on to clean greaseproof paper, and strip off the lining paper.

Spread one cake with apricot jam and place the second cake on top. Cut the cake into three equal strips, spread these with jam too and place on top of each other, to make six layers in all. Knead the almond paste and roll out to the size of the cake. Place on top of the cake,

cover with foil or greaseproof paper, weigh down with a heavy wooden board and leave for 24 hours. At the end of this time cut the cake into 3·5-cm/1½-inch squares or shapes.

For the icing, beat the sifted icing sugar with the water and rum until smooth. The icing should be of a thick flowing consistency. Use to coat the petits fours, colouring some of the icing with food colouring, if liked. Pipe over pretty decorations with the rest of the icing and decorate with glacé cherries, crystallised violets, chopped pistachios or silver balls, according to taste. Allow to dry out on a wire rack for 1–2 hours, and serve in small paper cases.

Cook's Tip

The key to success with these petits fours is to weigh the sponge cake layers down with a heavy board and leave for several hours. Otherwise the sponge will dry out and the petits fours will lose their delicious moistness.

Bath Buns

500 g/1 lb plain flour
30 g/1 oz fresh yeast
185 ml/6 fl oz lukewarm milk
120 g/4 oz butter, melted
2 eggs
80 g/3 oz castor sugar
100 g/4 oz chopped mixed peel
¼ teaspoon salt
½ teaspoon ground aniseed
pinch of ground cinnamon
grated rind of ½ lemon
80 g/3 oz raisins
GLAZE
1 egg yolk, beaten
60 g/2 oz sugar crystals

Sift the flour into a bowl and make a well in the centre. Cream the yeast with a little of the milk, pour into the well in the flour with the remaining milk, sprinkle over a little flour and leave for 15 minutes, until frothy. Add the melted butter, eggs and sugar and beat all together to a dough. Then work in the finely chopped peel, salt, spices, lemon rind and raisins. Cover and leave to rise until doubled in size, up to 1 hour.

Knead the dough on a lightly floured board until smooth. Shape into small buns and place well apart on greased baking trays. Leave to rise in a warm place until doubled in size.

Preheat the oven to moderately hot (200°C, 400°F, Gas Mark 6). Brush the buns with beaten egg yolk, sprinkle with sugar crystals and bake for 15–20 minutes.

Shrewsbury Biscuits

530 g/1¼ lb plain flour
300 g/12 oz castor sugar
2 eggs
pinch each of salt and ground cinnamon
300 g/12 oz butter, cut into flakes

Line two baking trays with greased greaseproof paper.

Sift the flour on to a working surface, make a well in the centre and add the sugar, eggs, salt and cinnamon. Dot the butter over the flour and quickly knead all the ingredients to a smooth dough. Wrap the mixture in foil and leave for 2 hours in the refrigerator.

Preheat the oven to moderate (180°C, 350°F, Gas Mark 4). Roll out the biscuit dough on a floured surface to a thickness of about 3 mm/⅛ inch. Cut out rounds measuring 6–7·5 cm/ 2½–3 inches in diameter. Place on the baking trays and bake for 15–20 minutes.

Allow the biscuits to cool on the trays before removing with a palette knife.

Entertaining

Shortbread Fingers

320 g/11 oz butter
180 g/6 oz castor sugar
¼ teaspoon salt
500 g/1 lb 2 oz plain flour
castor sugar to sprinkle

Cream the butter with the sugar and salt until pale and fluffy. Sift the flour and knead into the creamed ingredients to give a workable dough. Cover and leave for 2 hours in the refrigerator.

Preheat the oven to moderately hot (190°C, 375°F, Gas Mark 5). Roll out the mixture on a floured surface until 1·5 cm/¾ inch thick and place on a greased baking tray. Prick several times with a fork and bake for 25–30 minutes.

Whilst still warm, cut the shortbread into fingers with a sharp knife and sprinkle with castor sugar.

Teacakes

Prepare these using the recipe for Bath Buns (see left), but use 1 teaspoon of sugar to sweeten the mixture instead of 80 g/3 oz. Leave out the aniseed, cinnamon and lemon rind. Instead of using mixed peel and raisins, add 150 g/5 oz currants. Brush the risen teacakes with egg yolk before baking.

Finger Biscuits

4 eggs, separated, plus 2 egg
  yolks
125 g/4½ oz castor sugar
50 g/2 oz cornflour
100 g/4 oz plain flour
icing sugar to sprinkle

Grease non-stick baking trays
or line ordinary baking trays
with non-stick baking parchment and grease well. Preheat
the oven to moderately hot
(200°C, 400°F, Gas Mark 6).

Whisk all the egg yolks with
the sugar until pale and creamy.
Whisk the egg whites until stiff
and carefully fold into the egg
yolk mixture. Finally fold in
the sifted cornflour and flour.

Fill a piping bag fitted with a
large plain nozzle with this
biscuit dough. Pipe 8·5-cm/
3½-inch long fingers on to the
baking trays, allowing space
between each one for the mixture to spread during cooking.

Bake the biscuits for 7–10
minutes, until light golden
brown.

Allow to cool for a few
seconds on the baking trays
then transfer to a wire rack.
Sprinkle with sifted icing sugar
when cooled.

Cook's Tip

Using the same mixture,
you can pipe round
biscuits. When cool join
two together with melted
chocolate and decorate
the top of each pair with
a blob of chocolate.

Almond Macaroons

225 g/8 oz ground almonds
225 g/8 oz castor sugar
4 egg whites

Line one or two baking trays
with rice paper. Preheat the
oven to moderate (160°C,
325°F, Gas Mark 3).

Mix the ground almonds
with the sugar and unbeaten
egg whites, stirring to a smooth
mixture. Fill a piping bag fitted
with a plain nozzle with the
mixture and pipe small rounds
on to the rice paper, leaving
enough room for them to
spread during cooking. Bake
the macaroons for 15–20
minutes.

Leave to cool on the rice
paper, then cut round to trim
off excess paper.

Cook's Tip

These macaroons can
also be made with
ground hazelnuts instead
of almonds; for the best
possible taste use lightly
roasted nuts.

Marzipan Toasts

500 g/1 lb plain flour
30 g/1 oz fresh yeast
250 ml/8 fl oz lukewarm milk
50 g/2 oz butter or margarine
50 g/2 oz castor sugar
¼ teaspoon salt
grated rind of ½ lemon
2 eggs
TOPPING
100 g/4 oz ground almonds
80 g/3 oz icing sugar
1 egg white
1 tablespoon rum

Grease two cylindrical-shaped or Balmoral cake tins, or two 0·5 kg/1-lb loaf tins.

Sift the flour into a bowl and make a well in the centre. Cream the yeast with a little of the milk. Add the remaining milk and pour into the flour. Mix in a little flour, cover and leave in a warm place for 15 minutes, until frothy.

Melt the butter or margarine and mix with the sugar, salt, lemon rind and beaten eggs. Add these to the yeast mixture and work all the ingredients to a dry dough. Knead the dough until smooth and elastic then cover and leave to rise for 15 minutes. Knead again lightly and form into two rolls on a floured surface. Shape these to fit the prepared tins and leave to rise until the loaves have doubled in size.

Preheat the oven to hot (220°C, 425°F, Gas Mark 7) and bake the loaves for 25–35 minutes, until golden brown.

Turn out to cool on a wire rack and leave overnight.

Preheat the grill to the hottest setting. Cut the cooled loaves into thick slices, arrange them on the grill pan and toast on one side. Leave to cool. Meanwhile mix the ground almonds with the sifted icing sugar, egg white and rum, to make a smooth spreading consistency. Spread this mixture on to the untoasted sides of the bread slices and toast until lightly browned.

Cook's Tip

If you are in a hurry, use bought almond paste kneaded with a little rum.

These Marzipan Toasts make a delicious and speedy snack to serve at teatime or with morning coffee.

Turkish Fruit Cake

175 g/6 oz butter
100 g/4 oz castor sugar
1 tablespoon vanilla sugar
grated rind of 1 lemon
4 eggs
1 tablespoon Madeira
175 g/6 oz self-raising flour
50 g/2 oz cornflour
1 teaspoon baking powder
75 g/3 oz raisins
75 g/3 oz glacé cherries, washed
*   and roughly chopped*
100 g/4 oz pickled walnuts,
*   roughly chopped*
¼ teaspoon salt
½ teaspoon ground cinnamon
½ teaspoon ground cardamom
ICING
100 g/4 oz plain chocolate
50 g/2 oz pistachio nuts, chopped

Grease a 1-kg/2-lb loaf tin and
sprinkle with fine breadcrumbs.
Preheat the oven to moderate
(180°C, 350°F, Gas Mark 4).
  Cream the butter, sugar,
vanilla sugar and lemon rind
together until pale and soft.
Stir in the eggs and Madeira.
Sift the flour, cornflour and
baking powder together and
mix in the raisins, cherries,
pickled walnuts, salt, cinnamon
and cardamom. Fold this flour
mixture into the creamed mixture and turn into the prepared
tin. Bake for about 1 hour 5
minutes then turn on to a wire
rack to cool.
  Melt the chocolate in a basin
over a pan of hot water and use
to ice the cake all over.
Decorate with the chopped
pistachios before the icing sets.

Rum Butter Cake

180 g/6 oz butter
200 g/7 oz castor sugar
5 eggs
250 g/9 oz plain flour
80 g/3 oz maize flour
1 teaspoon baking powder
3 tablespoons rum
1 tablespoon lemon juice
1 tablespoon orange juice
grated rind of $\frac{1}{2}$ lemon
grated rind of $\frac{1}{2}$ orange

Grease a 1-kg/2-lb loaf tin and
sprinkle with flour. Preheat the
oven to moderately hot (190°C,
375°F, Gas Mark 5).
  Beat the butter and sugar
until pale and creamy then add
the eggs one at a time. Sift the
flour, maize flour and baking
powder together then carefully
fold into the mixture. Gradually fold in the rum, lemon and
orange juice and grated fruit
rinds. Place the mixture in the
tin, smooth over the top and
bake for 1¼ hours. Cover with
foil if becoming too brown.
  Turn out on to a wire rack
to cool.

Royal Fruit Loaf

50 g/2 oz candied lemon peel
100 g/4 oz blanched almonds
200 g/7 oz raisins
175 g/6 oz self-raising flour
175 g/6 oz butter or margarine
100 g/4 oz castor sugar
4 eggs
50 g/2 oz cornflour
1 teaspoon baking powder
1 tablespoon rum

Grease a 0·5-kg/1-lb loaf tin
and sprinkle with fine breadcrumbs. Preheat the oven to
moderate (180°C, 350°F, Gas
Mark 4).
  Chop the lemon peel and
almonds. Toss the raisins in a
little of the flour. Beat the
butter or margarine with the
sugar until pale and creamy,
then beat in one of the eggs.
Sift the flour, cornflour and
baking powder together and
fold in a little of this between
adding the remaining eggs.
Fold in the rest of the flour.
Add the lemon peel, almonds,
raisins and rum and fold into
the creamed mixture. Place in
the prepared tin, smooth over
the surface and bake for about
1 hour 5 minutes.
  Turn the cake on to a wire
rack to cool.

Teatime Treats

Crumble Puffs

1 (368-g/13-oz) packet frozen
   puff pastry
1 egg yolk
TOPPING
200 g/7 oz plain flour
100 g/3½ oz castor sugar
pinch of ground cinnamon
pinch of salt
150 g/5 oz butter
icing sugar to sprinkle

Allow the pastry to thaw for
1 hour at room temperature.
   Roll out the pastry on a
floured surface and cut into
5-cm/2-inch rounds. Then roll
in one direction only until
about 11·5 cm/4½ inches long
and leaf-shaped. Sprinkle a
baking tray with cold water,
arrange the elongated leaves on
it and brush with beaten egg
yolk. Leave to rest for 15
minutes. Preheat the oven to
moderately hot (200°C, 400°F,
Gas Mark 6).

Mix the sifted flour with the
sugar, cinnamon and salt. Melt
the butter and add to the dry
ingredients drop by drop, stirring continuously with the
blade of a knife. Rub the mixture to a crumble consistency
with the hands. Sprinkle this
over the leaves and bake for
12–15 minutes, until crisp and
brown.
   Leave the cooled crumble
puffs on a wire rack to become
completely cold then sprinkle
with sifted icing sugar.

Chinese Doughnuts

25 g/1 oz butter or margarine
175 g/6 oz castor sugar
1 egg
2 tablespoons water
350 g/12 oz plain flour
1 teaspoon baking powder
75 g/3 oz sesame seeds
oil or fat to deep fry

Mix the butter or margarine
with the sugar, then beat in the
egg and water until light. Sift
the flour with the baking
powder and work into the
mixture. Knead the dough well
and form into a 50-cm/20-inch
long roll. Cut 2·5-cm/1-inch
slices from the roll. Shape these
into small balls, dip them
briefly into cold water then toss
them in the sesame seeds.
   Heat the cooking oil or fat to
182°C/360°F. Cook 6–8
doughnuts at a time, turning
frequently, for about 5 minutes
until golden brown. Remove
from the hot fat with a draining
spoon and drain on absorbent
paper.

Butter Swirls

375 g/13 oz plain flour
250 g/9 oz butter, cut into flakes
125 g/4½ oz castor sugar
6 egg yolks
pinch of salt
grated rind of ¼ lemon
sugar crystals to sprinkle

Sift the flour into a bowl and dot with the butter. Form a well in the centre of the flour and add the sugar, 5 egg yolks, the salt and lemon rind. Knead all the ingredients together to obtain a smooth dough. Place the mixture in a piping bag fitted with a plain nozzle and at equal intervals pipe 'S' shapes on to two greased baking trays. Leave for 1 hour in a cool place.

Preheat the oven to moderately hot (190°C, 375°F, Gas Mark 5). Beat the remaining egg yolk and use to brush the biscuits. While still moist sprinkle with sugar crystals. If any sugar falls on to the baking tray remove with a pastry brush to avoid burning. Bake the biscuits for 8–10 minutes until golden.

Allow the biscuits to cool on the baking trays for about 5 minutes, then remove with a palette knife and leave until completely cool on a wire rack.

Aniseed Chräbeli

250 g/9 oz plain flour
250 g/9 oz castor sugar
2 eggs
1–2 teaspoons ground aniseed
grated rind of ½ lemon

Sift the flour into a bowl. Beat the sugar with the eggs until creamy and mix in the flour with a spoon. Finally add the aniseed and lemon rind. Form the dough into rolls of finger thickness. Cut the rolls into 7·5-cm/3-inch lengths and form each piece into a half-moon shape. Slit the outer edges of the half-moons three times horizontally with a sharp knife. Place on a floured baking tray, cover and leave to stand overnight at room temperature.

Preheat the oven to moderately hot (190°C, 375°F, Gas Mark 5) and bake for 12–15 minutes on the middle shelf. Remove from the baking tray while still warm and cool on a wire rack.

Cook's Tip

Half-moons are the traditional shape for Chräbeli. To save time you can simply cut the rolls into equal thick slices, make slits in these and continue as in the recipe.

Chocolate Almond Bars

250 g/9 oz butter
150 g/5 oz icing sugar
2 eggs
2 tablespoons milk
grated rind of 1 lemon
520 g/1 lb 2 oz plain flour
200 g/7 oz blanched almonds,
  coarsely chopped
TOPPING
100 g/4 oz plain chocolate
200 g/7 oz blanched almonds,
  cut into strips

Beat the butter, sifted icing sugar, eggs, milk and lemon rind together. Sift the flour and knead well into the butter mixture with the chopped almonds, to give a workable dough. Roll out half the dough with your hands, to make a long thin roll, about 2·5 cm/1 inch in width, and then press flat, to give a strip of dough about 3·5 cm/

1½ inches wide. Wrap in foil or cling film and leave for 2 hours in the refrigerator. Similarly roll and chill the remaining portion of dough.

Preheat the oven to moderately hot (200°C, 400°F, Gas Mark 6). Cut the strips of dough into pieces 6 cm/2½ inches long. Place these biscuits on greased baking trays and bake for 15 minutes, until golden brown. Allow to cool slightly before transferring to a wire rack with a palette knife.

Melt the chocolate in a basin over hot water and spread thickly over the biscuits. While the chocolate is still soft, toast the almond strips and sprinkle over. Allow the chocolate to set before storing the biscuits in an airtight container.

Sugar Pretzels

20 g/¾ oz fresh yeast
125 ml/4 fl oz lukewarm milk
80 g/3 oz butter or margarine
1 egg
¼ teaspoon salt
pinch of ground cardamom
320 g/11 oz plain flour
1 egg yolk, beaten to glaze
50 g/2 oz sugar crystals to
  decorate

Lightly grease a baking tray with butter or margarine.

Cream the yeast with the milk. Melt the butter and stir in the beaten egg, salt and cardamom. Sift the flour into a bowl, make a well in the centre and pour in the yeast and the butter mixture. Mix all together to a firm dough. Knead until smooth but do not leave to rise. Preheat the oven to hot (230°C, 450°F, Gas Mark 8).

Roll out the dough on a lightly floured surface to make

a thick long roll. Cut into 24 equal pieces and roll out each piece into a long thin strip, approximately 40 cm/16 inches in length. Form the strips into pretzel shapes, as illustrated. Brush these with beaten egg yolk and press the sugar crystals on to one side to decorate. Place on the tray and bake for 8–10 minutes.

Remove from the baking tray carefully and allow to cool on a wire rack. These pretzels taste best served fresh.

Orange and Nutmeg Biscuits

150 g/5 oz butter
100 g/4 oz castor sugar
pinch of salt
generous pinch of grated nutmeg
grated rind of 1 orange
2 egg yolks
250 g/9 oz plain flour
75 g/3 oz sugar crystals

Beat together the butter, sugar, salt, nutmeg, orange rind and 1 egg yolk, until pale and creamy. Add the sifted flour and knead in thoroughly to give a workable dough. Form the mixture into a roll measuring 4 cm/1¾ inches in diameter. Cover with foil and leave in the refrigerator for 2 hours.

Preheat the oven to moderately hot (200°C, 400°F, Gas Mark 6).

Beat the second egg yolk.

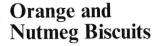

Brush the roll of dough with this and coat it all over with the sugar crystals, pressing in well. Cut into slices about 5 mm/¼ inch thick and lay flat on greased baking trays, leaving a little space between each one. Bake the biscuits for 12–15 minutes, until light brown.

Allow the biscuits to cool for 5 minutes, then carefully remove from the baking trays with a palette knife and cool completely on a wire rack.

Cats' Tongues

250 g/9 oz butter
220 g/8 oz icing sugar
¼ teaspoon vanilla essence
pinch of salt
1 egg plus 1 egg yolk
250 g/9 oz plain flour
ICING
100 g/4 oz nougat
75 g/3 oz plain chocolate

Grease two baking trays and dust with flour. Preheat the oven to moderately hot (200°C, 400°F, Gas Mark 6).

Beat the butter, sifted icing sugar, vanilla essence and salt together until pale and creamy. Beat in the egg and egg yolk separately and finally fold in the sifted flour. Using a piping bag fitted with a plain nozzle, pipe the biscuit mixture on to the trays. Shape into cats' tongues as you pipe (see illustration) and make each one about 7·5 cm/3 inches in

length. Leave enough space between each to allow for spreading during baking. Bake for 8–12 minutes, until golden brown, then transfer to a wire rack and allow to cool.

Melt the nougat with the chocolate in a basin over hot water. Spread this icing over the cats' tongues, pressing pairs lightly together (see illustration). Allow the nougat icing to harden before storing in an airtight tin.

Austrian Marble Cake

250 g/9 oz soft margarine
200 g/7 oz castor sugar
4 eggs
6 tablespoons milk
400 g/14 oz plain flour
100 g/4 oz cornflour
2 teaspoons baking powder
40 g/1½ oz cocoa powder
40 g/1½ oz icing sugar
icing sugar to sprinkle

Grease two small fluted savarin tins, each measuring 18 cm/ 7 inches in diameter, and sprinkle with fine breadcrumbs. Preheat the oven to moderately hot (200°C, 400°F, Gas Mark 6).

Beat the margarine and castor sugar together until pale and creamy. Beat in the eggs one by one, and finally add the milk. Sift the flour with the cornflour and baking powder and carefully fold into the creamed mixture.

Divide the mixture into two equal portions and half-fill the prepared tins with one portion. Mix the remaining portion with the sifted cocoa powder and icing sugar, and divide this also between both tins. Lightly blend the two mixtures in the tins by swirling carefully with a skewer. Place in the oven and bake for 1–1¼ hours.

Allow to cool on a wire rack then dust with sifted icing sugar.

Candied Fruit Loaf

300 g/11 oz plain flour
pinch of salt
30 g/1 oz fresh yeast
6 tablespoons lukewarm milk
400 g/14 oz candied fruit
  (cherries, angelica, pineapple, ginger, finely chopped)
80 g/3 oz soft margarine
50 g/2 oz castor sugar
4 eggs

Grease two 0·5-kg/1-lb loaf tins and sprinkle with flour.

Sift the flour and salt into a bowl. Cream the yeast with a little of the milk then add the remaining milk. Stir the candied fruit into the flour then make a well in the centre and pour in the yeast liquid. Sprinkle over a little flour and leave in a warm place for 15 minutes, until frothy.

Beat the margarine with the sugar and eggs and add to the bowl. Beat all the ingredients well together until bubbles appear. Cover and leave to rise in a warm place for a further 30 minutes. Beat well again and divide between the two tins. Stand in a warm place until the mixture has risen to approximately 1 cm/½ inch below the top of the tin. Preheat the oven to moderately hot (200°C, 400°F, Gas Mark 6).

Bake for 30–35 minutes then turn out to cool on a wire rack.

Fruit Flans

PASTRY
60 g/2 oz soft margarine
45 g/1½ oz icing sugar
few drops of vanilla essence
pinch of salt
1 small egg yolk
125 g/4½ oz plain flour
TOPPING
50 g/2 oz ground almonds
1 tablespoon rum
2 tablespoons sugar syrup
675 g/1½ lb prepared fresh or
*   drained canned fruit*
1 small packet quick-setting jel
*   mix (lemon)*
50 g/2 oz toasted flaked almonds

Knead together the margarine,
sifted icing sugar, vanilla
essence, salt, egg yolk and
sifted flour. Wrap in foil or
cling film and leave for 2 hours
in the refrigerator.

Preheat the oven to moderately hot (200°C, 400°F, Gas
Mark 6). Roll out the pastry on

a floured surface to line the
base of two 15-cm/6-inch flan
tins. Bake blind for 15 minutes
then allow to cool on a wire
rack.

Mix the ground almonds
with the rum and syrup, and
spread over the pastry bases
and sides. Arrange the prepared fruit attractively on top.
Prepare the quick-setting jel
mix, following the instructions
on the packet, and pour over
the fruit. Finally decorate the
sides of the flans with toasted
flaked almonds, pressing them
in well.

Iced Lemon Cake

CAKE MIXTURE
125 g/4½ oz soft margarine
grated rind of 1 lemon
100 g/4 oz castor sugar
2 eggs
3 tablespoons milk
200 g/7 oz self-raising flour
50 g/2 oz cornflour
¼ teaspoon baking powder
SYRUP
2 tablespoons water
juice of 1 lemon
50 g/2 oz sugar
1 tablespoon arrack or ouzo
ICING
100 g/4 oz icing sugar
2 tablespoons lemon juice
strip of lemon peel

Grease a 20-cm/8-inch round
cake tin and sprinkle with fine
breadcrumbs. Preheat the oven
to moderately hot (190°C,
375°F, Gas Mark 5).

Beat together the margarine,
lemon rind and sugar until pale

and creamy. Stir in the eggs
and milk then fold in the sifted
flour, cornflour and baking
powder. Turn into the prepared
cake tin, smooth over the surface, and bake for 40–50
minutes. Turn on to a wire
rack to cool.

Bring the water to the boil
with the lemon juice and sugar.
Add the arrack or ouzo and
pour slowly over the cake,
allowing the syrup to soak well
in.

Mix the sifted icing sugar
with the lemon juice until
smooth and spread thickly on
top of the cake, allowing it to
fall over the sides. Shred the
strip of lemon peel and
sprinkle over the icing before
it sets.

Quiche Lorraine

PASTRY
200 g / 7 oz plain flour
½ teaspoon salt
100 g / 3½ oz butter or margarine,
  cut into flakes
2–3 tablespoons water
FILLING
225 g / 8 oz streaky bacon
4 eggs, separated
250 ml / 8 fl oz single cream
pinch of white pepper
¼ teaspoon salt
125 g / 4½ oz Edam cheese, grated

Grease and flour one loose-bottomed 25-cm/10-inch flan tin or two 18-cm/7-inch tins.

Sift the flour and salt into a mixing bowl and add the butter and water. Knead to a dough. Wrap the pastry in foil or cling film and leave in the refrigerator for 2 hours.

Preheat the oven to moderately hot (200°C, 400°F, Gas Mark 6). Roll out the pastry on a floured surface to about 4 mm/⅛ inch thick and use to line the base and sides of the flan tin. Prick the base of the pastry all over with a fork.

Coarsely chop the bacon rashers and scatter over the pastry base. Whisk the egg yolks with the cream, pepper and salt, and mix in the grated cheese. Whisk the egg whites until stiff and fold into the cheese mixture. Pour into the pastry case, smooth the surface and bake for 30–40 minutes.

When cooked, allow the quiche to cool for a while in the tin, then transfer to a serving plate and cut while still warm. Accompany the quiche with wine – a dry white Alsace is especially good.

Cook's Tip

Bacon, combined with eggs and cream, is the traditional filling for a Quiche Lorraine. Equally delicious quiche fillings include smoked or flaked fresh salmon, mushrooms tossed in a little butter, cooked chopped spinach or drained canned asparagus spears.

Cheese Puffs

1 (368-g/13-oz) packet frozen
   puff pastry
80 g/3 oz Gruyère cheese, grated
2 tablespoons milk
1 egg yolk
80 g/3 oz Emmenthal cheese,
   grated
$\frac{1}{2}$ teaspoon paprika pepper

Allow the puff pastry to thaw, then divide in half.

To make cheese bows, sprinkle some of the Gruyère cheese over the pastry board and roll out one-half of the puff pastry on it, to a thickness of 5 mm/$\frac{1}{4}$ inch. Whisk together the milk and egg yolk and use to brush the surface of the pastry. Sprinkle with more of the Gruyère cheese, fold the pastry up and roll it out again. Sprinkle the rest of the cheese over the surface, fold up and finally roll the pastry out to 3 mm/$\frac{1}{8}$ inch thick. Cut into 7·5-cm/3-inch strips and lay them four strips on top of one another. Cut 5-mm/$\frac{1}{4}$-inch wide slices from these and twist to form bows. Sprinkle a baking tray with cold water, arrange the bows on it and leave to rest for 15 minutes. Preheat the oven to hot (220°C, 425°F, Gas Mark 7), and bake the cheese bows for 8–10 minutes.

Repeat the same process with the second half of the pastry, but this time sprinkle the pastry with the grated Emmenthal and paprika mixed together. Cut into 10-cm/4-inch long narrow strips. Brush these with the rest of the egg yolk glaze and sprinkle with the rest of the cheese. Bake these cheese straws as above.

Cook's Tip

Delicious canapés can be made with a variation of these cheese puffs.
Form the cheese pastry into small oval shapes. When cool, sandwich pairs of these together with beaten and piped cream cheese, softened with a little cream. Sprinkle with poppy seeds or caraway seeds and garnish as illustrated.

Bacon and Mushroom Pasties

1 (368-g/13-oz) packet frozen
puff pastry
1 egg, beaten to glaze
FILLING
100 g/4 oz streaky bacon
1 small onion
175 g/6 oz button mushrooms
2 teaspoons tomato purée
¼ teaspoon celery salt
¼ teaspoon white pepper
25 g/1 oz butter

Allow the pastry to thaw for
1 hour at room temperature.
Preheat the oven to hot (220°C,
425°F, Gas Mark 7).
    Dice the bacon. Peel and
finely chop the onion. Clean
and slice the mushrooms. Fry
the bacon and onion together
until the bacon has rendered its
fat. Add the mushrooms,
tomato purée, celery salt,
pepper and butter, and fry
until the liquid evaporates.
Remove from the heat.
    Roll out the pastry on a
floured surface. Cut into eight
to ten 10-cm/4-inch circles.
Place a spoonful of filling on
one-half of each circle and fold
over the other half to cover,
forming a half-moon shape.
Press the edges together to seal,
using the prongs of a fork for
decorative effect. Brush with
beaten egg and place the pasties
on a dampened baking tray.
    Bake for 15–20 minutes and
serve hot or cold, garnished
with a sprig of parsley.

Savoury Tartlets

2 (212-g/7½-oz) packets frozen
shortcrust pastry
FILLINGS
175 g/6 oz lean minced beef
pinch of salt
pinch of white pepper
1 egg, beaten
pinch of dried mixed herbs
50 g/2 oz mushrooms
50 g/2 oz cheese, diced
50 g/2 oz tongue, diced
50 g/2 oz garlic sausage, diced
¼ cucumber
100 g/4 oz liver sausage
2 tablespoons chopped parsley

Allow the pastry to thaw for
1 hour at room temperature.
    Roll out the pastry on a
floured surface and use to line
twelve 10-cm/4-inch flan tins.
Preheat the oven to moderately
hot (200°C, 400°F, Gas Mark
6).
    Mix the minced beef with the
salt, pepper, egg and herbs, and
fill four of the tins with this
mixture. Chop the mushrooms.
Mix with the cheese, tongue
and garlic sausage and use to
fill four more tins. Grate the
cucumber coarsely. Mix with
the liver sausage and parsley
and use to fill the remaining
tins.
    Place the filled tartlet tins on
a baking tray and cook for 20
minutes. Carefully remove the
tartlets from their tins and
allow to cool on a wire rack.

Spiced Meat Pasties

PASTRY
300 g/11 oz plain flour
30 g/1 oz cornflour
pinch of salt
150 g/5½ oz butter
2–3 tablespoons cold water
FILLING
1 onion
30 g/1 oz butter
2 tablespoons plain flour
6 tablespoons meat stock
4 tablespoons double cream
*pinch each of salt, black pepper,
  sugar, curry powder, ground
  ginger and cayenne pepper*
150 g/5 oz cold roast pork
100 g/4 oz button mushrooms
1 tablespoon chopped parsley
1 egg yolk, beaten to glaze

Sift the flour, cornflour and
salt into a bowl. Rub in the
butter and mix with sufficient
water to form a pastry dough.

Cover and leave for 2 hours in
the refrigerator.

Chop the onion finely and
fry in the butter until light
golden. Stir in the flour, cook
for a few minutes then mix in
the meat stock and cream.
Bring to the boil, stirring continuously, and cook for 1
minute. Add seasoning, sugar
and spices to taste. Chop the
pork and mushrooms finely and
mix with the parsley. Preheat
the oven to moderately hot
(200°C, 400°F, Gas Mark 6).

Roll out the pastry until
3 mm/⅛ inch thick and mark
out circles measuring 10 cm/
4 inches in diameter. Place a
little of the filling on the centre
of each, brush the sides with
water and fold over, pressing
the edges together to seal.
Flute with a fork and brush the
pasties with beaten egg yolk.
Bake for 25–30 minutes and
serve hot.

Gypsy-Style Savouries

*1 (368-g/13-oz) packet frozen
  puff pastry*
FILLING
2 small onions
4 tomatoes
24 small slices salami
75 g/3 oz ham, chopped
freshly ground black pepper
¼ teaspoon paprika pepper
*¼ teaspoon mushroom powder
  (optional)*
*100 g/4 oz Cheddar cheese,
  diced*
3 tablespoons chopped parsley
3 tablespoons olive oil

Allow the frozen pastry to thaw
for 1 hour at room temperature. Rinse 12 tartlet tins in
cold water. Preheat the oven to
moderately hot (200°C, 400°F,
Gas Mark 6).

Roll out the pastry thinly
and use to line the tartlet tins.

Prick the bases all over with a
fork. Slice the onions into
rings and peel and slice the
tomatoes. Remove any rind
from the salami and place the
slices into the pastry cases. Add
the chopped ham and onion
rings, season with the pepper,
paprika and mushroom
powder, and arrange the
tomato slices on top. Dot with
the cheese and parsley and
finally sprinkle with oil.

Bake towards the top of the
oven for 20 minutes and serve
hot.

Piroshki

YEAST DOUGH
500 g/1 lb plain flour
30 g/1 oz fresh yeast
250 ml/8 fl oz lukewarm milk
50 g/2 oz butter, melted
pinch of sugar
¼ teaspoon salt
2 eggs
1 egg yolk, beaten to glaze
FILLING
1 leek, washed and trimmed
1 small onion, peeled
1 tablespoon oil
225 g/8 oz sausagemeat
2 tablespoons fresh white
  breadcrumbs

Sift the flour into a bowl and
form a well in the centre.
Cream the yeast with a little of
the milk. Add the remaining
milk, the butter, sugar, salt and
beaten eggs and pour into the
well in the flour. Sprinkle over
a little of the flour and leave in
a warm place for 15 minutes,
until frothy. Mix all together
to form a dough then knead
until smooth and elastic. Cover
and leave to rise in a warm
place for 1 hour.

Cut the leek into thin slices
and finely chop the onion. Heat
the oil in a pan and fry the leek
and onion for 5 minutes. Mix
with the sausagemeat and
breadcrumbs. Preheat the oven
to moderately hot (200°C,
400°F, Gas Mark 6).

Knead the dough lightly and
roll out to give a rectangle,
52·5 × 40 cm/21 × 16 inches.
Divide the dough lengthways
into seven long pieces measuring 7·5 × 40 cm/3 × 16 inches.
Cut each of these strips into
four identical pieces. Divide the
filling between these pieces of
dough, dampen the edges and
fold the longer side over the
filling to give 28 filled rectangles. Press the edges
together well to seal, brush
with beaten egg yolk and bake
for 30 minutes. Serve hot.

Savoury Choux Puffs

CHOUX PASTE
250 ml/8 fl oz water
60 g/2 oz butter
pinch of salt
190 g/7 oz plain flour
4 eggs
FILLING
100 g/4 oz cream cheese
¼ teaspoon paprika pepper
pinch of celery salt
1 tablespoon chopped chives
3–4 tablespoons milk
GARNISH
stuffed olives, gherkins, walnut
  halves, glacé cherries and red
  pepper strips

Preheat the oven to hot (220°C,
425°F, Gas Mark 7).

Put the water in a small pan
with the butter and a pinch of
salt. Heat gently to melt the
butter then bring to the boil.
Remove the pan from the heat
and add the flour all at once.
Mix with a wooden spoon to
form a paste. Return to the
heat and beat until the mixture
forms a smooth ball. Cool,
then beat in the eggs one at a
time. Pipe or spoon the mixture
in small balls on to a large
greased baking tray. Cook for
about 20 minutes, until well
risen and golden brown.

Remove, cut in half and
leave to cool on a wire rack.
Mix the ingredients together
for the filling and pipe some
into half the cheese puffs. Top
with the remaining puffs and
pipe over the rest of the filling.
Garnish as illustrated.

Crispy Cheese Biscuits

150 g/5 oz butter
180 g/6 oz Gruyère or
Emmenthal cheese, grated
6 tablespoons single cream
¼ teaspoon salt
1 teaspoon paprika pepper
½ teaspoon baking powder
250 g/9 oz plain flour
1 egg yolk, beaten to glaze
TOPPING
poppy seeds, sesame seeds,
caraway seeds, chopped
pistachio nuts, blanched
almonds

Soften the butter with a
wooden spoon. Gradually add
the cheese and beat thoroughly.
Stir in the cream, salt and
paprika. Sift the baking powder
with the flour and stir into the
mixture. Knead lightly to incorporate all the flour and give
a smooth dough. Cut the dough
into two or three pieces, wrap
in kitchen foil or cling film and
leave for 2 hours in the
refrigerator.
    Preheat the oven to moder-
ately hot (200°C, 400°F, Gas
Mark 6). On a floured board
roll out the pieces of dough one
at a time to a thickness of
about 5 mm/¼ inch. Cut into
biscuits of any shape, for
example rings, hearts, half-
moons or stars, and place on
greased baking trays. Brush
with the beaten egg yolk and
while still moist sprinkle with
poppy seeds, sesame seeds,
caraway seeds or chopped
pistachios, or top with a halved
almond. Bake the biscuits for

10–15 minutes.
    While the cheese biscuits are
still hot remove carefully from
the baking trays with a palette
knife and leave until warm on a
wire rack. Serve warm.

Cook's Tip

There is also an Italian
variety of these biscuits
made with Gorgonzola
cheese. Make the biscuits
as in the given recipe and
sprinkle half with sesame
seeds. Bake as above.
Finely grate 75 g/3 oz
Gorgonzola cheese and
mix with 125 g/5 oz
cream cheese, 1 egg yolk,
a pinch of salt and
cayenne pepper, and 1
teaspoon paprika pepper.
Fill a piping bag with the
cream cheese mixture
and with a star nozzle
decorate the remaining
cooked biscuits.

To Serve with Drinks

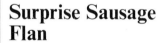

Surprise Sausage Flan

1 (368-g/13-oz) packet frozen
   puff pastry
FILLING
1 onion, sliced
2 tablespoons oil
1 clove garlic, crushed
½ teaspoon salt
¼ teaspoon black pepper
100 g/4 oz minced beef
100 g/4 oz minced pork
2 tablespoons fresh white
   breadcrumbs
few drops of anchovy essence
2 beef or pork sausages
50 g/2 oz garlic sausage, sliced
2 eggs
1 teaspoon dried marjoram
½ teaspoon dried thyme
3 tablespoons milk

Allow the pastry to thaw for
1 hour at room temperature.
Roll out on a floured surface
and use to line a 23-cm/9-inch
flan ring or tin. Preheat the
oven to moderately hot (200°C,
400°F, Gas Mark 6).
   Fry the onion in the oil until
soft. Add the garlic, salt and
pepper and fry for a further 5
minutes. Mix together the
minced beef and pork, the
breadcrumbs, anchovy essence
and the onion mixture. Spread
into the pastry case. Grill or
fry the sausages until well
browned, then slice. Arrange
the sausage and garlic sausage
slices over the minced meat
mixture. Whisk the eggs with
the herbs and milk and pour
over. Bake for 40 minutes and
serve hot.

Savoury Upside-Down Pie

1 (212-g/7½-oz) packet frozen
   puff pastry
TOPPING
675 g/1½ lb minced beef
1 teaspoon salt
½ teaspoon black pepper
1 large onion, chopped
3 egg yolks
100 g/4 oz mushrooms
50 g/2 oz blue cheese
100 g/4 oz streaky bacon rashers
1½ tablespoons each chopped
   sorrel and chervil

Allow the pastry to thaw for
1 hour at room temperature.
   Mix the minced beef with the
salt, pepper and onion; bind
with the egg yolks. Wash and
quarter the mushrooms and
crumble the cheese. Preheat the
oven to moderately hot (200°C,
400°F, Gas Mark 6).
   Cover the base of a 20-cm/

8-inch loose-bottomed cake tin
with the streaky bacon.
Arrange the cheese, herbs and
mushrooms on top. Cover with
the meat mixture, pressing it
down firmly and smoothing the
top.
   Roll out the pastry on a
floured surface to a circle large
enough to cover the filling.
Place over the filling and prick
the pastry with a fork. Bake for
40–50 minutes. Remove from
the oven, invert the tin over a
warm plate or wire rack and
turn out the pie.

Spicy Meat Pie

PASTRY
350 g/12 oz plain flour
150 g/5 oz butter or margarine,
cut into flakes
1 egg yolk
6 tablespoons lukewarm water
1 teaspoon salt
1 egg, beaten to glaze
FILLING
1 bread roll
6 tablespoons hot milk
1 onion
50 g/2 oz streaky bacon
350 g/12 oz minced pork and veal
1 tablespoon chopped parsley
6 tablespoons single cream
pinch each of salt, white pepper,
cayenne pepper, ground
allspice, ground cardamom
and dried basil
¼ teaspoon grated lemon rind

Sift the flour into a mixing bowl and dot with the butter. Form a well in the centre and add the egg yolk, water and salt. Starting at the centre, knead all the ingredients quickly together to form a pastry dough. Wrap in foil or cling film and leave for 2 hours in the refrigerator.

Crumble the bread roll into a basin and spoon the milk over it. Finely chop the onion. Dice the bacon and fry with the onion until golden brown, turning continuously. In a bowl mix the minced meats with the squeezed breadcrumbs, the bacon and onion mixture, parsley, cream, seasoning, spices and lemon rind. The mixture should be highly spiced.

Preheat the oven to hot (220°C, 425°F, Gas Mark 7). Roll out two-thirds of the dough on a floured board to line a 20-cm/8-inch sandwich cake tin, leaving a border of

about 3 mm/⅛ inch above the tin. Prick the pastry base in several places and spread the filling smoothly over it. Roll out the rest of the dough to the size of the tin, place over the filling and seal the edges well. Make a small hole in the centre. Brush the surface with beaten egg and pierce in several places with a skewer. From the remains of the pastry cut out flowers, leaves and stalks, and use to decorate the pie. Brush with beaten egg and bake the pie for about 1 hour. Cover with foil after 45 minutes. Place on a serving dish and serve hot.

Cook's Tip

Try the following variation occasionally. Use only 175 g/6 oz minced veal. Replace the minced pork with 175 g/6 oz finely diced calf's liver, fried lightly with a chopped onion. Add to the filling and continue as above.

Ham and Cheese Horns

1 (368-g/13-oz) packet frozen
*   puff pastry*
1 egg, beaten to glaze
FILLING
75 g/3 oz Gouda cheese
100 g/4 oz ham
1 egg yolk
1 tablespoon finely chopped
*   parsley*
1 tablespoon finely chopped
*   onion*
pinch each of pepper and dried
*   oregano*

Allow the pastry to thaw at room temperature for 1 hour.

On a floured board roll out the pastry into a sheet 58 × 25 cm/23 × 10 inches. Cut into 15 triangles, each with two very long sides (see illustration).

Finely dice the cheese and ham and mix with the egg yolk, parsley, onion, pepper and oregano. Place about 2 teaspoons of the filling towards the bottom of each triangle. Make a small cut in the short side of the triangle (see illustration) and roll the triangles into horn shapes; they should be loosely wrapped.

Sprinkle two baking trays with cold water and place the horns on them. Brush with beaten egg and leave in the refrigerator for 15 minutes. Preheat the oven to moderately hot (200°C, 400°F, Gas Mark 6) and bake the horns towards the top of the oven for 25 minutes. Serve warm.

Cook's Tip

Instead of horn shapes, the pastry may be cut into oblong pieces and used to make small rolls, which can be filled with well-seasoned minced beef instead of cheese and ham.

Cheese and Grape Puffs

2 (212-g/7½-oz) packets frozen
 puff pastry
2 eggs
2 tablespoons water
1 teaspoon paprika pepper
¼ teaspoon black pepper
1 teaspoon ground mixed spice
FILLING
225 g/8 oz Red Windsor or
 Cheddar cheese
100 g/4 oz white grapes
100 g/4 oz continental sausage,
 sliced

Allow the pastry to thaw for
1 hour at room temperature.
Preheat the oven to moderately
hot (200°C, 400°F, Gas Mark
6).

Roll out the pastry on a
floured surface to a rectangle
about 3 mm/⅛ inch thick and
cut into about forty 5-cm/2-
inch squares. Beat the eggs with
the water, paprika, black
pepper and spice, and brush
some of this mixture over the
pastry squares.

Cut the cheese into small
cubes. Halve the grapes and
remove the pips. Cut the
sausage slices into small pieces.
Place a cube of cheese, a grape
and a piece of sausage on each
pastry square. Bring the corners
of the pastry inwards to form
an envelope, and press together
firmly. Cut small rounds from
the pastry trimmings and press
on the envelopes to seal. Brush
with the remaining egg mixture.

Place on a baking tray
sprinkled with cold water and
bake in the oven for 15 minutes,
or until lightly browned. Serve
warm.

Surprise Tartlets

1 (368-g/13-oz) packet frozen
 puff pastry
FILLING
125 g/4 oz minced steak
¼ teaspoon salt
¼ teaspoon white pepper
1 egg
50 g/2 oz button mushrooms,
 finely chopped
50 g/2 oz Cheddar cheese, grated
50 g/2 oz liver sausage
50 g/2 oz German sausage, diced
3 tablespoons chopped parsley
75 g/3 oz walnuts, finely chopped

Allow the pastry to thaw for
1 hour at room temperature.

Sprinkle 12 small boat-
shaped and 18 round patty tins
with cold water. Preheat the
oven to moderately hot (200°C,
400°F, Gas Mark 6). Roll the
pastry out thinly and cut out to
line the patty tins. Prick the
pastry cases with a fork.

Mix the steak thoroughly
with a little salt and pepper and
the egg. Mix the mushrooms
with the cheese and liver
sausage and season lightly. Mix
the German sausage with the
parsley and walnuts and season
lightly. Use these mixtures to
fill the patty cases.

Bake the tartlets for 20
minutes and serve hot. Garnish
with tiny parsley sprigs, if
wished.

Savoury Snacks

Chicken Pasties

PASTRY
250 g/9 oz plain flour
125 g/4½ oz butter
1 small egg
pinch of salt
2–3 tablespoons water
1 egg yolk, beaten to glaze
FILLING
2 soft bread rolls
about 250 ml/8 fl oz milk
50 g/2 oz ground almonds
1 egg plus 1 egg yolk
50 g/2 oz minced chicken
pinch each of salt, white pepper,
nutmeg and cayenne pepper

Knead the sifted flour with the
butter, egg, salt and water.
Cover the pastry and leave for
2 hours in the refrigerator.
Crumble and soften the
bread in the milk. Mix the
almonds with the egg, egg yolk,
minced chicken, seasoning and
spices. Squeeze the bread rolls
and add to the mixture with

enough of the milk to give a
soft but not runny consistency.
Preheat the oven to hot (220°C,
425°F, Gas Mark 7).
Roll out the pastry to a
thickness of 3 mm/⅛ inch. Cut
out six to eight circles measuring 10 cm/4 inches in diameter
and six to eight circles measuring 6 cm/2½ inches in diameter.
Make a hole the size of a
thimble in the centre of the
smaller circles. Line patty tins
with the larger circles and
divide the chicken mixture
between them. Brush the edges
of the smaller circles with
beaten egg yolk and place over
the filling, sealing well to the
edges. Brush the tops with egg
yolk and decorate with the leftover pastry. Bake for 20–30
minutes and serve hot.

Emmenthal Tartlets

PASTRY
250 g/9 oz plain flour
125 g/4½ oz butter, cut into
flakes
1 small egg
pinch of salt
2–3 tablespoons water
FILLING
350 g/12 oz Emmenthal cheese,
finely grated
175 ml/6 fl oz milk or cream
2 eggs
generous pinch each of white
pepper and grated nutmeg

Sift the flour into a mixing
bowl. Add the butter, egg, salt
and water, and knead to a soft
pastry dough. Wrap in foil or
cling film and leave for 2 hours
in the refrigerator.
Preheat the oven to moderately hot (200°C, 400°F, Gas
Mark 6). Stir the cheese into

the milk or cream with the
beaten eggs and spices. Roll
out the dough on a floured
surface to a thickness of about
3 mm/⅛ inch. Cut out 16 circles,
10 cm/4 inches in diameter, and
use to line 16 patty tins. Press
down the edges well. Fill the
pastry cases to the brim with
the cheese mixture and smooth
the surface. Bake for 25–30
minutes in the centre of the
oven. These tartlets taste most
delicious served hot.

Cook's Tip

For an alternative filling,
use a mixture of 175 g/
6 oz grated cheese and
175 g/6 oz very finely
chopped ham.

Ham Pasties

1 (368-g/13-oz) packet frozen
  puff pastry
4–5 slices Parma ham
1 egg yolk, beaten to glaze

Allow the pastry to thaw at
room temperature for 1 hour.
  Roll out the pastry thinly on
a floured surface and cut into
eight to ten oblongs, measuring
5 × 10 cm/2 × 4 inches. Cut
each slice of ham in half lengthways and roll up. Place a rolled
slice of ham on each piece of
pastry. Brush the edges with
beaten egg yolk, fold over and
press together well. Brush the
surface of the pasties with egg
yolk. Cut very narrow strips of
pastry from the leftover trimmings and place in a cross on
the pasties. Brush with egg
yolk. Preheat the oven to hot
(220°C, 425°F, Gas Mark 7).
  Sprinkle a baking tray with
cold water, place the pasties on

it and leave in the refrigerator
for 15 minutes. Bake near the
top of the oven for 15–20
minutes and serve hot.

Cook's Tip
Instead of rolling the
ham, it can be finely
chopped.

Rich Game
Pasties

1 (368-g/13-oz) packet frozen
  puff pastry
1 egg yolk
1 tablespoon milk
FILLING
350 g/12 oz lean venison or
  pheasant
100 g/4 oz butter
100 g/4 oz mushrooms
juice of 2 oranges
¼ teaspoon dried marjoram
¼ teaspoon pepper
½ teaspoon salt
3 tablespoons brandy
4 tablespoons double cream
3 tablespoons chopped parsley

Allow the pastry to thaw at
room temperature for 1 hour.
  Mince the venison or
pheasant and brown in the
butter, stirring continuously.
Wash the mushrooms and chop
them. Add to the meat with the

orange juice, marjoram, pepper
and salt. Leave to cook until
most of the liquid has evaporated. Pour the brandy over the
mixture, heat slightly, flame
and allow to burn out. Leave
the filling to cool then stir in
the double cream and parsley.
  Roll out the pastry to 3 mm/
⅛ inch thick and cut into 12
equal squares. Divide the filling
between the squares, moisten
the edges of the pastry with a
little water and fold over to
enclose the filling. Press down
well to seal. Beat the egg yolk
with the milk and brush the
pasties with this mixture. Place
on a baking tray sprinkled with
cold water and leave in the
refrigerator for 15 minutes.
Preheat the oven to moderately
hot (200°C, 400°F, Gas Mark
6) and bake the pasties towards
the top of the oven for 20–25
minutes. Serve hot.

Pizzas

Bacon Pizza

PIZZA DOUGH
30 g/1 oz fresh yeast
250 ml/8 fl oz lukewarm milk
500 g/1 lb plain flour
pinch of sugar
60 g/2 oz butter
1 egg
½ teaspoon salt
TOPPING
500 g/1 lb streaky bacon
1 tablespoon caraway seeds
  (optional)

Lightly grease two 24-cm/9½-inch flan tins. Cream the yeast with a little of the lukewarm milk. Gradually add all the milk. Sift the flour into a bowl, make a well in the centre and pour in the yeast liquid and sugar. Sprinkle a little of the flour over the liquid and leave to stand in a warm place for 15 minutes, until frothy.

Melt the butter, stir the beaten egg and salt into it then add to the yeast liquid. Gradually mix in all the flour and knead the dough until it is smooth and springy (about 5–10 minutes). Cover and leave to stand in a warm place for 30 minutes.

Cut the bacon into small pieces. Lightly knead the dough then roll out on a floured board and line the flan tins. Spread the bacon pieces over the dough and brush the edges of the pizza with a little oil. Sprinkle with caraway seeds and leave to stand in a warm place for 15 minutes. Preheat the oven to hot (220°C, 425°F, Gas Mark 7). Bake for 25 minutes and serve hot.

Alternatively the dough may be rolled out to line one large baking tray.

Onion Pizza

PIZZA DOUGH
20 g/¾ oz fresh yeast
125 ml/4 fl oz lukewarm milk
300 g/11 oz plain flour
80 g/3 oz butter
1 teaspoon salt
TOPPING
25 g/1 oz butter
100 g/4 oz streaky bacon,
  chopped
1·5 kg/3 lb onions, thinly sliced
150 ml/¼ pint soured cream
2 eggs
pinch of salt
1 tablespoon caraway seeds
  (optional)

Grease a 31-cm/12½-inch square baking tray.

Cream the yeast with a little of the milk. Gradually add the remaining milk. Sift the flour into a bowl and make a well in the centre. Pour the yeast liquid into it and sprinkle with a little of the flour. Cover and leave to stand in a warm place for 15 minutes, until frothy.

Melt the butter and add to the yeast mixture with the salt, then stir in all the flour. Knead the dough until it is smooth and springy (5–10 minutes). Leave the yeast dough to stand in a warm place for 15 minutes. Preheat the oven to moderately hot (200°C, 400°F, Gas Mark 6).

Melt the butter in a frying pan, add the bacon and cook until lightly browned. Add the onion and cook until soft. Roll out the dough on a floured board and line the baking tray. Turn the edges of the dough up to form a rim. Beat the cream with the eggs, salt and caraway seeds. Mix in the onion and bacon and spread the mixture over the pizza dough. Leave to stand in a warm place for a further 15 minutes, then bake for 45 minutes.

Serve hot if possible.

Puff Pastry Pizzas

1 (368-g/13-oz) packet frozen
  puff pastry
TOPPING
1 small onion
1 clove garlic
1 tablespoon oil
1 (425-g/15-oz) can tomatoes,
  drained
1 teaspoon salt
½ teaspoon black pepper
1 tablespoon chopped herbs
200 g/7 oz Emmenthal cheese,
  grated
GARNISH
salami slices, stuffed olives,
  capers and chopped herbs
or mussels, paprika pepper,
  stuffed olives, mushrooms,
  onion rings and freshly
  ground black pepper
or strips of red pepper, black
  olives, cocktail onions and
  anchovy fillets

Allow the pastry to thaw at
room temperature for 1 hour.
  Finely chop the onion and
garlic and cook until soft in the
oil. Cut up the tomatoes and
stir into the onion mixture with
the salt and pepper. Simmer
gently in a covered pan for 15
minutes and finally stir in the
herbs.
  Roll out the pastry and cut
into 10-cm/4-inch squares.
Sprinkle a baking tray with
cold water and place the pastry
squares on it. Top each square
with the tomato mixture and
add the garnishing ingredients
according to taste. Sprinkle
thickly with cheese and leave to
stand for 15 minutes.
  Preheat the oven to hot
(220°C, 425°F, Gas Mark 7)
and bake the squares near the
top of the oven for 15–18
minutes. Serve straight from
the oven.

Pizzas

Seafood Pizza

1 (368-g/13-oz) packet frozen
  puff pastry
FILLING
1 (56-g/2-oz) can anchovy
  fillets
2 tablespoons milk
2 tablespoons oil
3 tablespoons tomato purée
100 g/4 oz stoned green olives
500 g/1 lb tomatoes
1 (99-g/3½-oz) can tuna
1 small onion, thinly sliced
2 tablespoons capers
1 (85-g/3-oz) can dressed crab
50 g/2 oz peeled prawns
pinch each of garlic salt and
  dried oregano

Allow the pastry to thaw at
room temperature for 1 hour.
Soak the drained anchovies in
the milk to remove excess
saltiness.

Preheat the oven to moderately hot (200°C, 400°F, Gas
Mark 6). On a floured surface
roll out the pastry to line a
25-cm/10-inch flan tin which
has been sprinkled with cold
water.

Stir 1 tablespoon of the oil
into the tomato purée. Use the
rest of the oil to brush the
pastry case. Slice the olives.
Peel and slice the tomatoes.
Cover the pastry base with the
tomato purée then add the
sliced tomatoes and olives.
Flake the tuna and spread over
the tomatoes together with the
sliced onion, drained anchovies,
capers, crabmeat and prawns.
Sprinkle the pizza with garlic
salt and oregano and bake
near the top of the oven for
35 minutes. Serve hot.

Note To peel tomatoes
successfully, place in a bowl
and pour over boiling water to
cover. Leave for about 1
minute then transfer to a bowl
of cold water. The skins should
then slip off easily.

Cook's Tip

In many places along the
Italian coast, Seafood
Pizza is filled with the
following ingredients:
225 g/8 oz smoked fish,
cut into pieces, 350 g/
12 oz peeled, diced
tomatoes, 100 g/4 oz
diced streaky bacon,
100 g/4 oz cubed cheese
and a finely chopped
onion. Beat 1 egg with 2
tablespoons olive oil,
½ teaspoon salt, a gener-
ous pinch of garlic salt
and 1 teaspoon paprika
pepper, and pour over
the filling. Bake as above.

Sicilian Sfincione

PIZZA DOUGH
500 g/1 lb plain flour
¼ teaspoon salt
30 g/1 oz fresh yeast
300 ml/½ pint lukewarm milk
1 egg
TOPPING
1 kg/2 lb tomatoes
2 cloves garlic, crushed
2 small onions, chopped
1 teaspoon salt
3 tablespoons olive oil
75 g/3 oz black olives, stoned
  and chopped
2 teaspoons dried oregano
100 g/4 oz Caciocavallo or
  Parmesan cheese

First prepare the topping. Peel and chop the tomatoes and place in a bowl. Add the garlic, onions, salt and olive oil to the tomatoes. Cover and leave to stand; the longer it stands the tastier will be the topping.

Sift the flour and salt into a bowl and make a well in the centre. Cream the yeast with a little of the milk then add the remainder. Pour the yeast liquid into the bowl, stir a little of the flour into it and leave until frothy. Add the egg and stir it into the yeast liquid. Gradually stir in all the flour. Knead the mixture to a smooth springy dough (5–10 minutes). Leave the dough to stand for about 25 minutes.

Grease two baking trays with oil. Preheat the oven to hot (220°C, 425°F, Gas Mark 7). Lightly knead the dough and divide into four to six pieces. Roll the pieces out into individual rounds and place on the baking trays. Top each round with the tomato mixture. Sprinkle the olives over the pizza with the oregano. Crumble or grate the cheese over all the ingredients and bake near the top of the oven for about 20 minutes. If liked, sprinkle with olive oil on removal from the oven.

Baking Tray Sfincione

The yeast dough should be rolled to the size of a large baking tray, approximately 33 cm/13 inches square. Prick the dough several times with a fork to avoid bubbling during baking. Prepare the tomato topping as in the previous recipe and spread over the dough. Sprinkle the surface with fresh, roughly chopped peppermint leaves and a teaspoon of chopped basil, if available. Use twice the quantity of black olives and sprinkle with 175 g/6 oz Mozzarella cheese. Bake the sfincione for 20–25 minutes in a hot oven (220°C, 425°F, Gas Mark 7).

Although sfincione are certainly similar to the Neapolitan pizza, it would be unforgivable to call this Sicilian speciality a pizza. Sfincione were originally made from local products and the Sicilians maintain that they were baking them before anyone in Italy had thought of making a pizza. Sfincione are typical of the baking of peasants and farm workers. Naturally the toppings and herbs can vary, but the basic ingredients always remain the same. Sometimes sfincione are simply sprinkled with oregano, sometimes with basil too; they may be baked in small round cakes or as one cake on a baking tray.

Pizzas

Anchovy Pizza

PIZZA DOUGH
225 g/8 oz plain flour
¼ teaspoon salt
15 g/½ oz fresh yeast
½ teaspoon sugar
150 ml/¼ pint lukewarm milk
2 tablespoons olive oil
TOPPING
8 ripe tomatoes
100 g/4 oz Gruyère cheese slices
2 (56-g/2-oz) cans anchovy
  fillets
1¼ teaspoons dried oregano
2 tablespoons olive oil

Sift the flour and salt into a bowl and make a well in the centre. Cream the yeast with the sugar, milk and a little of the flour. Pour into the well in the flour, sprinkle with flour then cover and leave in a warm place for 15 minutes, until frothy.

Gradually work in the rest of the flour with the olive oil and knead the dough for 5–10 minutes. Roll out two 18-cm/7-inch rounds of dough and place on a greased baking tray. Preheat the oven to moderate (180°C, 350°F, Gas Mark 4).

Peel and halve the tomatoes and place cut sides down on the pizza bases. Cut the cheese slices into squares and place between the tomato halves with the anchovy fillets. Sprinkle with the oregano and oil and leave for 15 minutes. Bake near the top of the oven for 40 minutes and serve hot.

Mushroom Pizza

PIZZA DOUGH
225 g/8 oz plain flour
¼ teaspoon salt
15 g/½ oz fresh yeast
½ teaspoon sugar
150 ml/¼ pint lukewarm milk
2 tablespoons olive oil
TOPPING
8 ripe tomatoes
225 g/8 oz button mushrooms
50 g/2 oz Gruyère cheese slices
2 tablespoons chopped parsley
2 tablespoons olive oil

Sift the flour and salt into a bowl and make a well in the centre. Cream the yeast with the sugar, milk and a little of the flour. Pour into the well in the flour, sprinkle with flour then cover and leave in a warm place for 15 minutes, until frothy.

Gradually work in the rest of the flour with the olive oil and knead the dough for 5–10 minutes. Roll out two 18-cm/7-inch rounds of dough and place on a greased baking tray. Preheat the oven to moderate (180°C, 350°F, Gas Mark 4).

Peel and slice the tomatoes. Cover the pizza bases with tomato slices, arrange the sliced mushrooms between them and cover with the sliced cheese. Sprinkle with the parsley and oil and leave for a further 15 minutes. Bake near the top of the oven for 40 minutes and serve hot.

Salami Pizza

PIZZA DOUGH
225 g/8 oz plain flour
¼ teaspoon salt
15 g/½ oz fresh yeast
¼ teaspoon sugar
150 ml/¼ pint lukewarm milk
2 tablespoons olive oil
TOPPING
6 ripe tomatoes
6 small red chilli peppers
(optional)
50 g/2 oz Gruyère cheese slices
225 g/8 oz salami, sliced
2 tablespoons olive oil
1 teaspoon dried basil
freshly ground black pepper

Grease two 15-cm/6-inch sandwich tins with oil.

Sift the flour and salt into a
bowl and make a well in the
centre. Cream the yeast with
the sugar, milk and a little of
the flour. Pour into the well in
the flour, sprinkle with flour
then cover and leave in a warm

place for 15 minutes, until
frothy.

Gradually work in the rest of
the flour with the olive oil and
knead for 5–10 minutes. Divide
the dough in half and roll out
to fit the sandwich tins. Preheat
the oven to moderate (180°C,
350°F, Gas Mark 4).

Peel and halve the tomatoes
and arrange on the pizza bases
with the cut sides uppermost.
Cut the stalks off the chilli
peppers, halve lengthways and
remove seeds. Cut the cheese
into 1-cm/½-inch wide strips.
Arrange the chillis, strips of
cheese and slices of salami
between and over the tomatoes.
Sprinkle with the oil, basil and
freshly ground black pepper.
Leave the pizzas for a further
15 minutes. Bake near the top
of the oven for 40 minutes and
serve hot.

Note The red chilli peppers
may be too hot for some tastes.

Neapolitan Pizza

PIZZA DOUGH
225 g/8 oz plain flour
¼ teaspoon salt
15 g/½ oz fresh yeast
¼ teaspoon sugar
150 ml/¼ pint lukewarm milk
2 tablespoons olive oil
TOPPING
4 tomatoes
1 teaspoon celery salt
1 teaspoon black pepper
2 teaspoons dried oregano
100 g/4 oz Mozzarella cheese
2 onions, chopped
10 anchovy fillets
1 tablespoon capers
2 tablespoons olive oil

Sift the flour and salt into a
bowl and make a well in the
centre. Cream the yeast with
the sugar, milk and a little of
the flour. Pour into the well,
sprinkle with flour then cover
and leave in a warm place
for 15 minutes, until frothy.

Gradually work in the rest of
the flour with the olive oil and
knead the dough for 5–10
minutes. Roll out thinly into
two 18-cm/7-inch rounds.
Place on a greased baking tray
and turn up the edges slightly.
Preheat the oven to moderate
(180°C, 350°F, Gas Mark 4).

Peel and slice the tomatoes
and place on the pizzas. Add
the celery salt, pepper, oregano
and slices of cheese. Scatter
over the onions, anchovies and
capers. Sprinkle with the oil
and leave the pizzas for 15
minutes. Bake near the top of
the oven for 40 minutes and
serve hot.

Spicy Flans

Mushroom and Cheese Flan

PASTRY
250 g/9 oz plain flour
125 g/4½ oz butter or margarine,
   cut into flakes
¼ teaspoon salt
2–3 tablespoons water
1 egg yolk
FILLING
1 leek
150 g/5 oz ham
225 g/8 oz button mushrooms
100 g/4 oz Camembert cheese
10 stuffed green olives
2 tablespoons oil
20 g/¾ oz butter
20 g/¾ oz plain flour
300 ml/½ pint milk
2 tablespoons chopped mixed
   herbs
¼ teaspoon each salt and pepper
1 egg yolk

Place the sifted flour in a mixing bowl with the butter or margarine, salt, water and egg yolk, and mix until a pastry dough is formed. Cover and leave for 2 hours in the refrigerator.

Trim and wash the leek. Dice the ham, leek, mushrooms and Camembert and slice the olives. Heat the oil and brown the diced ham. Add the leek and mushrooms and simmer for a further 10 minutes.

Melt the butter, cook the flour lightly in it, pour in the milk and bring to the boil, stirring continuously. Stir the herbs, seasoning, beaten egg yolk and diced Camembert into this sauce. Preheat the oven to hot (220°C, 425°F, Gas Mark 7).

Roll out the pastry to line a 25-cm/10-inch flan tin. Spread the mushroom filling over the base, pour on the sauce and sprinkle with the olives. Bake for 40–50 minutes and serve hot.

Country Leek Flan

PASTRY
200 g/7 oz plain flour
pinch of salt
1 egg
1–2 tablespoons water
100 g/3½ oz butter or margarine,
   cut into flakes
FILLING
450 g/1 lb leeks
175 g/6 oz streaky bacon
1 tablespoon oil
salt and freshly ground black
   pepper
pinch of curry powder
225 g/8 oz pork breakfast
   sausage, sliced
2 eggs
250 ml/8 fl oz soured cream

Place the sifted flour in a mixing bowl with the salt, egg, water and butter, and mix until a pastry dough is formed. Cover and leave for 2 hours in the refrigerator.

Trim, wash and slice the leeks. Dice the bacon and brown in the oil. Add the leeks, sprinkle with a pinch of salt, pepper and curry powder and cook gently for 10 minutes. Preheat the oven to moderately hot (200°C, 400°F, Gas Mark 6).

Roll out the pastry to line a 23-cm/9-inch flan tin. Prick the base several times with a fork. Remove the rind from the breakfast sausage and lay the slices over the pastry base. Spread with the leek filling. Beat the eggs with the soured cream and seasoning to taste and pour over the filling. Bake for 50–60 minutes and serve hot from the tin.

Piquant Cheese Flan

1 (368-g/13-oz) packet frozen
  puff pastry
FILLING
150 g/5 oz ham
450 g/1 lb cream cheese
1 tablespoon tomato purée
1 tablespoon paprika pepper
pinch each of salt, white pepper
  and sugar
few drops of Worcestershire
  sauce
1 small clove garlic
3 tablespoons chopped mixed
  herbs
12 small red chilli peppers
  (optional)
12 capers

Allow the puff pastry to thaw
for 1 hour at room temperature. Divide in half and roll out
each half into a 20-cm/8-inch
round. Sprinkle a baking tray
with cold water, place the
pastry rounds on it, prick
lightly with a fork and leave to
stand for 15 minutes.

Preheat the oven to hot
(220°C, 425°F, Gas Mark 7)
and bake the pastry near the
top of the oven for 10–15
minutes.

Finely chop the ham and mix
with half the cream cheese, the
tomato purée and paprika.
Season with salt, pepper, sugar
and Worcestershire sauce.
Crush the garlic and mix with
150 g/5 oz cream cheese, the
herbs and a little seasoning.
Beat the rest of the cream
cheese to soften it for piping.
Cover one pastry base with the
tomato, ham and cream cheese
mixture, place the second round
of pastry on top and cover with
the cream cheese containing the
herbs. Mark into twelve using
the blade of a knife. Decorate
the top with swirls of piped
cream cheese, topped with the
red chillis and capers.

Prawn and Artichoke Flan

1 (212-g/7½-oz) packet frozen
  puff pastry
TOPPING
100 g/4 oz frozen prawns
1 (200-g/7-oz) can artichoke
  hearts, drained
20 stuffed green olives
½ (184-g/6½-oz) can pimientos
1 (300-ml/½-pint) packet aspic
mayonnaise
2 tablespoons wholemeal
  breadcrumbs
2 eggs, hard-boiled
2 tablespoons caviar or lumpfish
  roe

Allow the pastry and the
prawns to thaw for 1 hour at
room temperature.

Preheat the oven to hot
(220°C, 425°F, Gas Mark 7).
Roll the pastry out to line the
base of a 25-cm/10-inch flan
ring and leave in the refrigerator for 15 minutes. Prick the
pastry all over with a fork and
bake towards the top of the
oven for 15 minutes. Leave to
cool.

Quarter the artichoke hearts,
slice the olives and cut the
pimientos into strips. Arrange
these ingredients over the
pastry base with the prawns.
Make up the aspic according to
the instructions on the packet.
When on the point of setting
pour over the flan and leave to
set. Remove the flan ring,
spread the sides with a little
mayonnaise and sprinkle with
the breadcrumbs. Garnish with
swirls of mayonnaise, quartered
eggs and caviar.

Chocolate Hedgehogs

SHORTBREAD BASE
100 g/3½ oz butter, cut into flakes
60 g/2 oz castor sugar
pinch of salt
160 g/5½ oz plain flour
TOPPING
1 (600-ml/1-pint) packet vanilla blancmange powder
450 ml/¾ pint milk
2 egg yolks
100 g/4 oz sugar
40 g/1½ oz cocoa powder
5 tablespoons boiling water
250 g/9 oz butter
1 sponge or sandwich cake (see page 228; use half quantities)
6 tablespoons water
DECORATION
100 g/4 oz blanched almonds, cut into quarters lengthways
350 g/12 oz plain chocolate

Knead the butter, sugar, salt and sifted flour together to give a firm, smooth dough. Wrap in foil or cling film and leave for 2 hours in the refrigerator.

Cut a cardboard pattern in the shape of a pointed oval, 8–9 cm/3½ inches long. Preheat the oven to moderately hot (200°C, 400°F, Gas Mark 6).

Roll out the shortbread to 5 mm/¼ inch thick and, using the cardboard pattern, cut out hedgehog-shaped pieces. Arrange on greased baking trays and bake for 10–12 minutes. Leave to cool on the baking trays for a minute then remove to a wire rack to cool completely.

Mix the blancmange powder to a smooth cream with 3 tablespoons milk and whisk in the egg yolks. Bring the rest of the milk to the boil with half the sugar. Pour into the blended blancmange powder, stir well and return to the saucepan. Bring to the boil, stirring con-tinuously, and cook for 1 minute until thick and smooth. Leave to cool, stirring occa-sionally to prevent a skin forming. Reserve 3 tablespoons of the blancmange to make the hedgehog eyes and noses. Cream the cocoa powder with the boiling water and beat into the blancmange. Cream the butter until soft and light. When the blancmange is cool, gradually beat the butter into it until smooth.

Cut the sponge or sandwich cake into 1-cm/½-inch cubes and place in a bowl. Dissolve the remaining sugar in the water and bring to the boil. Pour over the cake cubes, cover and leave for 30 minutes. Mix the cake cubes carefully into the chocolate mixture and chill in the refrigerator for 1 hour. When firm, pile this chocolate mixture on the shortbread bases to form a hedgehog shape, and smooth over with a knife. Stick the almond quar-ters into the hedgehogs all over but leave the heads as they are. Place the hedgehogs in the refrigerator for 1 hour to become firm.

Melt the chocolate in a basin over a pan of hot water. Stand the hedgehogs on greaseproof paper and coat them com-pletely with the chocolate. Make noses and eyes from the reserved blancmange, as illustrated.

Celebration Cakes

Marzipan Figures

1 kg/2 lb almond paste
COLOURING AND DECORATION
red and yellow food colouring
1 tablespoon cocoa powder
2 teaspoons boiling water
blanched halved almonds
50 g/2 oz icing sugar
1 egg white
100 g/4 oz plain chocolate

Knead the almond paste on a
surface sprinkled with a little
icing sugar, then divide into
four pieces of equal size. Leave
one quarter of the almond
paste as it is, colour one quarter with red food colouring and
another quarter with yellow
food colouring. Blend the
cocoa powder with the boiling
water then knead into the last
quarter. Wrap the marzipan in
cling film or foil until you are
ready to use it, to avoid drying
out.

Cut pieces of 75–150 g/3–
5 oz from the various coloured
marzipan pieces. Taking the
illustration as a guide, form
animals or figures from the
marzipan as you like. For the
piglet add feet and ears of
almond halves. The separate
parts of the figures should stick
together, but if not then use
cocktail sticks, making sure
they are removed before the
figures are eaten.

Sift the icing sugar and mix
with the lightly whisked egg
white. Melt the chocolate in a
basin over a pan of hot water.
Make two small piping bags
from greaseproof paper and cut
a tiny hole in the corners. Fill
with the two icings and use to
draw the faces, as illustrated.

Cook's Tip

When you wish to
decorate only one cake
with marzipan figures,
you can quarter or halve
the suggested quantities.
The colour of the almond
paste will vary depending
on the brand or whether
it is homemade. White
almond paste is made
with egg whites instead
of yolks.

Birthday Car

*1 (326-g/11¼-oz) packet lemon
  sponge cake mix*
175 g/6 oz raspberry jam
ICING AND DECORATION
100 g/4 oz icing sugar
1–2 tablespoons boiling water
1–2 teaspoons cocoa powder
Smarties and silver balls

Line the base of a 33 × 23-cm/
13 × 9-inch Swiss roll tin with
greased greaseproof paper. Preheat the oven to moderately
hot (200°C, 400°F, Gas Mark
6).

Prepare the cake mix according to the instructions on the
packet. Spread evenly over the
Swiss roll tin and bake for 15–
20 minutes. Turn out on to a
wire cooling rack, remove the
greaseproof paper and leave to
cool.

Cut the cake in half widthways and place the two halves
together. Using a cardboard

pattern, cut out the shape of a
car from the cake, cutting
through both cake layers. Cut
windows in one of the layers
and sandwich the cake layers
together with jam. Cut out two
extra wheels from the cake
trimmings and sandwich on to
the car wheels using jam.

Stir the sifted icing sugar
with the water until smooth.
Cover the car with white icing
then stir 1–2 teaspoons sifted
cocoa powder into the re-
mainder. Fill a greaseproof
paper piping bag with the
chocolate icing and decorate
the car as illustrated. Stick the
Smarties and silver balls into
the icing while still soft.

Children's Birthday Cake

*1 (326-g/11¼-oz) packet
  chocolate sandwich cake mix*
ICING AND DECORATION
50 g/2 oz butter
75 g/3 oz icing sugar
1 tablespoon cocoa powder
1 tablespoon boiling water
marshmallows
*Smarties and coloured sugar
  balls*

Grease and flour two 18-cm/
7-inch sandwich tins. Preheat
the oven to moderately hot
(200°C, 400°F, Gas Mark 6).

Prepare the chocolate cake
mix according to the instructions on the packet. Pour into
the prepared tins, smooth the
surface and bake for 15–20
minutes. Turn out and cool on
a wire rack.

Prepare the chocolate filling
from the packet according to

the instructions. Sandwich the
cake together with this filling.

Cream the butter with the
sifted icing sugar until pale and
soft. Blend the cocoa powder
with the water and stir into the
butter cream. Cover the top
and sides of the cake with this
cream, swirling it with a palette
knife. Make figures from the
marshmallows, as illustrated,
and join together with wooden
cocktail sticks. Before serving
decorate the cake with the
marshmallow figures, Smarties
and coloured sugar balls.

Mother's Day Cake

1 (326-g/11½-oz) packet orange
  sponge cake mix
DECORATION
50 g/2 oz plain chocolate
2 teaspoons chopped pistachio
  nuts
12 sugar daisies (bought or
  made from almond paste)

Grease a 20-cm/8-inch cake
tin. Preheat the oven to moderately hot (200°C, 400°F, Gas
Mark 6).
  Make up the orange cake
mix according to the instructions on the packet. Turn into
the cake tin, smooth the surface and bake for about 25–30
minutes. Cool on a wire rack.
  Make up the icing from the
packet, according to the instructions. Cover the cake with
the icing. Melt the chocolate in
a basin over hot water and

place in a greaseproof paper
piping bag. Pipe rings round
the edge of the cake and
sprinkle with the pistachios.
Stick the sugar daisies on to
the chocolate rings at equal
intervals, using a little melted
chocolate to seal.

Cook's Tip

Any of these recipes
using packet mixes can
also be made from the
basic sponge and sand-
wich cake mixtures given
at the end of the book.

Sweetheart Cakes

1 (326-g/11½-oz) packet plain
  sponge cake mix
100 g/4 oz raspberry jam
ICING AND DECORATION
1 (44-g/1½-oz) packet dessert
  topping mix
6 tablespoons cold milk
2 tablespoons chopped nuts
sugar flowers and ladybirds
100 g/4 oz icing sugar
1–2 tablespoons water
crystallised violets, silver balls

Grease two heart-shaped cake
tins about 15 cm/6 inches in
length. Preheat the oven to
moderately hot (200°C, 400°F,
Gas Mark 6).
  Prepare the cake mix according to the instructions on the
packet. Pour into the greased
tins and bake for about 15–20
minutes. Turn out and cool on
a wire rack.

Cut one of the cakes through
to make two layers. Spread
with the raspberry jam and
sandwich together.
  Prepare the dessert topping
mix according to the instructions on the packet, using the
milk. Completely cover the
sandwiched cake, spreading
smoothly with a palette knife.
Pipe rosettes of the mix around
the top and decorate with
chopped nuts, sugar flowers
and ladybirds, as illustrated.
  Blend the sifted icing sugar
with the water and use to ice
the top of the second cake,
decorating it attractively with
crystallised violets and silver
balls.

Doughnut Mice

500 g/1 lb plain flour
30 g/1 oz fresh yeast
300 ml/½ pint lukewarm milk
25 g/1 oz castor sugar
50 g/2 oz raisins
100 g/4 oz candied peel
2 egg yolks
½ teaspoon salt
DECORATION
32 blanched almonds, halved
64 raisins
icing sugar to sprinkle
oil or fat to deep fry

Sift the flour into a bowl and make a well in the centre. Cream the yeast with a little of the milk then add the remaining milk. Stir in 1 teaspoon sugar and pour into the well. Stir in a little of the flour and leave for about 15 minutes, until frothy.

Pour boiling water over the raisins and leave to drain in a sieve, then dry well on absorbent paper. Finely chop the raisins and candied peel and sprinkle on to the flour. Beat the egg yolks with the salt and remaining sugar, stir into the yeast liquid and gradually work in the flour. Knead all the ingredients together for 5–10 minutes to obtain a smooth elastic dough. Cover and leave to stand in an oiled bowl in a warm place for a further 20 minutes.

Lightly knead the dough and shape into a long roll. Cut into 32 equal pieces. With floured hands make a small mouse

shape from each piece, as illustrated. Stick two almond halves in the heads for ears and two raisins for eyes. Place the mice when ready on a floured baking tray and leave to stand for a further 15 minutes.

Heat the oil or fat in a deep-frying pan to 175°C/347°F, and cook the mice a few at a time. After 2 minutes turn them with a draining spoon and cook for a further 2 minutes until golden brown all over. Lift out with a draining spoon and drain on absorbent paper.

Make a small tail for each mouse from string. Knot the string, stick a cocktail stick through the knot and use this to secure the tail to the mouse. Sprinkle the mice with icing sugar and serve warm. Be careful to remove the tails and cocktail sticks before eating the mice.

Cook's Tip

If it is too much trouble to make the mouse tails from string, you can simply spear a wooden cocktail stick into the mouse. This way you can use the stick to hold the doughnut mouse while you eat it.

Celebration Cakes

Chocolate Faces

CAKE MIXTURE
*4 eggs, separated, plus 2 egg
    whites*
120 g/4½ oz castor sugar
grated rind of ½ lemon
1 tablespoon water
50 g/2 oz plain flour
60 g/2½ oz cornflour
ICING AND DECORATION
100 g/4 oz apricot jam
100 g/4 oz plain chocolate
1 egg white
50 g/2 oz icing sugar
1 tube Smarties

Line a baking tray with non-
stick baking parchment. Preheat the oven to moderate
(180°C, 350°F, Gas Mark 4).
  Beat the egg yolks with 25 g/
1 oz sugar, the lemon rind and
water until frothy. Whisk the
egg whites until stiff, whisk in
the remaining sugar and fold
into the egg yolk mixture. Sift
over the flour and cornflour

and fold in well. Turn this mixture into a piping bag fitted
with a large plain nozzle and
pipe quite large half-spheres on
to the non-stick paper. Bake
for 12–15 minutes then leave
to cool on a wire rack.
  Remove the paper and stick
two halves together with a little
jam. Melt the chocolate in a
basin over hot water and use to
cover the cakes. Add sufficient
lightly whisked egg white to the
sifted icing sugar until the icing
is of a piping consistency. Pipe
faces on to the cakes, as illustrated, using coloured Smarties
to represent the eyes.

Alphabet Biscuits

180 g/6 oz plain flour
1 egg
90 g/3 oz castor sugar
25 g/1 oz vanilla sugar
60 g/2 oz butter, cut into flakes
ICING
200 g/7 oz icing sugar
2–3 tablespoons lemon juice
50 g/2 oz jelly bears

Sift the flour on to a pastry
board and knead to a dough
with the egg, sugar, vanilla
sugar and butter. Wrap in
foil or cling film and leave for
2 hours in the refrigerator.
  Preheat the oven to
moderately hot (200°C, 400°F,
Gas Mark 6). Cut small pieces
from the biscuit dough and
form into sausage shapes
about 1 cm/½ inch in diameter.
Make a letter from each
sausage and flatten slightly.

Place on a greased baking
tray and bake in the centre of
the oven for 8–10 minutes.
  Stir the sifted icing sugar
with enough lemon juice to
give a thick icing, but thin
enough to spread. Ice the
letters with it while still warm
and stick the jelly bears on to
the icing before it sets.

Cook's Tip

When you are making
the letters for older
children or adults, use
candied coffee beans for
the decoration.

Chocolate Ice Waffles

WAFFLE BATTER
60 g/2 oz butter
25 g/1 oz castor sugar
1 tablespoon vanilla sugar
pinch of salt
2 eggs
125 g/4 oz plain flour
¼ teaspoon baking powder
175 ml/6 fl oz buttermilk
FILLING AND TOPPING
150 ml/¼ pint double cream
1 tablespoon castor sugar
100 g/4 oz plain chocolate
1 (483-ml/17-fl oz) block chocolate ripple ice cream
20 g/¾ oz pistachio nuts, chopped

Beat the butter with the sugar, vanilla sugar and salt until pale and creamy. Beat in the eggs one at a time then add the sifted flour and baking powder. Mix in the buttermilk

to give a thick batter. Heat the waffle iron and brush lightly with melted butter. Cook the waffles individually until golden brown.

Whip the cream with the sugar until stiff and use to fill a piping bag fitted with a star nozzle. Melt the chocolate in a basin over a pan of hot water and allow to cool but not set. Just before serving, place a wedge of ice cream on half the waffles and cover each with a second waffle. Decorate as illustrated with rosettes of piped cream, chocolate icing and chopped pistachios.

Ice Cream Roll

SPONGE MIXTURE
4 eggs, separated, plus 2 egg yolks
100 g/4 oz castor sugar
80 g/3 oz plain flour
20 g/1 oz cornflour
FILLING
350 g/12 oz orange jelly marmalade
150 ml/¼ pint double cream
1 tablespoon castor sugar
1 (483-ml/17-fl oz) block Neapolitan ice cream

Line a 34 × 24-cm/13½ × 9½-inch Swiss roll tin with greased greaseproof paper. Preheat the oven to hot (220°C, 425°F, Gas Mark 7).

Beat all the egg yolks with half the sugar until pale and creamy. Whisk the egg whites until stiff, slowly add the rest of the sugar and whisk until smooth and glossy. Fold into the egg yolks. Sift the flour

and cornflour together and fold carefully into the egg mixture. Spread evenly into the tin and bake for 10–12 minutes.

Turn out, while still hot, on to a tea towel sprinkled with castor sugar. Remove the lining paper and trim the edges of the cake. Sieve the marmalade and spread it evenly over the cake. With the help of the tea towel, roll the cake up firmly and cool on a wire rack. Whip the cream and sugar until stiff and place in a piping bag fitted with a star nozzle.

When the roll is cool, cut into 1-cm/½-inch slices and sandwich a 1-cm/½-inch slice of ice cream between each pair of slices until both roll and ice cream are used up. Decorate with rosettes of cream.

Coffee Meringue Kisses

MERINGUE
1½ tablespoons instant coffee
   powder
8 egg whites
200 g/7 oz castor sugar
150 g/5 oz icing sugar
30 g/1 oz cornflour
FILLING
2 teaspoons cornflour
1 (213-g/7½-oz) can cherries
50 g/2 oz sugar
¼ teaspoon ground cinnamon
300 ml/½ pint double cream
1 tablespoon castor sugar

Dissolve the coffee powder in just enough hot water to blend it. Allow to cool. Line two baking trays with non-stick baking parchment or grease-proof paper. (If using the latter, grease lightly.) Preheat the oven to very cool (120°C, 250°F, Gas Mark ½).

Whisk the egg whites until stiff and slowly add the castor sugar, whisking continuously. Sift the icing sugar and corn-flour on to the egg whites and fold in together with the blended coffee. Fill a piping bag fitted with a star nozzle with the meringue mixture and pipe rosettes on to the baking trays. Bake for 3–4 hours with the door slightly open. Remove from the trays and strip off the paper.

Blend the cornflour with a little of the drained cherry juice. Bring the rest of the cherry juice to the boil with the sugar and cinnamon, add the blended cornflour and stir until thickened. Add the stoned cherries, bring back to the boil then leave to cool.

Whip the cream with the sugar. Pipe a ring of cream on to the flat side of half the meringues, fill the centre with the cherry sauce and place a second meringue on top.

Banana Meringues

MERINGUE
4 egg whites
100 g/3½ oz castor sugar
70 g/2½ oz icing sugar
15 g/½ oz cornflour
FILLING AND TOPPING
300 ml/½ pint double cream
3 tablespoons icing sugar
1 tablespoon cocoa powder
100 g/4 oz plain chocolate
6 bananas
50 g/2 oz soft brown sugar

Line a baking tray with non-stick baking parchment or greaseproof paper. (If using the latter, grease lightly.) Preheat the oven to very cool (120°C, 250°F, Gas Mark ½).

Whisk the egg whites until stiff then slowly add the castor sugar, whisking continuously. Sift over the icing sugar and cornflour and fold in. Fill a piping bag fitted with a plain nozzle with the meringue mixture and pipe 12 banana shapes on to the prepared baking tray. Bake for 3–4 hours with the oven door slightly open.

Remove the meringues from the baking tray and peel off the paper. Leave to cool.

Whip the cream with the sifted icing sugar until stiff then stir in the sifted cocoa powder. Using a star nozzle, pipe this cocoa cream on to the meringues. Melt the chocolate in a basin over a pan of hot water and allow to cool slightly. Peel the bananas and cut in half lengthways. Place a halved banana on each cream-topped meringue and pour over the chocolate icing. Sprinkle with brown sugar before the icing sets.

Traditional Wedding Cake

CAKE MIXTURE
250 g/9 oz butter
250 g/9 oz castor sugar
5 eggs
grated rind and juice of 1 lemon
1 tablespoon rum
250 g/9 oz plain flour
¼ teaspoon ground cinnamon
generous pinch of grated nutmeg
150 g/5 oz glacé cherries washed, dried and roughly chopped
400 g/14 oz currants
400 g/14 oz raisins
200 g/7 oz chopped mixed peel
50 g/2 oz blanched almonds, chopped
ROYAL ICING
3 large egg whites
675 g/1½ lb icing sugar
1 teaspoon lemon juice
sugar flowers to decorate

Grease a 25-cm/10-inch cake tin with butter or margarine. Line the greased tin with greaseproof paper and grease this thoroughly. Preheat the oven to cool (140°C, 275°F, Gas Mark 1).

Beat the butter with the sugar until pale and creamy. Beat in the eggs one at a time with the lemon rind and juice and the rum. Add a little flour if necessary to prevent the mixture curdling. Sift the remaining flour and mix with the cinnamon, nutmeg, cherries, currants, raisins, chopped peel and almonds. Add to the creamed mixture, folding it all in thoroughly. Pour into the cake tin and smooth the surface. Wrap a double thickness of brown paper or newspaper around the tin and secure it with string. This will prevent the outside of the cake from becoming overcooked before the middle is cooked through.

Bake the cake for 4½–5½ hours. It is essential to test with a skewer (see page 225) before removing the cake from the oven. If necessary continue baking for a little longer. Leave to cool for a short while in the tin then turn out on to a wire rack.

Lightly whisk the egg whites and brush a little over the surface of the cake. Gradually beat the sifted icing sugar and lemon juice into the remaining egg white to give a firm icing. Ice the top and sides of the cake, spreading smoothly with a palette knife. Place the rest of the icing in a piping bag fitted with a small star nozzle and decorate as illustrated.

Note To make the variation on the jacket, bake the cake mixture in a 25-cm/10-inch round fluted cake tin. When cool, brush over a very thin glacé icing and decorate with candied fruits and angelica.

Cook's Tip

The wedding cake will taste best if baked at least 3–4 weeks before the wedding and kept well wrapped in foil. Ice and decorate it just before using.

If well wrapped, the cake will keep for up to 1 year. In England it is customary in many families to make a two or three-tier wedding cake and to keep the second tier for the christening of the first child.

The traditional wedding cake is often covered with a layer of almond paste before the royal icing; this gives a smoother surface on which to ice.

Three-Tier Wedding Cake

For this wedding cake you will need twice the ingredients given in the recipe for Traditional Wedding Cake (left)

DECORATION
coloured sugar balls, crystallised violets, glacé cherries, angelica and round wafer biscuits

Generously grease and line with greased greaseproof paper three 25-cm/10-inch, 18-cm/7-inch, 13-cm/5-inch cake tins. Preheat the oven to cool (140°C, 275°F, Gas Mark 1) and prepare the cake mixture as in the preceding recipe. Bake the cakes, checking the smallest after 2½–3 hours and the middle size after 3-4 hours. Before removing from the oven test each of the cakes with a skewer (see page 225) and if necessary bake for a little longer.

Leave to cool on a wire rack, wrap in foil and keep for 3–4 weeks.

Lightly whisk the egg whites and brush over the surface of the cakes. Sift the icing sugar and mix to a firm icing with the lemon juice and the remaining egg whites. Cover the top and sides of all three cakes with the icing and when completely set place one upon the other.

Place the rest of the icing in a piping bag fitted with a small star nozzle and in a small greaseproof paper piping bag. Using the illustration as a guide, decorate the cake with piped icing, sugar balls, glacé cherries, crystallised violets and angelica. Cut some of the wafer biscuits into quarters, cover thinly with icing and use to decorate the cake as illustrated. Place three iced wafers on top of the cake to form a crown and decorate.

Fleurons

1 (368-g/13-oz) packet frozen
  puff pastry
1 egg yolk, beaten to glaze

Allow the pastry to thaw for
1 hour at room temperature.
  Roll out the pastry to
5 mm/¼ inch thick. With a
round pastry cutter or a glass,
cut half-moon shapes from
the pastry, starting at the edge.
Place the remains of the pastry
in a pile, press firmly together,
roll out and cut more half-
moons. Sprinkle a baking tray
with cold water, place the
half-moons on it and brush
with egg yolk. Lightly mark a
lattice pattern on top of each
with a knife and chill in the
refrigerator for 15 minutes.
  Preheat the oven to hot
(220°C, 425°F, Gas Mark 7).
Bake the fleurons for 15
minutes towards the top of the
oven and serve warm.

Cook's Tip
Fleurons can be served to
accompany a special
soup or to garnish a
particularly delicious fish
dish.

Cheese Twists

1 (368-g/13-oz) packet frozen
  puff pastry
1 egg
salt and pepper
50 g/2 oz Emmenthal cheese,
  finely grated

Allow the pastry to thaw at
room temperature for 1 hour.
  Divide the pastry into thirds
and roll each piece out to give
an oblong of 35 × 13 cm /
14 × 5 inches. Brush each
piece of pastry generously with
the seasoned, beaten egg and
sandwich the three pieces
together with the cheese. Press
together well and cut into thin
strips measuring approxi-
mately 5 mm/¼ inch wide.
Twist the strips and place on
baking trays which have been
sprinkled with cold water.
Leave to stand in a cool place
for 15 minutes.
  Preheat the oven to moderately hot (200°C, 400°F, Gas
Mark 6) and bake the cheese
twists for 15 minutes. Serve at
once if possible.

Cook's Tip
When baking puff
pastry, always sprinkle
the baking tray or tin
with cold water before
beginning. The steam
from the water helps the
pastry to rise.

Favourite Savouries

American Muffins

250 ml/8 fl oz milk
50 g/2 oz cornmeal
30 g/1 oz self-raising flour
2 teaspoons baking powder
1 teaspoon salt
2 teaspoons sugar
1 egg
50 g/2 oz butter, softened

Grease 10–12 patty tins with butter or margarine. Preheat the oven to moderately hot (200°C, 400°F, Gas Mark 6).

Bring the milk to the boil, sprinkle the cornmeal into it and cook, stirring, for a few minutes, until the mixture leaves the sides of the pan. Sift the flour and baking powder into the mixture and stir in with the salt, sugar, egg and softened butter. Three-quarters fill the prepared tins and bake for 20–30 minutes.

Remove from the tins immediately and serve hot with butter.

Cook's Tip
These American muffins are served at a celebration meal in place of ordinary white bread rolls.

Anchovy Bites

1 (368-g/13-oz) packet frozen puff pastry
1 (56-g/2 oz) can anchovy fillets
1 egg yolk, beaten to glaze
1–2 tablespoons sea salt

Allow the pastry to thaw for 1 hour at room temperature. Roll out on a floured board to 5 mm/¼ inch thick and cut into 6-cm/2½-inch rounds with a fluted cutter. Place a halved anchovy fillet on half the pastry rounds. Brush the edges of each round with egg yolk and sandwich together in pairs, sealing the edges well. Brush the tops with egg yolk and sprinkle with the salt.

Sprinkle a baking tray with cold water, arrange the pastry rounds on it and chill in the refrigerator for 15 minutes. Preheat the oven to hot (220°C, 425°F, Gas Mark 7) and bake towards the top of the oven for 10–15 minutes.

These are best eaten while still warm.

Cook's Tip
Sardines can be used instead of anchovies for the filling.

Vol au Vent Pastry Case

1 (368-g/13-oz) packet frozen
*   puff pastry*
1 egg, beaten

Allow the pastry to thaw at room temperature for about 1 hour. Line a 1·5-litre/2½-pint pudding basin with foil. Fill with crumpled absorbent paper, pressing down lightly. Fold the foil over and lightly secure. Turn out this foil mould. Sprinkle a large baking tray with cold water and pre-heat the oven to hot (220°C, 425°F, Gas Mark 7).

Roll out the pastry to a rectangle approximately 50 × 30 cm / 20 × 12 inches. Cut out a round measuring approximately 19 cm / 7½ inches in diameter and place on the baking tray. Stand the foil mould in the middle of this pastry round, with the narrow end at the top. Cut out another pastry round large enough to cover the mould (approximately 33 cm/13 inches in diameter). Brush the edges of both pastry rounds with beaten egg. Carefully place the large round of pastry

over the foil mould and seal the edges to the pastry base. Flute the edges with a knife, as illustrated, and brush all over with beaten egg. Cut out shapes from the remaining pastry trimmings and use to decorate the pastry case. Glaze these with beaten egg and bake the vol au vent for 15–20 minutes.

Remove from the oven and, using a sharp pointed knife, cut a round lid from the top of the pastry case. Remove this lid carefully and cut a hole in the foil underneath. Carefully remove the absorbent paper then crumple the foil and remove this also from the pastry shell. Fill and serve immediately if required warm, or allow to cool and then fill.

Cook's Tip

The vol au vent case can be filled with a hot chicken, veal or mush-room mixture, with cold lobster cocktail or with a crab and prawn mousse. For a dessert, fill with a sweet custard or cream.

The vol au vent case can be reheated success-fully if you wish to make it in advance and still serve it hot. Heat the filling separately and fill the case just before serv-ing, or heat the vol au vent case already filled.

Hot or cold, sweet or savoury, this vol au vent makes a spectacular buffet party dish.

Favourite Savouries

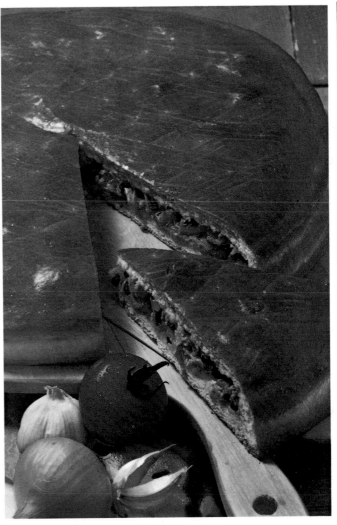

Royal Vols aux Vents

1 (368-g/13-oz) packet frozen puff pastry
1 egg yolk, beaten to glaze

To make these vols aux vents you will need two sharp pastry cutters: one 6 cm/2½ inches in diameter and one 3·5 cm/1½ inches in diameter.

Allow the pastry to thaw at room temperature for 1 hour.

Roll the pastry out to 5 mm/¼ inch thick. Cut out an even number of rounds using the 6-cm/2½-inch cutter. Cut out the centre of half the rounds using the 3·5-cm/1½-inch cutter. Brush the rounds with water and place the rings on top then lightly mark a circle inside the hole with a pointed knife. Brush with beaten egg yolk and leave in the refrigerator for 30 minutes. Preheat the oven to hot (220°C, 425°F, Gas Mark 7).

Bake for 15–20 minutes then cool on a wire rack and fill according to taste.

Cook's Tip

Prepare a chicken filling for the vols aux vents as illustrated. Make up a thick white sauce, using half chicken stock and half milk. Fold in diced cooked chicken and frozen green peas, heating through completely. Season to taste and spoon into the vol au vent cases.

Basque Chicken Pie

500 g/1 lb risen white bread dough, made with 500 g/1 lb flour, etc. (see page 226)
1 egg, beaten to glaze
FILLING
1 red pepper
1 green pepper
1 large onion
225 g/8 oz tomatoes
50 g/2 oz ham
350 g/12 oz cooked chicken
2 tablespoons oil
¼ clove garlic, crushed
1 teaspoon salt
¼ teaspoon pepper

Preheat the oven to moderately hot (200°C, 400°F, Gas Mark 6).

First prepare the filling. Remove cores, pith and seeds from the peppers, then chop finely. Peel and chop the onion and tomatoes. Dice the meats.

Heat the oil and fry the peppers, onion and garlic gently for 10 minutes. Add the tomatoes, ham and chicken and bring to a simmer. Stir in the salt and pepper and remove from the heat.

Divide the bread dough in half and roll out on a floured surface into two rounds, each about 30 cm/12 inches in diameter. Place one round on a greased baking tray. Spread over the chicken mixture to within 1 cm/½ inch of the edge. Place the second round on top and press the edges together to seal. Score with a knife, brush with the beaten egg and bake for 45 minutes.

Desserts with a Difference

Raspberry Ice Cream Cake

SPONGE MIXTURE
3 eggs, separated
65 g/2¼ oz castor sugar
pinch of salt
50 g/2 oz plain flour
25 g/1 oz cornflour
25 g/1 oz ground almonds
25 g/1 oz butter, melted
FILLING AND TOPPING
1 tablespoon Kirsch
225 g/8 oz raspberries
600 ml/1 pint double cream
250 g/9 oz castor sugar
chocolate caraque (see page 231)

Grease and flour a 20-cm/8-inch cake tin. Preheat the oven to moderately hot (190°C, 375°F, Gas Mark 5).

Beat the eggs with the sugar and salt until pale and creamy. Sift the flour with the cornflour and fold into the mixture with the ground almonds and butter.

Place in the cake tin and bake for 25–30 minutes.

Turn on to a wire rack to cool for 24 hours then cut into two layers. Line the sides of the cake tin with foil and place one of the layers over the base.

Spoon the Kirsch over the raspberries, cover and leave for 1 hour. Keep a few whole raspberries for decoration and crush the remainder lightly.

Whip the cream with the sugar until stiff. Reserve approximately a quarter of this cream and stir the raspberries into the remainder. Pour into the cake tin and place the second cake layer on top. Freeze for 5–10 hours in a freezer or in the freezing compartment of a refrigerator.

Leave at room temperature for 15 minutes then turn out. Spread a little of the reserved cream thinly over the top and sides of the cake and decorate as illustrated.

Hazelnut Ice Cream Cake

SPONGE MIXTURE
3 eggs, separated
65 g/2¼ oz castor sugar
25 g/1 oz plain flour
30 g/1 oz cornflour
75 g/3 oz toasted hazelnuts,
  finely ground
FILLING AND TOPPING
600 ml/1 pint double cream
225 g/8 oz castor sugar
75 g/3 oz toasted hazelnuts,
  ground
few whole hazelnuts

Grease and flour a 20-cm/8-inch cake tin. Preheat the oven to moderately hot (190°C, 375°F, Gas Mark 5).

Whisk the eggs with the sugar until pale and creamy. Sift the flour with the cornflour and carefully fold in with the ground hazelnuts. Pour into the cake tin and bake for

25–30 minutes.

Turn on to a wire rack to cool. Leave the cake for 24 hours then cut it through into two layers. Line the sides of the cake tin with foil and place one of the layers over the base.

Whip the cream with the sugar until stiff. Reserve a third of this cream then add 50 g/ 2 oz ground hazelnuts to the remainder. Spread over the cake base and place the second cake layer on top. Freeze the cake for 5–10 hours in the freezer or in the freezing compartment of the refrigerator.

Leave at room temperature for 15 minutes then turn out and decorate. Use a little of the reserved cream to spread thinly over the top and sides of the cake then sprinkle with the remaining grounds nuts. With the rest of the cream, pipe rosettes on the cake and top these with whole hazelnuts. Serve at once.

Baked Alaska

SPONGE BASE
1 egg
25 g/1 oz castor sugar
25 g/1 oz plain flour
TOPPING
50 g/2 oz ground almonds
50 g/2 oz apricot jam
1 tablespoon rum
50 g/2 oz candied lemon peel
4 egg whites
150 g/5 oz castor sugar
1 block each raspberry ripple
  and raspberry ice cream
8 glacé cherries
2 teaspoons flaked almonds

Preheat the oven to 190°C,
375°F, Gas Mark 5. Grease and
flour a 15-cm/6-inch sandwich
tin. Whisk the egg with the
sugar until pale. Fold in the
sifted flour and turn into the
tin. Bake for 20–25 minutes
then cool.

Mix the ground almonds
with the jam, rum and chopped
peel. Whisk the egg whites
until stiff, fold in the sugar and
place in a piping bag.

Spread the almond mixture
over the cake base. Place the
raspberry ripple ice cream on
the centre and surround with
the raspberry ice cream cut into
pieces. Smooth over. Place in a
freezer for 30 minutes until
firm. Preheat the oven to
240°C, 475°F, Gas Mark 9.

Cover the cake completely
with the whisked egg white,
decorate with glacé cherries
and flaked almonds and brown
in the oven for 3–4 minutes.
Serve at once.

Baked Chocolate Alaska

Make a sponge base as above,
using twice the quantity of
ingredients, and bake in a
15 × 23-cm/6 × 9-inch
shallow tin. Trim to fit a block
of Neapolitan ice cream,
spread with 2 tablespoons
redcurrant jelly and place the
ice cream on top. Whisk 4 egg
whites with 150 g/5 oz castor
sugar as above, adding 1 teaspoon sifted cocoa powder.
Pipe all over and brown in a
very hot oven (240°C, 475°F,
Gas Mark 9) for 3–4 minutes.
Sift over chocolate powder
before serving at once.

Desserts with a Difference

Cherry Meringue Nests

MERINGUE
6 egg whites
225 g/8 oz castor sugar
75 g/3 oz icing sugar
30 g/1 oz cornflour
TOPPING
1 tablespoon instant coffee
powder
250 ml/8 fl oz double cream
2 tablespoons castor sugar
1 (425-g/15-oz) can red
cherries
1 (483-ml/17-fl oz) block
vanilla ice cream

Line a baking tray with non-stick baking parchment or lightly greased greaseproof paper. Preheat the oven to very cool (110°C, 225°F, Gas Mark ¼).

Whisk the egg whites until stiff then whisk in the castor sugar until stiff and glossy.

Fold in the sifted icing sugar and cornflour. Fill a piping bag fitted with a star nozzle with the meringue mixture and pipe rosette shapes on to the baking tray. Leave to dry out in the oven with the door slightly open for 3–4 hours.

Dissolve the coffee powder in 1 tablespoon boiling water and leave to cool. Whip the cream with the sugar until stiff and stir in the coffee. Pipe rings of coffee cream on to the meringue nests. Drain the cherries and pat dry. Place a few cherries in the coffee cream, top with a scoop of ice cream and decorate with the rest of the cherries. Serve at once.

Orange Cream Tartlets

PASTRY
200 g/8 oz plain flour
100 g/4 oz icing sugar
100 g/4 oz butter
2 egg yolks
few drops of vanilla essence
pinch of salt
1 tablespoon water
FILLING AND TOPPING
1 (178-ml/6¼-fl oz) can frozen
concentrated orange juice
3 tablespoons white wine
100 g/4 oz castor sugar
15 g/½ oz powdered gelatine
300 ml/½ pint double cream
50 g/2 oz drinking chocolate
powder
1 (483-ml/17-fl oz) block
raspberry ice cream
50 g/2 oz toasted flaked
almonds

Sift the flour and icing sugar into a bowl and work in the

butter, egg yolks, vanilla essence, salt and water, to make a firm dough. Cover and refrigerate for 2 hours.

Preheat the oven to moderately hot (200°C, 400°F, Gas Mark 6). Roll out the pastry thinly and use to line twelve 7·5-cm/3-inch tartlet tins. Bake blind for 10 minutes, remove the cases from the tins and cool on a wire rack.

Heat the orange juice with the wine and sugar, add the gelatine and warm gently to dissolve it. Leave to cool then place in the refrigerator. Whip the cream until it stands in peaks. As the jelly begins to set, fold in half the cream. Use to fill the tartlet cases and leave to set completely.

Mix the remaining cream with the sifted drinking chocolate powder. Just before serving, place a slice of ice cream on each tartlet, pipe a chocolate cream rosette and sprinkle with almonds.

Desserts with a Difference

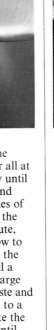

Strawberry Cream Puffs

CHOUX PASTE
125 ml/4 fl oz water
30 g/1 oz butter
pinch of salt
95 g/3½ oz plain flour
2 eggs, beaten
FILLING
225 g/8 oz frozen strawberries
2 tablespoons castor sugar
1 tablespoon rum
150 ml/¼ pint double cream
3 tablespoons icing sugar
1 (483-ml/17-fl oz) block
    strawberry ice cream

Mix the strawberries with the castor sugar and rum and leave to defrost. Preheat the oven to hot (220°C, 425°F, Gas Mark 7).

Place the water, butter and salt in a saucepan and heat gently until the butter has melted. Bring quickly to the boil then remove from the heat. Add the sifted flour all at once and beat vigorously until the dough forms a ball and comes away from the sides of the pan clean. Return to the heat and cook for 1 minute, stirring all the time. Allow to cool slightly then beat in the eggs a little at a time. Fill a piping bag fitted with a large fluted nozzle with the paste and pipe 16 small rosettes on to a greased baking tray. Bake the rosettes for 20 minutes until puffed and golden.

Cut a lid from each of the choux puffs then leave to cool. Fill the bottom half of the puffs with the soaked strawberries. Whip the cream stiffly with 1 tablespoon sifted icing sugar. With a shallow spoon cut scoops of ice cream and place on the strawberries. Pipe cream on to the ice cream, top with the lids and sift the remaining icing sugar over the top. Serve at once.

Exotic Fruit Meringues

6 egg whites
100 g/4 oz castor sugar
100 g/4 oz icing sugar
30 g/1 oz cornflour
40 g/1½ oz cocoa powder
250 ml/8 fl oz double cream
2 tablespoons icing sugar
6 Chinese gooseberries
1 (483-ml/17-fl oz) block ice
    cream (flavour of your
    choice)

Line a baking tray with greased greaseproof paper or non-stick baking parchment. Preheat the oven to very cool (110°C, 225°F, Gas Mark ¼).

Whisk the egg whites until stiff then whisk in the castor sugar. Sift the icing sugar with the cornflour and cocoa powder and fold into the whisked egg whites. Place in a piping bag fitted with a plain nozzle and pipe 14 oval meringues on to the baking tray.

Leave the meringues to dry out overnight in the centre of the oven, keeping the door slightly ajar with a wooden spoon.

Whip the cream with the sifted icing sugar until stiff and place in a piping bag fitted with a star nozzle. Pipe rings of cream on to the cooled meringues. Peel and slice the Chinese gooseberries and arrange on top of the cream. Place slices of ice cream over the gooseberries and serve immediately.

Fruit and Rum Babas

SAVARIN DOUGH
350 g/12 oz plain flour
20 g/¾ oz fresh yeast
250 ml/8 fl oz lukewarm milk
4 eggs
40 g/1½ oz castor sugar
25 g/1 oz vanilla sugar
½ teaspoon salt
150 g/5 oz butter
SYRUP
150 g/5 oz granulated sugar
250 ml/8 fl oz water
grated rind of 1 lemon
4 tablespoons rum
6 tablespoons white wine
FILLING
250 ml/8 fl oz double cream
1 tablespoon icing sugar
1 teaspoon cocoa powder
350 g/12 oz drained canned
fruit (pineapple, goose-
berries, cherries, kumquats,
Chinese gooseberries)
50 g/2 oz flaked almonds

Grease about twenty-four
7·5-cm/3-inch savarin tins with
butter and sprinkle with flour.

Sift the flour into a bowl and
make a well in the centre.
Cream the yeast with a little
of the milk, then gradually add
the remainder. Pour into the
well in the flour, cover and
leave in a warm place for 15
minutes, until frothy.

Whisk the eggs with the
sugar until frothy, add the
vanilla sugar and salt. Melt the
butter without allowing it to
become hot and add to the egg
mixture. Pour into the yeast
mixture in the bowl and beat
in the rest of the flour to give a
loose dough. Cover and leave
to stand for a further 10
minutes. Half-fill the savarin
tins with the dough mixture,
cover and leave to rise for
15 minutes.

Preheat the oven to moderately hot (200°C, 400°F, Gas
Mark 6) and bake for 30
minutes in the centre of the

oven. Turn the savarins out on
to a wire rack and allow to
cool.

Dissolve the sugar in the
water with the lemon rind,
rum and white wine, stirring
continuously over a low heat
until the sugar has completely
dissolved. Bring to the boil and
cook for 5–10 minutes. Place
the babas upside down on a
plate and spoon over the warm
syrup; they must be completely
soaked.

Whip the cream with the
sifted icing sugar until stiff and
divide in half. Mix one half
with the sifted cocoa powder.
Fill a piping bag fitted with a
star nozzle with the plain and
chocolate cream one after the
other, and pipe a rosette of
cream into the centre of each
baba.

Cut the fruit into small
pieces and decorate the babas
with the fruit and flaked
almonds.

Cook's Tip

If you have only 12
savarin tins you must
bake the babas in two
lots. Instead of savarin
tins you can use ring
moulds or make more
savarin tins out of
aluminium foil.

Italian Cassata

1 sandwich cake (see below)
FILLING
350 g/12 oz curd cheese
2 tablespoons double cream
60 g/2 oz castor sugar
1 tablespoon orange liqueur
2 tablespoons finely chopped
  glacé fruit
ICING
225 g/8 oz plain chocolate
4–5 tablespoons strong black
  coffee
100 g/4 oz butter
glacé fruit to decorate

Make the sandwich cake
according to the basic recipe
(see page 228), then turn into a
greased 1-kg/2-lb loaf tin.
Bake in a moderate oven
(160°C, 325°F, Gas Mark 3)
for 45 minutes and leave to
cool on a wire rack. Trim the
cake if necessary and cut into
four layers horizontally.

Sieve the cheese and stir
until smooth with the cream,
sugar and orange liqueur. Add
the chopped glacé fruit. Cover
three layers of the cake with
this filling and place one upon
the other. Top with the final
cake layer, pressing the cake
down slightly so that it is
compact in shape. Leave to
stand for 2 hours in the
refrigerator.

Break the chocolate into
small pieces and stir into the
coffee over a moderate heat
until melted. Stir in the butter
in small pieces until a completely smooth creamy mixture
is obtained. Place in the
refrigerator until it begins to
set. Cover the sides and top of
the cake with this chocolate
cream.

Fill a piping bag fitted with
a star nozzle with the remainder of the cream and
decorate the cake with rosettes
and garlands, as illustrated.
Top the rosettes of cream with
glacé fruit cut into small
pieces. Wrap the cake carefully in foil and leave for 1
day in the refrigerator before
serving.

Christmas Baking Begins Early

Christmas Stollen

1 kg/2¼ lb plus 200 g/7 oz
  plain flour
100 g/4 oz fresh yeast
450 ml/¾ pint lukewarm milk
100 g/4 oz castor sugar
2 eggs
few drops of vanilla essence
grated rind of 1 lemon
¼ teaspoon salt
400 g/14 oz butter
350 g/12 oz raisins
100 g/4 oz blanched almonds,
  chopped
100 g/4 oz candied lemon peel,
  chopped
50 g/2 oz candied orange peel,
  chopped
1 tablespoon rum
TOPPING
150 g/5 oz butter, melted
150 g/5 oz icing sugar

Line a baking tray with buttered greaseproof paper.
  Sift the 1 kg/2¼ lb flour into a large bowl and make a well in the centre. Cream the yeast with a little milk then gradually add the remaining milk. Stir in a little sugar, pour into the well and sprinkle with a little of the flour. Cover and leave in a warm place for 15 minutes, until frothy. Mix the rest of the sugar with the eggs, vanilla, lemon rind and salt, add to the yeast mixture and work in with the rest of the flour to give a dry firm dough. Knead until smooth then cover and leave to rise for 1 hour.
  Work the butter and the remaining 200 g/7 oz flour together, knead into the risen dough, cover and leave to stand for a further 15 minutes. Meanwhile, mix the raisins, almonds and chopped peel together, sprinkle with the rum, cover and leave to steep. Then quickly work this fruit

mixture into the dough, cover and leave to stand in a warm place for a further 15 minutes.
  Divide the dough into three portions and roll each piece into a 30-cm/12-inch length. Roll gently so that the dough is thinner in the middle than at the ends. Fold the dough over lengthways, making a 15-cm/6-inch length – this gives the typical stollen shape – and place on the baking tray. Repeat using the other two pieces of dough. Cover the loaves and leave to stand for a further 20 minutes, until increased in size. Preheat the oven to moderately hot (200°C, 400°F, Gas Mark 6).
  Bake the loaves for 25–30 minutes. While still hot, brush with the melted butter and dredge generously with sifted icing sugar.

Almond Stollen

Omit the raisins, almonds, lemon peel, orange peel and rum. Prepare the dough as for the Christmas Stollen, and after the second rising knead in 250 g/9 oz chopped blanched almonds and 250 g/9 oz chopped candied lemon peel. Leave to stand for a further 15 minutes then continue as for Christmas Stollen.

Christmas Baking Begins Early

Traditional Fruit Loaf

75 g/3 oz dried stoned prunes
175 g/6 oz dried pears
75 g/3 oz dried figs
50 g/2 oz raisins
50 g/2 oz currants
50 g/2 oz chopped mixed peel
300 ml/½ pint hot black tea
50 g/2 oz sugar
½ teaspoon ground cinnamon
pinch each of ground cloves,
  ground aniseed and salt
2 tablespoons rum
2 tablespoons lemon juice
200 g/7 oz plain flour
50 g/2 oz hazelnuts, finely
  chopped
50 g/2 oz walnuts, finely
  chopped
STARTER DOUGH
2 tablespoons milk
4 tablespoons water
1 teaspoon oil
1 teaspoon dried yeast
2 tablespoons lukewarm water

1 teaspoon castor sugar
2 teaspoons salt
50 g/2 oz strong plain flour
50 g/2 oz rye flour
DECORATION
25 g/1 oz blanched almonds,
  halved
glacé cherries
angelica

First make the starter dough.
Combine the milk, 4 tablespoons water and the oil in a
saucepan and bring to the boil.
Allow to cool until lukewarm.
Blend the yeast with 2 tablespoons lukewarm water and the
sugar and leave for 5 minutes.
Add to the milk mixture with
the salt. Stir this liquid into the
plain and rye flours until well
blended. Cover and leave to
stand for 12–18 hours.
  Meanwhile chop the prunes,
pears and figs. Place in a bowl
with the raisins, currants and
mixed peel. Pour on the freshly
made tea, cover and leave to
soak overnight. Add the sugar,

spices, salt, rum and lemon
juice to the fruit. Stir all the
ingredients well, cover and
leave to stand for a further
30 minutes.
  Grease a 20-cm/8-inch cake
tin with butter or margarine.
Preheat the oven to moderate
(180°C, 350°F, Gas Mark 4).
  Add the fruit mixture to the
starter dough with the sifted
flour and chopped nuts. Mix
all thoroughly until well
combined and place in the cake
tin. Decorate with almond
halves, glacé cherries and strips
of angelica, as illustrated. Bake
for 1 hour 10 minutes.

Cook's Tip

This fruit loaf is
especially delicious made
with the given mixture
of various fruits. Should
you not have one kind of
dried fruit, you can in-
crease the quantity of the
other fruits accordingly.
Take care that your fruit
is made up of a mixture
of light and dark fruits.
Fruit loaves keep fresh
and moist for a long time
if stored in an airtight
container or wrapped
tightly in foil.

Christmas Baking Begins Early

Baking for Festive Occasions

Christmas Loaf

400 g/14 oz dried pears
300 g/11 oz dried prunes
400 g/14 oz dried figs
150 g/5 oz walnuts
100 g/3½ oz raisins
125 g/4½ oz sultanas
100 g/4 oz chopped mixed peel
200 g/7 oz castor sugar
2 teaspoons ground cinnamon
1 teaspoon each ground cloves,
   aniseed and salt
2 tablespoons rum
1 kg/2¼ lb plain flour
40 g/1½ oz fresh yeast
1 teaspoon sugar
RYE BREAD DOUGH
900 g/2 lb rye flour
150 ml/¼ pint hot milk
25 g/1 oz fresh yeast
2 teaspoons castor sugar
1 teaspoon salt
25 g/1 oz butter, melted
1 tablespoon oil

Soak the pears and prunes in
900 ml/1½ pints water, cover
and cook until soft. Drain and
reserve the liquor. Stone the
prunes and coarsely chop with
the pears, figs and walnuts.
Add the raisins, sultanas,
mixed peel, sugar, spices, salt
and rum and cover.
   Gradually whisk 300 ml/
½ pint hot water into 50 g/2 oz
of the rye flour. Cover and
leave for 1½ hours then stir in
the hot milk. Cream the yeast
with the sugar and 150 ml/¼ pint
lukewarm water and leave for 10
minutes. Stir into the flour paste
with the salt, butter and oil.
Work in the remaining rye flour.
Cover and leave until risen.
   Sift the plain flour into a
bowl and form a well. Cream
the yeast with the sugar and
400 ml/14 fl oz of the cooled
fruit liquor; pour into the well.
Sprinkle over a little of the
flour and leave until frothy.
Add the fruit and nut mixture,
work to a dough. Leave for
15 minutes then shape into four
oval loaves.
   Divide the rye bread dough
into four and roll out each
quarter into an oval large
enough to enclose a fruit loaf.
Brush each fruit loaf with
water and wrap in the rye
dough, sealing the edges with
water. Place on greased baking
trays and brush with water.
Leave to stand for 15 minutes.
Preheat the oven to moderately
hot (190°C, 375°F, Gas Mark
5) and bake for 1¼–1½ hours.

Christmas Baking Begins Early

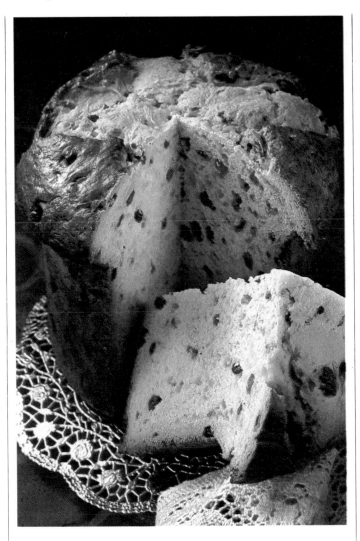

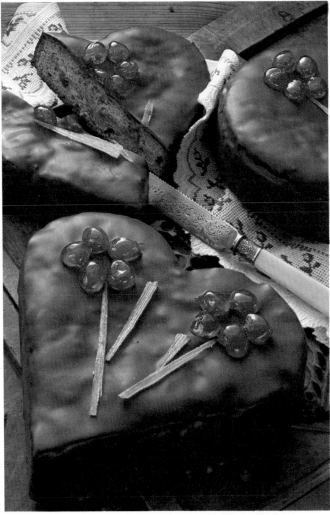

Italian Panettone

400 g / 14 oz plain flour
25 g / 1 oz fresh yeast
50 g / 2 oz castor sugar
150 ml / ¼ pint lukewarm milk
100 g / 4 oz butter, melted
3 egg yolks
1 teaspoon salt
pinch of grated nutmeg
grated rind of ½ lemon
100 g / 4 oz chopped mixed peel
50 g / 2 oz raisins
1 egg yolk, beaten to glaze

Line a deep 18-cm/7-inch cake tin with buttered greaseproof paper.

Sift the flour into a bowl and make a well in the centre. Cream the yeast with a little of the sugar and the milk and pour into the well. Sprinkle with a little of the flour and leave in a warm place for 15 minutes, until frothy. Add the remaining sugar, the melted butter, egg yolks, salt, nutmeg and lemon rind and beat in all the flour until the mixture forms a soft dough. Knead the dough for about 10 minutes then cover and leave to rise until doubled in size (about 1 hour). Turn on to a lightly floured board and knead in the chopped peel and raisins. Form the dough into a ball, place in the tin, cover and leave to stand until the dough reaches the top of the tin. Preheat the oven to moderately hot (200°C, 400°F, Gas Mark 6).

Brush the cake with beaten egg yolk, cut a cross on the top and bake for 20 minutes. Reduce the oven temperature to moderate (180°C, 350°F, Gas Mark 4) and continue to bake for a further 45 minutes. Allow the cake to cool slightly in the tin, then turn out on to a wire rack and leave until completely cold. Remove the greaseproof paper just before cutting the cake.

Honey Cakes

500 g / 1 lb honey
6 tablespoons water
500 g / 1 lb black treacle
700 g / 1½ lb wholemeal flour
300 g / 10 oz rye flour
1 tablespoon baking powder
1 teaspoon bicarbonate of soda
1 tablespoon milk
FILLING
100 g / 4 oz almond paste
130 g / 4½ oz castor sugar
1 egg white
1 tablespoon rum
100 g / 4 oz candied fruit,
   chopped
100 g / 4 oz blanched almonds,
   chopped
milk to brush
ICING
300 g / 11 oz plain chocolate
glacé cherries and angelica

Melt the honey and gradually bring to the boil with the water and treacle. Leave to cool. Work in the flours and the baking powder. Dissolve the bicarbonate of soda in the milk and stir into the mixture. Wrap in foil and leave for 2 days at room temperature.

Break the almond paste into small pieces and mix with the sugar, egg white, rum, candied fruit and almonds. Stand over a pan of hot water and mix well.

Preheat the oven to moderately hot (190°C, 375°F, Gas Mark 5). Grease three baking trays. Divide the cake dough into three portions. Roll each piece out to a thickness of 1·5 cm/¾ inch and cut out two heart shapes from each portion. Spread the marzipan filling over the centre of half the hearts, brush the edges with milk, top with a second heart and press the edges well together.

Bake the cakes for 30–35 minutes then leave to cool. Melt the chocolate in a basin over hot water, ice the cakes all over and top with cherries and angelica as illustrated.

Gingerbread House

1 kg/2 lb thick honey
250 ml/8 fl oz water
650 g/1½ lb rye flour
500 g/1 lb plain wholemeal flour
200 g/7 oz chopped mixed peel
1 teaspoon ground ginger
1 teaspoon ground cinnamon
¼ teaspoon grated nutmeg
1 teaspoon bicarbonate of soda
DECORATION
20–30 blanched almonds
2 egg whites
500 g/1 lb icing sugar
1 tablespoon lemon juice
coloured sugar balls

Bring the honey to the boil with the water, stirring continuously, then leave to cool. Place the flours in a large mixing bowl and sprinkle with the mixed peel and spices. Form a well in the centre and pour in the honey which should be almost cold. Knead all the ingredients to obtain a soft dough. Finally mix the bicarbonate of soda into the dough. Place the dough in a polythene bag, seal and leave to stand for 1–2 days; this will make the gingerbread more tasty.

To construct the house it is advisable to cut out a cardboard pattern for the walls and roof, corresponding in size with the illustration. Lightly grease two baking trays. Preheat the oven to moderately hot (200°C, 400°F, Gas Mark 6). Roll part of the honey dough into 18 long sausage shapes, 40 cm/16 inches long and 1·5 cm/¾ inch in diameter.

Place side by side on one of the baking trays, leaving about 3 mm/⅛ inch between each. They should form a rectangle 40 × 25 cm/16 × 10 inches. During baking the gaps close up and form the walls of the log cabin. Bake in the centre of the oven for 20–30 minutes.

Roll out the rest of the dough to 1 cm/½ inch thick. Cut out one piece of about 25 × 15 cm/10 × 6 inches and a second piece 35 × 28 cm/14 × 11 inches. Place these pieces on the baking tray, prick with a fork and bake for 12–18 minutes in the centre of the oven. From the 40 × 25-cm/16 × 10-inch piece which was baked first, cut out with a sharp knife the front, back and side walls of the house, using the cardboard pattern. Cut out a door and window in the front wall. From the flat pieces of dough cut out a base and two roof pieces using the cardboard pattern as a guide. Roll out

the rest of the dough to 5 mm/¼ inch thick, cut out 20 small biscuits and place an almond on each. Also cut out pieces for the chimney and strips for the fence as illustrated and bake for 12–15 minutes.

Lightly whisk the egg whites until frothy, then gradually beat in the sifted icing sugar until a thick icing is obtained. Finally beat in the lemon juice. Assemble the sections of the house, using the icing to hold the pieces together; leave the icing to dry completely at each stage before constructing the next section. Coat the roof and chimney with icing to resemble freshly fallen snow. Decorate the house as you choose or as illustrated with the ginger biscuits, sugar balls and almonds.

Christmas Treats for Children

Gingerbread Family

90 g/3½ oz margarine
275 g/10 oz clear honey
115 g/4½ oz castor sugar
1½ teaspoons ground ginger
¼ teaspoon ground allspice
¼ teaspoon ground cinnamon
7 g/¼ oz cocoa powder
675 g/1½ lb plain flour
1 teaspoon bicarbonate of soda
pinch of salt
2 eggs
ICING
1 egg white
175–225 g/6–8 oz icing sugar
75 g/3 oz plain chocolate
blanched almonds, pistachio
  nuts, glacé cherries, raisins,
  etc., to decorate

Stir the margarine, honey, sugar, spices and cocoa powder together and warm over a low heat until the sugar is completely dissolved. Leave to cool.

Sift the flour and bicarbonate of soda into a bowl and knead in the salt, eggs and honey mixture to obtain a smooth dough. Cover and leave to stand overnight at room temperature.

Grease two baking trays. Preheat the oven to moderately hot (200°C, 400°F, Gas Mark 6). Roll out the dough to 5 mm/¼ inch thick and cut out figures using a gingerbread cutter. Place on the trays and bake for 12–15 minutes in the centre of the oven. Remove from the baking tray while still warm and cool on a wire rack.

Whisk the egg white stiffly with the sifted icing sugar. Decorate the figures with the piped icing, melted chocolate and the nuts and fruit, as illustrated.

Shortbread Christmas Tree

SHORTBREAD
300 g/11 oz plain flour
100 g/4 oz icing sugar
150 g/5½ oz butter, softened
1 egg
FILLING
250 ml/8 fl oz milk
1 tablespoon sugar
2 tablespoons custard powder
2 egg whites
2 tablespoons icing sugar
DECORATION
4 tablespoons apricot jam
100 g/4 oz desiccated coconut
chocolate and coloured icing,
  hundreds and thousands,
  silver balls and chopped nuts

Cut out from cardboard a Christmas tree pattern 33 cm/13 inches high and 28 cm/11 inches wide at the widest point. Sift the flour and icing sugar into a bowl with the butter

and egg, and mix until a dough is formed. Cover and leave for 2 hours in the refrigerator.

Prepare a custard from the milk, sugar and custard powder, following the instructions on the packet. Leave to cool. Whisk the egg whites until stiff then whisk in the sifted icing sugar. Fold into the cooled custard. Preheat the oven to moderately hot (190°C, 375°F, Gas Mark 5).

Roll out the shortbread dough, cut out two trees, and from the trimmings cut several small shapes for decoration. Bake for 15–20 minutes. While still warm cover one tree with the custard filling and place the second tree on top. Leave to cool.

Warm the jam, spread on the tree and sprinkle generously with desiccated coconut. Ice and decorate the small biscuit shapes and attach to the Christmas tree with jam.

Christmas Baking from Abroad

Austrian Jam Rings

400 g/14 oz plain flour
200 g/7 oz butter, cut into flakes
3 egg yolks
100 g/4 oz castor sugar
25 g/1 oz vanilla sugar
grated rind and juice of 1 lemon
50 g/2 oz ground hazelnuts
100 g/4 oz strawberry jam
icing sugar to sprinkle

Sift the flour into a mixing bowl and add the butter. Put the egg yolks, sugar, vanilla sugar, lemon rind and hazelnuts in the centre and knead all the ingredients to a pastry dough. Wrap in foil or cling film and leave in the refrigerator for 2 hours.

Preheat the oven to moderately hot (200°C, 400°F, Gas Mark 6). Roll out the pastry on a floured surface to a thickness of about 5 mm/¼

inch, and cut into an equal number of 6-cm/2½-inch circles and rings. Place on a greased baking tray and bake for 10 minutes, until golden brown.

Carefully lift the circles and rings from the baking tray with a palette knife and leave to cool on a wire rack. Mix the jam with the lemon juice. Sift icing sugar generously over the ring biscuits. Spread the round biscuits with the jam and put a ring biscuit on the top of each.

Almond Ring Biscuits

4 hard-boiled egg yolks
200 g/7 oz butter, softened
80 g/3 oz icing sugar
few drops of vanilla essence
pinch of salt
300 g/10¼ oz plain flour
120 g/4 oz almonds
100 g/3½ oz castor sugar
2 egg yolks
6 tablespoons redcurrant jelly
icing sugar to sprinkle

Press the hard-boiled egg yolks through a sieve and beat with the butter and sifted icing sugar until well mixed. Add the vanilla essence, salt and sifted flour and mix all the ingredients to a firm dough. Wrap in foil or cling film and leave for 2 hours in the refrigerator.

Blanch the almonds in boiling water, peel and chop

coarsely, then toss in the sugar.

Preheat the oven to moderately hot (200°C, 400°F, Gas Mark 6). Roll out the dough to 3 mm/⅛ inch thick and with a biscuit ring cutter, cut out rings about 5 cm/2 inches in diameter. Beat the fresh egg yolks, brush one side of the rings and sprinkle with the sugared almond mixture. Place on a baking tray with the almond side uppermost and bake for 10–15 minutes. Remove with a palette knife and cool on a wire rack.

Sandwich the rings together with redcurrant jelly and sprinkle with sifted icing sugar.

Christmas Baking from Abroad

Swiss Honey Bars

350 g/12 oz thick honey
350 g/12 oz sugar
90 g/3¼ oz blanched almonds
90 g/3¼ oz hazelnuts
90 g/3¼ oz walnuts
250 g/9 oz chopped mixed peel
grated rind of 1 lemon
575 g/1¼ lb plain flour
1 teaspoon ground cinnamon
2 teaspoons ground cloves
generous pinch of grated nutmeg
¼ teaspoon bicarbonate of soda
2 tablespoons arrack or ouzo
2 tablespoons cherry brandy

Bring the honey to the boil with 250 g/9 oz of the sugar, stirring continuously. Finely chop the almonds, hazelnuts and walnuts. Combine the nuts with the mixed peel, lemon rind and sifted flour. Stir in the cinnamon, cloves, nutmeg and bicarbonate of soda and mix well with the hot honey mixture. Knead in the arrack and cherry brandy, form into a ball and leave to stand at room temperature for 1 day.

Preheat the oven to moderate (180°C, 350°F, Gas Mark 4). Grease a baking tray and roll out the dough to 1 cm/½ inch thick. Place on the baking tray and bake for 30–35 minutes in the centre of the oven. Bring the remaining sugar to the boil with a little water. Spread quickly over the cake while still warm and cut into bars on the baking tray. Leave to cool.

Viennese Vanilla Crescents

50 g/2 oz blanched almonds
50 g/2 oz hazelnuts
280 g/10 oz plain flour
70 g/2½ oz castor sugar
pinch of salt
200 g/7 oz butter, cut into flakes
2 egg yolks
75 g/3 oz vanilla sugar
25 g/1 oz icing sugar

Finely grate the almonds and hazelnuts. Place the sifted flour in a mixing bowl with the nuts, sugar, salt, butter and egg yolks, and knead to a soft dough. Wrap in foil or cling film and leave for 2 hours in the refrigerator.

Preheat the oven to moderately hot (190°C, 375°F, Gas Mark 5). Form the dough a little at a time into small rolls the thickness of a pencil. Cut the rolls into 5-cm/2-inch pieces and curve in crescents. Bake in the centre of the oven for 10 minutes until golden. Mix the vanilla sugar with the sifted icing sugar and toss the biscuits in this while still warm.

Cook's Tip

To store the biscuits, place in layers between greaseproof paper in a tin; this will avoid breakage.

American Ginger Slices

6 whole preserved gingers
150 g/5¼ oz butter or margarine
100 g/4 oz castor sugar
1 egg
pinch of salt
¼ teaspoon ground ginger
300 g/11 oz plain flour
1 egg yolk to glaze

Very finely chop 3 of the whole gingers and dice the remainder. Cream the butter or margarine with the sugar, egg, salt, ground ginger and finely chopped ginger. Sift in the flour and work quickly together to obtain a smooth dough. Form into a ball, wrap in foil or cling film and leave for 2 hours in the refrigerator.

Preheat the oven to moderately hot (200°C, 400°F, Gas Mark 6). Divide the dough into three and roll out one piece at a time on a floured board to about 5 mm/¼ inch thick. Cut out oblongs about 6 × 3.5 cm/2½ × 1½ inches. Place on a baking tray. Beat the egg yolk with a little water. Brush the biscuits with egg yolk, sprinkle with the diced ginger and bake in the centre of the oven for 15 minutes. Remove from the baking tray with a palette knife and leave to cool on a wire rack.

Danish Cookies

250 g/8 oz butter or margarine
200 g/7 oz sugar
125 g/4 oz golden syrup
75 g/2½ oz blanched almonds, chopped
75 g/2½ oz candied lemon peel, chopped
¼ teaspoon ground cloves
2 teaspoons ground cinnamon
½ teaspoon ground ginger
½ teaspoon bicarbonate of soda
500 g/1 lb plain flour

Melt the butter or margarine with the sugar and syrup. Remove from the heat and stir in the almonds, chopped peel, cloves, cinnamon and ginger.

Dissolve the bicarbonate of soda in a little boiling water, stir into the syrup mixture and leave to cool. Sift and knead in the flour. Form the dough into two rolls, wrap in foil or cling film and leave for 24 hours in the refrigerator.

Grease two baking trays. Preheat the oven to moderately hot (200°C, 400°F, Gas Mark 6). Cut the rolls of dough into slices 5 mm/¼ inch thick. Place on the baking trays, allowing room for spreading, and bake for 8–10 minutes. Remove from the baking trays with a palette knife and leave to cool on a wire rack.

Christmas Baking from Abroad

Norwegian Christmas Rings

3 eggs
1 egg yolk
160 g/5¼ oz icing sugar
250 g/9 oz butter, softened
few drops of vanilla essence
350 g/12 oz plain flour
1 egg yolk, beaten to glaze
sugar crystals to sprinkle

Boil the eggs for 10–12 minutes, plunge into cold water and shell. Press through a fine sieve and stir into the fresh egg yolk with the sifted icing sugar. Gradually work in the softened butter and the vanilla essence. Finally add the sifted flour and knead the ingredients to a soft dough. Wrap in foil or cling film and leave for 3 hours in the refrigerator.

Preheat the oven to moderately hot (190°C, 375°F,

Gas Mark 5). Divide the dough into small pieces and form each into a roll about 10 cm/4 inches in length. Brush the strips at each end with beaten egg yolk and join into rings. Generously brush the tops with egg yolk and sprinkle with sugar crystals. Place on a baking tray and bake for 10–12 minutes.

Remove from the baking tray with a palette knife and leave to cool on a wire rack.

Swedish Yule Biscuits

250 g/9 oz butter, softened
125 g/4½ oz castor sugar
1 egg
400 g/14 oz plain flour
1 teaspoon baking powder
¼ teaspoon salt
1 egg white, beaten to glaze
¼ teaspoon ground cinnamon
50 g/2 oz granulated sugar

Beat the butter with the sugar and egg until light and fluffy. Sift the flour with the baking powder and mix in the salt. Gradually add the flour to the butter mixture and knead all together. Form the dough into a ball, wrap in foil or cling film and leave for 3 hours in the refrigerator.

Preheat the oven to moderately hot (200°C, 400°F, Gas Mark 6). Divide the dough into three portions and

knead each in turn. Take each portion of dough from the refrigerator as required and roll out to a thickness of 3 mm/⅛ inch on a floured board. Cut out 6-cm/2½-inch round biscuits and place on a baking tray.

Brush the biscuits with beaten egg white and sprinkle generously with the mixed cinnamon and sugar. Bake for 8–10 minutes then cool on a wire rack.

Cook's Tip

When sprinkling the biscuits with cinnamon and sugar some will fall on to the baking tray. Before baking remove this with a pastry brush, so it does not burn.

Christmas Baking from Abroad

Dutch Zebras

250 g/9 oz butter
200 g/7 oz castor sugar
¼ teaspoon salt
4 egg yolks
250 g/9 oz plain flour
100 g/3½ oz cornflour
¼ teaspoon baking powder
2 tablespoons rum
4 tablespoons cocoa powder
2 tablespoons sugar crystals

Cream the butter with the
sugar and salt until light and
fluffy. Add the egg yolks one
at a time and beat well until
smooth. Sift the flour with the
cornflour and baking powder,
add to the butter mixture and
knead to a firm dough. Halve
the dough; mix the rum into
one half and the sifted cocoa
powder into the other. Cover
both portions and leave for 1
hour in the refrigerator.
Preheat the oven to moderately hot (190°C, 375°F, Gas

Mark 5). Roll out the light and
dark dough separately on a
floured board until very thin
(1·5 mm/$\frac{1}{16}$ inch). Halve each
portion and place the pieces of
light and dark dough alternately one upon the other, to
make four striped layers. Press
together well and cut into
small oblong shapes. Sprinkle
each with the sugar crystals
and press the sugar in slightly.
Place on greased baking trays
and bake for 15–20 minutes.
Remove from the baking
trays with a palette knife and
leave to cool on a wire rack.

French Madeleines

125 g/4 oz castor sugar
125 g/4 oz self-raising flour
125 g/4 oz butter
3 eggs
pinch of salt
60 g/2 oz ground almonds
2 teaspoons orange flower water
¼ teaspoon vanilla essence

For Madeleines you will need
the traditional small shell-
shaped tins. Grease the tins
with butter.
Mix the sugar and sifted
flour together in a bowl. Melt
but do not brown the butter.
Mix the eggs into the flour and
sugar with a wooden spoon
and gradually add the cooled
butter, salt, ground almonds,
orange flower water and vanilla
essence. Cover and leave to
stand for 1 hour in the
refrigerator.

Preheat the oven to
moderately hot (200°C, 400°F,
Gas Mark 6). Half-fill the
greased tins with the cake
mixture and bake for 10–15
minutes.

Cook's Tip

If you have no Madeleine
tins, use individual patty
or brioche tins.

Christmas Baking from Abroad

Apricot Rings

400 g/14 oz plain flour
120 g/4 oz castor sugar
pinch of salt
grated rind of 1 lemon
25 g/1 oz vanilla sugar
1 egg
2 tablespoons rum
250 g/9 oz butter, cut into flakes
icing sugar to sprinkle
225 g/8 oz apricot jam

Sift the flour into a mixing bowl. Make a well in the centre and add the sugar, salt, lemon rind, vanilla sugar, egg and rum. Dot the butter over the flour and knead all the ingredients to a soft dough. Wrap in foil or cling film and leave for 2 hours in the refrigerator.

Preheat the oven to moderate (180°C, 350°F, Gas Mark 4). Roll out the dough a little at a time on a floured board, to a thickness of

3 mm/⅛ inch. Using a plain and ring cutter of the same size, cut out equal quantities of rounds and rings. Place all on greased baking trays and bake for 10–15 minutes.

Remove from the baking tray with a palette knife and leave to cool on a wire rack. Sift icing sugar generously on to the rings. Warm the jam over a low heat and spread smoothly on to the rounds. Place the rings on top. Add a little more jam to the centre of the rings and cool completely before storing in an airtight tin.

Italian Biscotti

150 g/5 oz butter
200 g/7 oz castor sugar
few drops of vanilla essence
½ egg
1½ tablespoons milk
generous pinch each of ground
*   cardamom and ground*
*   cinnamon*
grated rind of ½ lemon
15 g/½ oz ground almonds
150 g/5 oz plain flour
100 g/4 oz plain chocolate

Beat the butter in a mixing bowl with the sugar and vanilla essence until pale and creamy. Add the egg, milk, spices, lemon rind and almonds and knead the sifted flour into this mixture. Form the dough into rectangular blocks, about 3·5 cm/1½ inches in diameter, wrap in foil and leave in the refrigerator for 2 hours.

Preheat the oven to moderately hot (190°C, 375°F,

Gas Mark 5). Cut the blocks of dough into 5-mm/¼-inch slices, place on a baking tray and bake for 15 minutes.

Remove the biscuits with a palette knife and cool on a wire rack. Melt the chocolate in a basin over a pan of hot water. Dip the biscuits into the chocolate so that they are half-coated diagonally and leave to dry on greaseproof paper.

Honeycake Hearts

115 g/4½ oz castor sugar
40 g/1½ oz butter
225 g/8 oz honey
1 large egg
pinch of salt
25 g/1 oz chopped mixed peel
½ teaspoon ground cinnamon
¼ teaspoon ground cloves
450 g/1 lb plain flour
1 teaspoon baking powder
FILLING AND ICING
100 g/4 oz redcurrant jelly
100 g/4 oz plain chocolate

Grease one or two baking trays with butter or margarine. Preheat the oven to hot (220°C, 425°F, Gas Mark 7).

Heat the sugar and butter with the honey, stirring continuously until all the ingredients have melted to give a smooth mixture. Remove from the heat and stir fre-quently until lukewarm. Beat the egg with the salt. Add the mixed peel to the honey mixture with the beaten egg, cinnamon, cloves and the flour sifted with the baking powder.

Knead well and roll out to about 5 mm/¼ inch thick on a floured pastry board. Cut out small heart shapes, place on the baking trays and bake for 8–10 minutes in the centre of the oven. While still warm sandwich the hearts together with redcurrant jelly. Melt the chocolate in a basin over a pan of hot water and dip one half of the cooled biscuits into the chocolate.

Note To make the variation illustrated on the jacket, do not sandwich pairs of biscuits together, but simply coat one side of each with melted chocolate and sprinkle with chopped pistachios.

Almond Spice Bars

4 eggs
250 g/9 oz castor sugar
400 g/14 oz plain flour
½ teaspoon baking powder
400 g/14 oz ground almonds
100 g/4 oz chopped mixed peel
1 teaspoon ground cinnamon
generous pinch each of ground
  cloves, nutmeg and allspice
1 egg yolk, beaten to glaze
blanched almonds, halved

Beat the eggs with the sugar until pale and creamy. Sift the flour with the baking powder and mix with the ground almonds, chopped peel and spices. Stir all these ingredients into the egg mixture to form a dough. Wrap in foil or cling film and leave for 2 hours in the refrigerator.

Preheat the oven to moderate (180°C, 350°F, Gas Mark 4).

Roll out the dough on a floured board to about 5 mm/¼ inch thick and cut into equal-sized bars. Place on greased baking trays. Thin the beaten egg yolk with a little water and use to brush the bars. Place an almond half in each corner and bake for 20 minutes, until golden. Remove from the baking tray with a palette knife and leave to cool on a wire rack.

Baking Tray Honey Cake

500 g/1 lb clear or thick honey
125 ml/4 fl oz oil
250 g/8 oz castor sugar
700 g/1½ lb plain flour
1 tablespoon baking powder
250 g/8 oz ground almonds
2 teaspoons ground cinnamon
¼ teaspoon ground allspice
pinch of ground cloves
pinch of salt
3 eggs
200 g/7 oz chopped mixed peel
2 tablespoons evaporated milk
almond halves, candied lemon
*   peel and glacé cherries to*
*   decorate*

Bring the honey to the boil with the oil and sugar, stirring continuously. Allow to cool. Sift the flour with the baking powder and mix with the ground almonds, spices, salt, eggs and mixed peel. Add the honey mixture and knead well. If the dough is too soft, add a little more flour. Cover and leave for 1 hour in the refrigerator.

Preheat the oven to moderately hot (190°C, 375°F, Gas Mark 5) and grease two 33 × 23-cm/13 × 9-inch Swiss roll tins. With floured hands press the mixture into the prepared tins, smooth the surface and brush with the evaporated milk. Lightly cut 7·5-cm/3-inch squares in the mixture with a sharp knife. Decorate each square with almonds, cherries and pieces of candied lemon peel, as illustrated. Bake in the centre of the oven for 25–30 minutes. Leave to cool slightly then remove from the baking tray and divide into squares.

Christmas Cakes and Biscuits

Coconut Macaroons

5 egg whites
250 g/9 oz icing sugar
225 g/8 oz ground almonds
225 g/8 oz desiccated coconut
grated rind of ½ lemon
1 tablespoon rum
icing sugar to sprinkle
100 g/4 oz plain chocolate

Line a large baking tray with rice paper. Preheat the oven to cool (150°C, 300°F, Gas Mark 2).

Whisk the egg whites until stiff. Fold in half the sifted icing sugar and the ground almonds. Add the coconut, remaining icing sugar, lemon rind and rum and work all together to a sticky dough. Put the mixture into a piping bag fitted with a large plain nozzle, and pipe walnut – sized drops on to the rice

paper. Sprinkle the macaroons with icing sugar and bake in the centre of the oven for 20 minutes. They should have a golden crust on the outside but remain soft inside. Allow to cool on a wire rack.

Melt the chocolate in a basin over hot water and dip a third of each macaroon in it to coat the end. Leave the chocolate icing to set before serving.

Iced Pretzels

200 g/7 oz butter
100 g/4 oz icing sugar
1 egg yolk
pinch of salt
few drops of vanilla essence
300 g/11 oz plain flour
ICING
1 egg white
3 tablespoons rum
2 teaspoons lemon juice
200 g/7 oz icing sugar

Cream the butter with the sifted icing sugar to a smooth paste, then add the egg yolk, salt and vanilla. Sift the flour and knead it into the mixture. Wrap the pastry dough in foil or cling film and leave in the refrigerator for 2 hours.

Preheat the oven to moderate (180°C, 350°F, Gas Mark 4). Cut off one piece of pastry at a time and shape, leaving the rest of the dough in the refrigerator. Roll each piece

in turn until pencil thin, to a length of 25 cm/10 inches, and make into a pretzel, as illustrated. Place the shaped pretzels on a baking tray and bake in the centre of the oven for 12–15 minutes.

Mix the egg white with the rum, lemon juice and sifted icing sugar. Allow the pretzels to cool a little then remove them from the baking tray with a palette knife. Place on a wire rack and brush the tops as thickly as possible with the rum icing.

Cook's Tip

If you wish to vary the flavour, you could make the icing with arrack instead of rum.

Christmas Cakes and Biscuits

Marshmallow Crescents

175 g/6 oz white marshmallows
100 g/3½ oz butter, softened
1 egg
1 tablespoon vanilla sugar
generous pinch of salt
300 g/10½ oz plain flour
¼ teaspoon baking powder
ICING
50 g/2 oz plain chocolate

Beat the marshmallows with the softened butter until pale and creamy. Add the egg, vanilla sugar and salt and mix well. Sift the flour with the baking powder and gradually stir into the marshmallow mixture. Form into a ball, wrap in foil and chill in the refrigerator until firm.

Preheat the oven to moderate (180°C, 350°F, Gas Mark 4). Quarter the dough and roll each piece into a long thin strip. Cut into 10-cm/4-inch lengths, form into small crescents and place on a baking tray. Bake for 10–15 minutes, until golden.

Carefully remove from the baking tray with a palette knife and leave to cool on a wire rack. Melt the chocolate by standing in a basin over hot water and dip the tips of the crescents into the chocolate. Allow the chocolate to dry thoroughly before storing the biscuits in an airtight tin.

Cinnamon Stars

4 small egg whites
225 g/8 oz icing sugar
300 g/11 oz ground almonds
1½ tablespoons ground cinnamon
grated rind of ½ lemon
castor sugar

Put the egg whites into a heatproof bowl. Whisk until frothy, then add the sifted icing sugar. Place over a pan of simmering water and continue whisking until the meringue is thick and holds its shape. Remove the bowl from the pan. Put 3–4 tablespoons of the meringue to one side. Fold the ground almonds, cinnamon and lemon rind into the remaining meringue mixture and leave to cool for 1 hour.

Preheat the oven to moderate (160°C, 325°F, Gas Mark 3). Grease and flour two baking trays.

Sprinkle a work surface with castor sugar and roll out the mixture until about 5 mm/¼ inch thick. The mixture will be soft and must be rolled out very carefully. Cut into stars with a biscuit cutter and place on the baking trays. Spread the reserved meringue carefully over the stars and bake for 15–20 minutes, until just firm. Transfer the stars carefully to a wire rack and leave to cool.

Chequered Biscuits

300 g/10 oz butter, softened
150 g/5 oz icing sugar
pinch of salt
400 g/14 oz plain flour
30 g/1 oz cocoa powder
1 egg white

Beat the softened butter with the sifted icing sugar and salt until pale and creamy. Knead in the sifted flour and divide the dough in half. Knead the sifted cocoa powder into one portion. Wrap both portions in foil or cling film and leave for 2 hours in the refrigerator.

Divide each piece of dough into five portions. Roll out one colour into five long thin rolls. With the other colour, roll out four pieces into long thin rolls. Arrange these rolls into a chequerboard design, brushing and sealing with a little beaten egg white. Roll out the remaining portion of dough large enough to wrap around the assembled dough. Seal with beaten egg white, wrap in foil or cling film and chill in the refrigerator until firm, about 1 hour.

Preheat the oven to moderately hot (190°C, 375°F, Gas Mark 5). Cut the dough into 5-mm/¼-inch thick slices, place on a baking tray and bake for 10–15 minutes. Remove the biscuits with a palette knife and cool on a wire rack.

Note To make the pinwheel biscuits illustrated on the jacket, shape the chilled dough into long rolls. Using one roll as the centre, shape two more rolls around it to make a complete circle, alternating the colours. Seal with beaten egg white and continue as above.

Cinnamon Spice Cookies

500 g/1 lb clear or thick honey
300 g/10 oz castor sugar
3 eggs
2 teaspoons bicarbonate of soda
1 teaspoon ground cinnamon
¼ teaspoon ground cloves
generous pinch each of ground
*   nutmeg, coriander, ginger,*
*   allspice and cardamom*
1 teaspoon white pepper
1 kg/2 lb plain flour
100 g/4 oz icing sugar

Grease two baking trays.
Warm the honey over a low heat until liquid then stir in the sugar, eggs, bicarbonate of soda and all the spices. Mix in the flour gradually at first and then knead it in thoroughly. Preheat the oven to moderately hot (190°C, 375°F, Gas Mark 5).

Form the dough into small balls about 2·5 cm/1 inch in diameter and place at intervals on the baking tray. Bake for 10–15 minutes until golden brown then cool on a wire rack. Blend the sifted icing sugar with a little water, bring to the boil, stirring continuously, and coat the biscuits with this icing.

Christmas Cakes and Biscuits

Aniseed Biscuits

4 eggs, separated
225 g/8 oz icing sugar
pinch of salt
300 g/11 oz plain flour
2 teaspoons ground aniseed

Grease a baking tray and
sprinkle with flour.
Cream the egg yolks with the
sifted icing sugar and salt
until pale and light. Whisk the
egg whites until very stiff, then
fold into the yolk mixture. Sift
the flour and aniseed on to
this mixture and fold in quickly
but thoroughly. Fill a piping
bag fitted with a plain nozzle
with the biscuit mixture and
pipe in small rounds on to the
baking tray. Leave to dry out
overnight.
    Preheat the oven to
moderate (160°C, 325°F, Gas
Mark 3), and bake towards the
top of the oven for 20 minutes.
Cool on a wire rack.

Cook's Tip

To make Cinnamon
Biscuits, substitute 2
teaspoons ground cinna-
mon for the ground
aniseed.

Chocolate Macaroons

100 g/4 oz plain chocolate
4 egg whites
200 g/7 oz castor sugar
225 g/8 oz ground almonds

Line a baking tray with non-
stick baking parchment or rice
paper. Preheat the oven to
moderate (180°C, 350°F, Gas
Mark 4).
    Grate the chocolate. Whisk
the egg whites until stiff. Add
the sugar gradually and
continue whisking until the
mixture is thick and glossy.
Fold in the ground almonds
and grated chocolate. Drop
spoonfuls of the mixture on to
the baking tray, leaving space
between each biscuit. Bake for
15–20 minutes. Do not let the
macaroons become too dark or
they will taste bitter.
    Cool on the baking tray,

then carefully peel the
macaroons off the non-stick
paper or cut around each
biscuit on the edible rice
paper.

Nutmeg Biscuits

125 g/4 oz butter
125 g/4 oz castor sugar
1 egg
grated rind of ½ lemon
generous pinch of grated nutmeg
pinch each of ground cinnamon
*   and ground cloves*
125 g/4 oz plain flour
125 g/4 oz hazelnuts, finely
*   chopped*
125 g/4 oz fresh white
*   breadcrumbs*
1 egg yolk, beaten to glaze
50 g/2 oz blanched almonds

Beat the butter with the sugar,
egg, lemon rind and spices.
Mix the sifted flour with the
hazelnuts and breadcrumbs,
add to the butter mixture and
knead all the ingredients
quickly to a dough. Cover and
leave for 2 hours in the
refrigerator.
   Preheat the oven to
moderately hot (200°C, 400°F,
Gas Mark 6). Roll out the
dough to 5 mm/¼ inch thick.
Cut out small scalloped arcs
6 cm/2½ inches long and
2·5 cm/1 inch wide. Place on
greased baking trays and brush
with beaten egg yolk. Place a
blanched almond on each
biscuit and bake for 10–15
minutes.

Cook's Tip

If you do not have the
proper biscuit cutter,
make a cardboard pattern
and use it to help you
cut out the arcs.

Iced Lemon Bars

150 g/5 oz butter
125 g/4 oz castor sugar
1 egg
generous pinch each of ground
*   cinnamon, ground cloves and*
*   grated nutmeg*
grated rind of 1 lemon
125 g/4 oz plain flour
125 g/4 oz ground almonds
125 g/4 oz fresh white
*   breadcrumbs*
ICING
200 g/7 oz icing sugar
2–3 tablespoons lemon juice
30 g/1 oz candied lemon peel
30 g/1 oz candied orange peel

Beat the butter with the sugar
until pale and creamy. Stir in
the egg, spices and lemon rind.
Sift in the flour, gradually add
the almonds and breadcrumbs
and knead to a smooth soft
dough. Wrap in foil or cling
film and leave for 2 hours in
the refrigerator.

   Preheat the oven to
moderately hot (200°C, 400°F,
Gas Mark 6). Roll out the
dough on a floured board to
5 mm/¼ inch thick and cut out
bars 2·5 × 6 cm/1 × 2½ inches.
Place on greased baking trays,
allowing room between each
for spreading. Bake for 10–15
minutes then remove with a
palette knife and place on a
wire rack.
   Sift the icing sugar and stir
in the lemon juice until smooth.
Use to thickly ice the biscuits
when they are slightly cooled.
Cut the lemon and orange peel
into thin strips and place on the
icing while still soft.

Christmas Cakes and Biscuits

Chocolate Orange Cookies

100 g/4 oz plain chocolate
125 g/4½ oz butter or margarine
125 g/4½ oz castor sugar
pinch of salt
1 egg
grated rind of 1 orange
200 g/7 oz plain flour
1 teaspoon baking powder
ICING
100 g/4 oz icing sugar
1–2 tablespoons orange juice

Coarsely grate the chocolate. Beat the butter or margarine with the sugar, salt, egg and orange rind. Sift in the flour with the baking powder, add the grated chocolate and quickly knead all the ingredients to a workable dough. Form into a ball, wrap in foil or cling film and leave for 2 hours in the refrigerator.

Preheat the oven to moderately hot (200°C, 400°F, Gas Mark 6). Roll out the dough on a floured board to 5 mm/¼ inch thick and cut out rounds 5 cm/2 inches in diameter. Place on greased baking trays, allowing room for spreading, and bake for 10–15 minutes. Carefully remove from the baking trays with a palette knife and leave to cool on a wire rack.

Sift the icing sugar and stir in the orange juice until smooth. Spread this icing over the top of the cookies and leave to set.

Crumbly Almond Hearts

250 g/9 oz butter
120 g/4½ oz icing sugar
2 egg yolks
100 g/4 oz ground almonds
350 g/12 oz plain flour
40 blanched almonds, halved

Beat the butter with the sifted icing sugar and 1 egg yolk until pale and creamy. Add the ground almonds and sifted flour and knead quickly to a firm dough. Form into a ball, wrap in foil or cling film and leave for 2 hours in the refrigerator.

Preheat the oven to moderately hot (200°C, 400°F, Gas Mark 6). Roll out the dough on a floured board to 5 mm/¼ inch thick and cut out 40 small heart shapes. Place on a large baking tray, beat the second egg yolk, brush the

biscuits with this and place two almond halves on each. Bake for 10–12 minutes.

Allow the biscuits to cool slightly on the baking tray, then remove to a wire rack and leave until completely cool.

Christmas Night Gâteau

SPONGE MIXTURE
4 eggs, separated
3 tablespoons water
180 g/6 oz castor sugar
1 tablespoon vanilla sugar
150 g/5¼ oz plain flour
100 g/3½ oz cornflour
2 teaspoons baking powder
FILLING AND TOPPING
7 g/¼ oz powdered gelatine
600 ml/1 pint double cream
150 g/5 oz castor sugar
40 g/1½ oz cocoa powder
1 tablespoon boiling water
1 tablespoon rum
3 tablespoons cranberry jelly
DECORATION
100 g/4 oz plain chocolate
8 glacé cherries
1 teaspoon icing sugar
25 g/1 oz toasted flaked almonds

Grease the base of a 23-cm/9-inch cake tin with butter or margarine. Preheat the oven to moderately hot (190°C, 375°F, Gas Mark 5).

Beat the egg yolks with the water, half the sugar and the vanilla sugar until pale and creamy. Whisk the egg whites until stiff and fold in the remaining sugar, then carefully fold into the egg yolk mixture. Sift the flour with the cornflour and baking powder and carefully fold into the mixture. Turn into the prepared tin, smooth the surface and bake for 30–40 minutes. Cool on a wire rack. Leave the cake to stand overnight if possible then cut through twice to make three layers.

Dissolve the gelatine in 2 tablespoons water over a gentle heat. Whip the cream with the sugar until stiff. Cream the cocoa powder with the boiling water and rum, cool and mix a quarter of the

cream with it. Spread this chocolate cream thickly on the first layer of cake and place the second layer on top. Warm the cranberry jelly, cool slightly and mix with the dissolved gelatine into a second quarter of the cream. Cover the second cake layer with this mixture and top with the last cake layer. Cover the cake all over with some of the remaining cream, place the rest in a piping bag fitted with a star nozzle and pipe 16 rosettes around the top of the cake.

Melt half the chocolate by standing in a basin over a pan of hot water and spread thinly on to greaseproof paper or foil. When the chocolate has set, dip a small star-shaped cutter into hot water and cut out 16 star shapes. Place a chocolate star and halved glacé cherry on each rosette. Coarsely grate the remaining chocolate. Sprinkle over the centre of the cake, sift lightly

with icing sugar and decorate the sides of the cake with flaked almonds.

Cook's Tip

From the block of chocolate you can also make chocolate caraque, as illustrated. Spread the melted chocolate on to a clean flat surface. When the chocolate has just set, scrape off shavings with the blade of a knife. Leave the shavings to set hard then sprinkle on to the cake.

Chocolate Log

SPONGE MIXTURE
*4 eggs, separated, plus 2 egg
   yolks*
80 g/3 oz castor sugar
grated rind of ½ lemon
80 g/3 oz plain flour
FILLING AND TOPPING
350 g/12 oz plain chocolate
225 g/8 oz butter
125 g/4½ oz icing sugar
1 tablespoon rum
3 glacé cherries
*1 teaspoon chopped pistachio
   nuts*

Line a 33 × 23-cm/13 × 9-inch
Swiss roll tin with greased
greaseproof paper. Preheat the
oven to hot (220°C, 425°F,
Gas Mark 7).

Beat all the egg yolks with 1
tablespoon sugar and the lemon
rind until pale and creamy.
Whisk the egg whites until
stiff, fold in the remaining
sugar then fold into the egg
yolks. Carefully fold in the
sifted flour. Spread this
mixture evenly over the Swiss
roll tin and bake near the top
of the oven for 10–12 minutes.

Turn the cake out on to a
clean tea towel sprinkled with
sugar, remove the greaseproof
lining paper and trim off the
edges of the sponge. Cover
with a clean piece of greaseproof
paper and carefully roll up the
cake with the help of the tea
towel, keeping the clean
greaseproof inside. Cool.

Melt the chocolate in a
basin over hot water. Spread
approximately a quarter of the
chocolate thinly over greaseproof paper and leave to set.
Allow the melted chocolate to
cool. Beat the butter with the
sifted icing sugar until pale
and creamy; keep 2 table-
spoons to one side. Beat the
cooled melted chocolate and
rum into the rest of this butter
cream. Carefully unroll the
cooled cake and spread two-
thirds of the chocolate cream
over it. Roll up again and pipe
the rest of the cream in stripes
along the length of the cake.

From the thin sheet of
chocolate cut out small leaves,
using a warmed knife. Decorate
the log with the reserved butter
cream, the halved glacé
cherries, chocolate leaves and
pistachio nuts, as illustrated.
Cut off one slice and place
beside the cake.

Fairy Tale Fir Cone Cake

*2 (18-cm/7-inch) sandwich
  cakes (see method)*
25 g/1 oz cornflour
2 egg yolks
300 ml/½ pint milk
100 g/4 oz castor sugar
250 g/9 oz butter
50 g/2 oz plain chocolate
50 g/2 oz cocoa powder
*3 small packets chocolate
  buttons*

Make a sandwich cake following the basic recipe on page 228. Bake in two 18-cm/7-inch greased sandwich tins in a moderately hot oven (190°C, 375°F, Gas Mark 5) for 25 minutes. Cut the cooled cakes into the oval shape of a large fir cone.

Blend the cornflour with the egg yolks and a little of the milk. Dissolve the sugar in the remaining milk and bring to the boil. Pour on to the cornflour mixture, stirring continuously. Return to the heat and bring to the boil, stirring until thickened, then leave to cool. Beat the butter until pale and creamy then gradually stir in the cooled cornflour custard, beating well with each addition. Melt the chocolate in a basin over hot water and mix into the butter cream with the sifted cocoa powder.

Cut horizontally through each cake once to give four layers in all. Sandwich the cakes together with the chocolate butter cream and spread it over the top and sides. Press chocolate buttons over the surface of the cake, slightly overlapping, to cover it completely.

Brussels Fruit Cake

200 g/7 oz crystallised pineapple
200 g/7 oz crystallised pears
90 g/3 oz candied lemon peel
*250 g/9 oz red and green glacé
  cherries, halved*
*225 g/8 oz walnuts, finely
  chopped*
*110 g/4 oz pecan nuts, finely
  chopped*
*110 g/4 oz almonds, finely
  chopped*
*110 g/4 oz hazelnuts, finely
  chopped*
400 g/14 oz raisins
5 tablespoons sherry
225 g/8 oz butter
450 g/1 lb castor sugar
*pinch each of salt and grated
  nutmeg*
6 eggs
450 g/1 lb self-raising flour
sherry to moisten
*crystallised and glacé fruit
  to decorate*

Finely dice the pineapple, pears and candied peel and mix with the cherries, nuts, raisins and sherry. Leave to stand overnight.

Line two 1-kg/2-lb loaf tins with buttered greaseproof paper. Preheat the oven to moderate (160°C, 325°F, Gas Mark 3).

Beat the butter with the sugar, salt and nutmeg until pale and creamy, then beat in the eggs one at a time. Fold in the sifted flour and finally stir in the fruit and nut mixture. Turn into the prepared tins and bake for 2–2¼ hours.

Remove the cakes from the tins when cool and strip off the greaseproof paper. Wrap each cake in a muslin cloth moistened in sherry, then wrap in foil and leave in the refrigerator for 4 weeks. Every week moisten the muslin with sherry again. Finally decorate the cakes with crystallised and glacé fruit.

Christmas Specialities

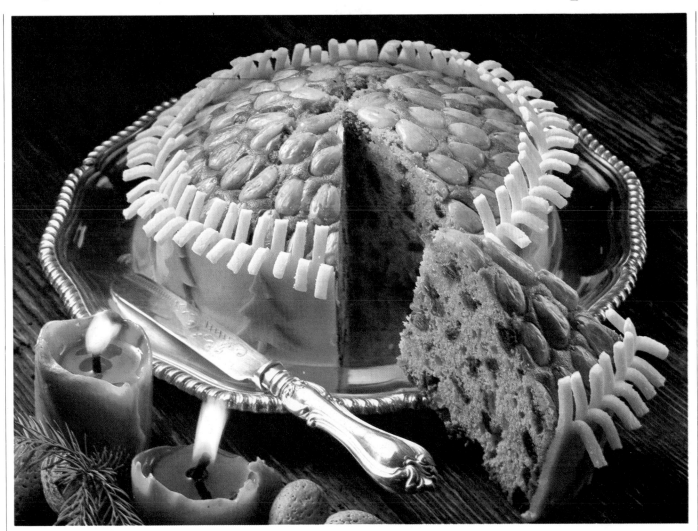

Festive Light Christmas Cake

250 g / 9 oz butter
250 g / 9 oz castor sugar
¼ teaspoon vanilla essence
generous pinch of salt
1 tablespoon rum
6 eggs
350 g / 12 oz plain flour
1 teaspoon baking powder
400 g / 14 oz sultanas
50 g / 2 oz ground almonds
100 g / 4 oz candied lemon peel,
  chopped
100 g / 4 oz blanched almonds,
  halved
GLAZE AND DECORATION
2 tablespoons granulated sugar
4 tablespoons water
225 g / 8 oz almond paste
2 tablespoons apricot jam
food colourings

Line a 23-cm/9-inch round cake tin with greased greaseproof paper. Preheat the oven to cool (150°C, 300°F, Gas Mark 2).

Beat the softened butter with the castor sugar, vanilla essence, salt and rum until pale and creamy. Stir in the eggs one at a time. If the eggs should curdle the mixture slightly, add a tablespoon of flour. Sift the remaining flour with the baking powder and mix with the sultanas, ground almonds and chopped peel. Fold this flour mixture gradually into the creamed mixture. Turn into the prepared tin, smooth the surface with the back of a wet spoon and arrange the almond halves in a circular pattern on top. Bake the cake for 4¼–4¾ hours. Before removing from the oven test with a skewer; if the skewer comes out clean from the centre, then the cake is cooked through. Allow to stand

in the tin for about 15 minutes then place on a wire cooling rack, leaving the greaseproof paper on the cake.

Heat the sugar and water, stirring continuously until the sugar is completely dissolved. Boil for 2–3 minutes. Cover the top of the cake with this glaze and leave to cool.

Spread the sides of the cake with the warmed jam. Roll out the almond paste thinly. Cut pieces to cover the sides of the cake, cutting into strips at the top, as illustrated. Colour the rest of the marzipan with the food colouring of your choice, cut out small Christmas tree shapes and attach to the cake with unbeaten egg white.

Cook's Tip

If you tie a double thickness of brown paper around the outside of the cake tin before baking, this will prevent the edges of the cake becoming brown and overcooked before the inside is cooked through.
The undecorated cake will keep well if wrapped in greaseproof paper and stored in an airtight tin.

Date and Almond Stollen

500 g/1 lb plain flour
30 g/1 oz fresh yeast
250 ml/8 fl oz lukewarm milk
60 g/2 oz castor sugar
2 eggs
150 g/5 oz butter, cut into flakes
50 g/2 oz blanched almonds,
  chopped
grated rind of 1 lemon
pinch of salt
FILLING
25 g/1 oz cornflour
450 ml/¾ pint milk
1 egg yolk
100 g/3½ oz castor sugar
250 g/8 oz dates, finely chopped
15 g/½ oz butter
ICING
200 g/7 oz icing sugar
1 egg white
juice of 1 lemon
2 tablespoons toasted flaked
  almonds

Grease a baking tray with butter or margarine.

Sift the flour into a bowl and form a well in the centre. Cream the yeast with a little of the milk and 1 tablespoon of the sugar. Add the remaining milk and pour into the flour. Sprinkle a little flour over it, cover and leave to stand for 15 minutes in a warm place, until frothy.

Beat the eggs and mix with the remaining sugar, the butter, almonds, lemon rind and salt. Add to the flour and yeast mixture and knead all the ingredients well for 5–10 minutes, to form a smooth elastic dough. Cover and leave to rise for 30 minutes.

Blend the cornflour with a little of the milk, the egg yolk and sugar. Bring the dates to the boil in the remaining milk. Stir the milk and dates into the cornflour mixture then add the butter. Return to the heat and bring to the boil, stirring

continuously until thickened. Leave the mixture to cool, stirring occasionally to prevent a skin forming.

Lightly knead the dough and roll out to 1 cm/½ inch thick on a floured board. Spread the date mixture evenly over it. Turn both side edges over twice towards the centre and press together. Place on the baking tray and leave to stand for a further 20 minutes.

Preheat the oven to moderately hot (200°C, 400°F, Gas Mark 6) and bake the stollen for 1 hour. Sift the icing sugar and beat into the egg white with the lemon juice. Ice the stollen while still warm and sprinkle flaked almonds on to the icing before it sets.

Cook's Tip

This stollen tastes best when eaten fresh. However, if well wrapped in foil, it will keep for 3–4 days.

Christmas Specialities

Apricot Plait

500 g/1 lb plain flour
30 g/1 oz fresh yeast
250 ml/8 fl oz lukewarm milk
60 g/2 oz castor sugar
150 g/5 oz dried apricots, finely
    chopped
100 g/3½ oz blanched almonds,
    chopped
50 g/2 oz candied lemon peel,
    chopped
25 g/1 oz candied orange peel,
    chopped
1 tablespoon arrack or ouzo
2 eggs, beaten
150 g/5 oz butter, cut into flakes
grated rind of 1 lemon
pinch of salt
TOPPING
50 g/2 oz butter
icing sugar to sprinkle

Grease a narrow 1-kg/2-lb
loaf tin and sprinkle with flour.

Sift the flour into a bowl and
form a well in the centre.
Cream the yeast with a little
of the milk and 1 teaspoon of
the sugar. Stir in the remaining
milk and pour into the flour.
Sprinkle a little of the flour
over the liquid and leave for
15 minutes, until frothy.

Mix the apricots with the
almonds, chopped peel and
arrack. To the flour and yeast
mixture add the eggs, remaining
sugar, the butter, lemon rind and
salt, and knead together until
smooth and elastic. Knead in
the fruit mixture, cover and
leave to rise in a warm place
for 30 minutes.

Divide the dough into three
and form into long rolls.
Weave into a plait, place in the
loaf tin, cover and leave to
stand in a warm place for a
further 20 minutes. Preheat
the oven to moderately hot
(190°C, 375°F, Gas Mark 5).

Bake for 30–40 minutes.
While still warm brush with
the melted butter and sift
icing sugar generously over the
top and sides.

Soft Fruit Loaf

500 g/1 lb cottage cheese
500 g/1 lb plain flour
2 teaspoons baking powder
2 eggs
150 g/5 oz castor sugar
1 tablespoon vanilla sugar
pinch of salt
1 tablespoon grated lemon rind
1 tablespoon chopped almonds
1 tablespoon raisins
2 tablespoons chopped mixed
    candied fruit
2 tablespoons chopped mixed
    peel
TOPPING
15 g/½ oz butter, melted
1 tablespoon icing sugar
1 tablespoon vanilla sugar

Grease a baking tray with
butter or margarine and
sprinkle with flour. Preheat the
oven to moderately hot (190°C,
375°F, Gas Mark 5).

Press the cottage cheese
through a sieve or liquidise.
Sift the flour with the baking
powder on to a pastry board
and form a well in the centre.
Add the cottage cheese, eggs,
sugar, vanilla sugar, salt,
lemon rind, nuts, fruit and
peel. Mix to a firm dough,
knead lightly and form into a
loaf. Place on a baking tray
and bake for 50–60 minutes.

Transfer the loaf to a wire
cooling rack and brush with
melted butter while still hot.
Mix the icing sugar and vanilla
sugar and sift generously over
the loaf.

Rich Chocolate Fudge

50 g/2 oz butter
2 egg yolks
100 g/4 oz icing sugar
grated rind of ½ orange
350 g/12 oz plain chocolate
*6 tablespoons strong black tea,
cooled*
*50 g/2 oz drinking chocolate
powder*

Line an 18-cm/7-inch shallow
square tin with foil or greaseproof paper. Beat the butter
with the egg yolks and sifted
icing sugar until pale and
creamy. Stir in the grated
orange rind. Coarsely chop the
chocolate and melt in a basin
over a pan of hot water. Stir
the cooled tea and melted
chocolate into the butter
mixture and pour into the
prepared tin. Place in the
refrigerator to set.

When firm cut into 2·5-cm/
1-inch squares and dip in the
sifted chocolate powder.

Cook's Tip

This fudge is delicious
flavoured with 2 tea-
spoons rum in place of
the grated orange rind.
Add the rum to the
melted chocolate then
continue as above.

Quince Diamonds

1·75 kg/4 lb fresh quinces
300 ml/½ pint water
grated rind of 1 orange
grated rind of 1 lemon
1 teaspoon ground cinnamon
1 tablespoon cherry brandy
about 1 kg/2 lb granulated sugar
100 g/4 oz chopped mixed peel

Rub the quinces well with a
damp cloth, quarter, remove
their stalks and the cores. Place
in a pan with the water and
cook over a gentle heat for
45 minutes. Press through a
sieve and weigh the sieved
pulp. Add the orange and
lemon rind, cinnamon and
cherry brandy. Cover and leave
to stand overnight.

Add 300 g/10 oz sugar for
every 500 g/1 lb of pulp, mix
well and heat until the sugar
dissolves, then reduce to a
thick consistency when the
pulp should come away from

the sides of the pan. Stir
occasionally during cooking.

Line two 18 × 28-cm/
7 × 11-inch Swiss roll tins
with greaseproof paper and
grease well. Mix the chopped
peel into the quince pulp and
divide the mixture between the
two tins, smoothing over.
Leave to dry out for 3–4
hours in a very cool oven
(110°C, 225°F, Gas Mark ¼)
with the door slightly open.
Leave to cool completely then
cut into diamond shapes and
coat in the remaining sugar.

Christmas Sweets and Candies

Marzipan Fig Balls

1 tablespoon arrack or rum
250 g/9 oz almond paste
8 dried figs
3 tablespoons orange jelly
*   marmalade*
100 g/4 oz demerara sugar

Knead the arrack or rum into the almond paste on a clean surface sprinkled with a little icing sugar. Quarter the figs. Wrap each piece of fig in marzipan and shape into a ball. Gently heat the marmalade and stir until smooth.

Roll the marzipan balls first in the marmalade then in the demerara sugar. Leave until completely dry on greaseproof paper then put into paper sweet cases.

Store the fig balls in an airtight tin between layers of greaseproof paper.

> **Cook's Tip**
>
> Instead of figs, you can stuff the marzipan balls with diced dried apricots, diced dates or a glacé cherry.

Caramel Creams

300 g/10 oz granulated sugar
125 ml/4 fl oz boiling water
25 g/1 oz butter
125 ml/4 fl oz double cream
1 tablespoon vanilla sugar

Line an 18-cm/7-inch shallow square tin with foil and brush with oil.

Carefully cook the sugar in a frying pan over a very low heat, stirring continuously until it forms a caramel. Gradually add the boiling water, then stir in the butter, cream and vanilla sugar. Bring this mixture to boiling point and continue to cook until a 116°C/240°F is reached.

Pour the mixture into the prepared tin. When it begins to set, cut into 1·5-cm/¾-inch squares with a sharp pointed knife. Separate the sweets so they do not stick together and leave to cool completely.

> **Cook's Tip**
>
> If the caramels are intended as a gift, it is especially nice to wrap each sweet in a piece of coloured cellophane paper.

Christmas Sweets and Candies

Apricot Coins

200 g/7 oz dried apricots
250 g/9 oz desiccated coconut
juice of 1 lemon
200–300 g/7–11 oz icing sugar

Place the apricots in a sauce-pan and cover with boiling water. Cover the pan and simmer for about 2 hours. Check the pan at intervals to make sure that there is suffi-cient water left.

Drain the apricots well and mince finely. Mix with 200 g/7 oz desiccated coconut and mince again. Alternatively the apricots and coconut may be processed in a liquidiser. Combine the apricot and coconut mixture with the lemon juice and enough sifted icing sugar to give a workable dough.

Form the dough into a roll about 3·5 cm/1½ inches in diameter and cut off 'coins',

5 mm/¼ inch thick. Sprinkle the remaining coconut on to a plate and turn the apricot coins in it until well coated. Place between layers of grease-proof paper in a tin and leave to dry out for at least 2 days.

Cook's Tip

Instead of apricots you can make the coins with dried plums. If using plums with stones, allow twice the amount and stone the plums after weighing.

Chocolate Almond Crisps

100 g/4 oz raisins
1–2 tablespoons rum
400 g/14 oz milk chocolate
150 g/5 oz toasted almonds, chopped
30 g/1 oz candied lemon peel, finely chopped

Line a baking tray with a sheet of foil or greaseproof paper. Spoon the rum over the raisins, cover and leave to steep overnight.

Melt the chocolate in a basin over a pan of hot water, allow to cool slightly then mix with the raisins, rum, almonds and chopped peel. Take small amounts of the mixture with a teaspoon and place in mounds on the lined baking tray. Allow to dry slightly and then place in the refrigerator to set completely.

Cook's Tip

Instead of raisins soaked in rum you can also make the crisps with 2 cups of meringue crumbs (crush about 6 meringues with a rolling pin). These make deliciously light sweets.

Christmas Sweets and Candies

Chocolate Ducats

300 g/10 oz plain sweet biscuits
80 g/3 oz plain chocolate
100 g/4 oz butter
200 g/7 oz castor sugar
1 egg
50 g/2 oz cocoa powder
1 tablespoon cherry brandy

Crush the biscuits in a poly-thene bag with a rolling pin. Break up the chocolate and melt in a basin over a pan of hot water. Beat the butter with the sugar and egg until pale and creamy. Add the melted chocolate, sifted cocoa powder, cherry brandy and biscuit crumbs, and mix all together well.

Chill slightly then form into a roll about 5 cm/2 inches in diameter. Wrap in cling film or foil and leave to stand in the refrigerator for at least 12 hours until completely set.

Cut 1-cm/½-inch slices from the roll and carefully wrap the ducats in gold wrapping paper or foil.

Cook's Tip

This chocolate mixture also makes a deliciously rich dessert. Turn into a 0·5-kg/1-lb foil-lined loaf tin and chill as above. Serve cut in thin slices and accompany with cream.

Chocolate Cherry Nougat

300 g/12 oz nougat
100 g/4 oz milk chocolate
100 g/4 oz flaked almonds
40 g/1½ oz pistachio nuts,
  chopped
50 g/2 oz candied lemon peel,
  finely chopped
100 g/4 oz glacé cherries,
  coarsely chopped
2 teaspoons cherry brandy
200 g/8 oz plain chocolate

Line a 0·5-kg/1-lb loaf tin with foil.

Melt the nougat with the milk chocolate in a basin over a pan of hot water. Stir the flaked almonds, pistachios, chopped peel, glacé cherries and cherry brandy into the chocolate mixture. Fill the loaf tin, smooth the surface and leave to set in the refrigerator.

Melt the plain chocolate in a basin over hot water. Remove the chocolate nougat from the tin when set and strip off the foil. Coat all over with the plain chocolate icing and leave to set. Before serving cut into 5-mm/¼-inch slices.

Marzipan Hearts

500 g/1 lb almond paste
300 g/11 oz icing sugar
2 egg whites
1 egg yolk, beaten to glaze
glacé cherries
candied orange and lemon peel

Preheat the oven to hot (220°C, 425°F, Gas Mark 7).
Work the almond paste and 200 g/7 oz of the sifted icing sugar together. Roll out on a surface dusted with icing sugar until 1 cm/½ inch thick. Cut out small heart shapes with a biscuit cutter. With the remaining marzipan mixture, cut thin strips long enough to form the outline of the heart. Brush the edges of the hearts with egg white, then place the strips on top to form a raised border. Flute with the prongs of a fork, then brush the borders with beaten egg yolk. Place the hearts on a baking tray and bake for 3–5 minutes.
Mix together the remaining egg white and icing sugar and ice over the centres of the hearts. Leave to set then decorate with the cherries and strips of candied peel.

Cook's Tip

Use a selection of biscuit cutters to make different marzipan shapes.

Marzipan Pralines

80 g/3 oz walnuts, finely chopped
1 tablespoon rum
1 tablespoon Maraschino
400 g/14 oz almond paste
400 g/14 oz plain chocolate
40 walnut halves

Knead the walnuts, rum and Maraschino into the almond paste on a clean surface sprinkled with a little icing sugar. Roll out to 1 cm/½ inch thick and with a sharp knife cut out trapezium shapes as illustrated.
Break up the chocolate and melt in a basin over a pan of hot water. Leave to cool until almost set and then warm again gently. Spear the marzipan pieces on to a fork and dip in the chocolate until thoroughly coated. Leave to drain slightly on a wire rack and press a walnut half into the icing while still soft. Allow the chocolate icing to dry and then place in the refrigerator until completely set.

Cook's Tip

Omit the chocolate icing and simply top each marzipan praline with a whole almond.

Christmas Sweets and Candies

Chocolate Fruits

200 g / 7 oz plain chocolate
250 g / 9 oz crystallised
*   pineapple rings*
250 g / 9 oz dried apricots
60 g / 2 oz blanched almonds

Break up the chocolate and melt in a basin over a pan of hot water. Leave the chocolate to cool until it is just about to set and then warm again gently. Cut the pineapple rings into trapezium shapes.

Dip the pineapple pieces and apricots into the chocolate to half-coat the fruit and drain on a wire rack. Stick an almond on to each apricot while the icing is still moist.

Cook's Tip

These fruit sweets will taste even better if you make the fruit mixture yourself from raspberries, strawberries or oranges, following the recipe for Quince Diamonds (see page 134). Mix the raspberry or strawberry purée with a little grated lemon rind and lemon juice; mix the orange pulp with chopped pistachio nuts and Cointreau liqueur. After drying out the fruit mixture in the oven, cut into quite large diamond or trapezium shapes and coat with chocolate.

Stuffed Dates

225 g / 8 oz dates
100 g / 4 oz almond paste
40 g / 1½ oz pistachio nuts, finely
*   chopped*
1 tablespoon orange liqueur
1–2 tablespoons granulated
*   sugar*

Stone the dates. Knead the almond paste with the pistachios and liqueur on a clean surface sprinkled with a little icing sugar. Form the marzipan into small balls and dip in the granulated sugar.

Press the marzipan balls into the stoned dates, mark into ridges with a knife and sprinkle with a little extra sugar.

Cook's Tip

The stuffed dates have a really festive air if half-dipped in melted chocolate. You can also mix about 100 g / 4 oz finely chopped crystallised pineapple into the marzipan mixture, form into small balls and coat in melted chocolate.

Jam Doughnuts

500 g/1 lb plain flour
30 g/1 oz fresh yeast
250 ml/8 fl oz lukewarm milk
50 g/2 oz castor sugar
1–2 tablespoons oil
2 egg yolks
¼ teaspoon salt
1 tablespoon rum
3–4 tablespoons plum jam
icing sugar to sprinkle
oil or fat to deep fry

Sift the flour into a bowl and make a well in the centre. Cream the yeast with a little of the milk then gradually add the remaining milk and a little sugar. Pour into the well and sprinkle a little of the flour over the top. Cover and leave to stand for 15 minutes, until frothy.

Work the rest of the sugar, the oil, egg yolks, salt and rum into the yeast mixture with the rest of the flour and beat until

light. Cover and leave to stand for a further 20 minutes. Roll out the dough to 2·5 cm/1 inch thick and cut out 6·5-cm/2¾-inch rounds. Place a teaspoonful of jam on each round, draw the dough together very carefully over the jam and leave the doughnuts to stand for a further 15 minutes.

Heat the oil for frying to 182°C/360°F. When the doughnuts have risen, place smooth side down in the hot oil. Cover and cook for 3 minutes, turning until golden brown all over. Drain the doughnuts on absorbent paper and sift icing sugar over the tops.

Deep-Fried Pretzels

500 g/1 lb plain flour
30 g/1 oz fresh yeast
250 ml/8 fl oz lukewarm milk
50 g/2 oz castor sugar
100 g/3½ oz margarine
1 egg
¼ teaspoon salt
grated rind of ½ lemon
generous pinch each of ground allspice and ground ginger
castor sugar to sprinkle
oil or fat to deep fry

Sift the flour into a bowl and make a well in the centre. Cream the yeast with the milk and a little sugar. Pour into the well and sprinkle over a little of the flour. Cover and leave to stand in a warm place for 15 minutes, until frothy.

Melt the margarine and beat with the rest of the sugar, the egg, salt, lemon rind and spices,

until fluffy. Add to the yeast liquid and beat in the rest of the flour to obtain a soft light dough. Cover and leave to stand for a further 20 minutes.

Divide the dough into 50-g/2-oz pieces and with floured hands form into balls. From the balls roll 40-cm/16-inch lengths and form these into pretzel shapes, as illustrated. Leave to stand for 15 minutes on a floured board. Heat the oil for frying to 182°C/360°F. Place three pretzels at a time in the hot oil and fry until crisp and golden all over. Drain on absorbent paper and while still hot sprinkle with castor sugar.

New Year's Eve Specials

Piped Choux Rings

CHOUX PASTE
250 ml/8 fl oz water
60 g/2 oz butter
pinch of salt
150 g/5 oz plain flour
4 eggs
ICING
150 g/5 oz icing sugar
2 tablespoons rum
1 tablespoon water
oil or fat to deep fry

Cut a sheet of greaseproof paper to fit into a deep-frying pan and brush with oil.

Heat the water gently with the butter and salt until the butter is melted, then bring to the boil. Add the sifted flour all at once, remove from the heat and stir until the dough comes away from the sides of the pan and forms a ball. Return to the heat and cook for 1 minute stirring continuously. Place in a bowl, leave to cool slightly, then stir in the beaten eggs one after the other.

Heat the oil or fat to 182°C/360°F in the deep-frying pan. Place the choux paste in a piping bag fitted with a large star nozzle and pipe rings on to the greaseproof paper; the rings should not be too large. Place the paper with the rings attached into the hot oil in the pan, with the rings under the paper. Remove the paper when the rings become free of it. Fry the rings on both sides until golden then drain on absorbent paper. Repeat until all the rings are cooked.

Blend the sifted icing sugar with the rum and water and thinly ice the choux rings.

Almond Doughnuts

500 g/1 lb plain flour
30 g/1 oz fresh yeast
250 ml/8 fl oz lukewarm milk
80 g/3 oz castor sugar
60 g/2 oz margarine
3 eggs
40 g/1½ oz ground almonds
½ teaspoon salt
ICING
70 g/3 oz icing sugar
1 egg white
1 tablespoon rum
2 tablespoons toasted flaked almonds
oil or fat to deep fry

Sift the flour into a bowl and form a well in the centre. Cream the yeast with the milk and a little of the sugar. Pour into the well and sprinkle over a little flour. Cover and leave in a warm place for 15 minutes, until frothy.

Melt the margarine and beat with the rest of the sugar, the eggs, ground almonds and salt until frothy. Pour into the flour and beat all together to a soft, light dough. Cover and leave to stand for 20 minutes.

Knead well then divide the dough into 50-g/2-oz pieces and form each piece into a ball. Make a hole in the middle of each ball with a wooden spoon handle, twisting the spoon to form the doughnuts into rings. Leave the rings to stand for a further 15 minutes.

Heat the oil for frying to 182°C/360°F in a deep-frying pan. Place four doughnuts at a time in the hot oil and fry on both sides until crisp and golden. Drain on absorbent paper.

Stir the sifted icing sugar into the egg white with the rum. Ice the cooled doughnuts and sprinkle with toasted flaked almonds.

141

New Year's Eve Specials

Brandy Fritters

400 g/14 oz plain flour
¼ teaspoon baking powder
30 g/1 oz butter or margarine,
* cut into flakes*
50 g/2 oz castor sugar
pinch of salt
2 eggs
6 tablespoons milk
1 tablespoon Grappa (Italian
* brandy)*
icing sugar to sprinkle
oil or fat to deep fry

Sift the flour with the baking
powder into a bowl. Dot over
the butter. Add the sugar, salt,
eggs, milk and Grappa, and
knead all the ingredients to a
smooth dough.

Heat the oil or fat for frying
to 182°C/360°F. Roll out the
dough on a floured board to
3 mm/⅛ inch thick and cut into
3·5-cm/1½-inch squares. Add
ten fritters at a time to the hot
oil and fry for 4–6 minutes
until golden: turn halfway
through cooking with a
draining spoon.

Lift out the fritters when
cooked and drain on absorbent
paper. Sift icing sugar over
them while still warm.

Rhine Rum Fritters

80 g/3 oz butter or margarine
50 g/2 oz castor sugar
1 egg
2 tablespoons rum
250 g/9 oz plain flour
3 tablespoons milk
pinch of salt
icing sugar to sprinkle
oil or fat to deep fry

Melt the butter or margarine,
remove from the heat and beat
with the sugar, egg and rum
until frothy. Sift the flour into a
bowl, form a well in the centre
and add the milk, salt and the
butter mixture. Knead to a
workable dough.

Heat the oil or fat to 182°C/
360°F in a deep-frying pan.
Roll out the dough on a
floured board to 3 mm/⅛ inch
thick. Using a pastry wheel,
cut out diamond shapes. Add
six fritters at a time to the hot
oil and fry for 4–5 minutes
until golden: turn halfway
through cooking with a
draining spoon.

Lift out the cooked fritters
and drain on absorbent paper.
Sift icing sugar over them
while still warm.

Cinnamon Balls

80 g/3 oz butter or margarine
80 g/3 oz castor sugar
grated rind of ½ lemon
pinch of salt
4 eggs
400 g/14 oz plain flour
1 teaspoon baking powder
100 g/4 oz sugar to sprinkle
2 teaspoons ground cinnamon
oil or fat to deep fry

Beat the butter or margarine with the sugar until light and creamy. Beat in the lemon rind and salt, and the eggs, one at a time. Sift the flour with the baking powder and fold into the mixture with a metal spoon.

Heat the oil or fat to 182°C/360°F in a deep-frying pan. Using two floured teaspoons form the dough into small balls and fry about eight balls at a time in the hot oil until golden. This will take about

5–6 minutes: turn halfway through cooking.

Remove with a draining spoon and drain on absorbent paper. Mix the sugar with the cinnamon and sprinkle over the balls while still warm.

Dutch Raisin Doughnuts

500 g/1 lb plain flour
40 g/1½ oz fresh yeast
100 g/3½ oz castor sugar
6 tablespoons lukewarm milk
pinch of salt
grated rind of 1 lemon
grated rind of 1 orange
2 eggs
75 g/3 oz butter, cut into flakes
100 g/3½ oz raisins
50 g/2 oz currants
75 g/3 oz candied orange peel,
  finely chopped
oil or fat to deep fry

Sift the flour into a bowl and make a well in the centre. Cream the yeast with a little of the sugar and half the milk and pour into the well. Sprinkle with a little of the flour, cover and leave to stand in a warm place for 15 minutes.

Mix the rest of the sugar

with the remaining milk, the salt, lemon and orange rinds, eggs and flaked butter, and beat into the flour. Mix all the ingredients to a stiff dough. Knead for a few minutes then leave to stand in a warm place for 15 minutes. Simmer the raisins and currants for 2 minutes in hot water, drain and mix into the dough with the candied orange peel. Leave the dough to stand for a further 30 minutes.

Heat the oil for frying to 160°C/320°F. Using two floured tablespoons, cut the dough into small doughnuts and fry six at a time in the oil for about 10 minutes, until golden brown. Halfway through the frying time turn the doughnuts with a draining spoon.

Lift out the cooked doughnuts with the draining spoon and drain on absorbent paper.

Easter Bread

BASIC YEAST DOUGH
1 kg/2¼ lb plain flour
50 g/2 oz fresh yeast
550 ml/18 fl oz lukewarm milk
200 g/7 oz butter, melted
100 g/3½ oz castor sugar
2 eggs
pinch of salt
grated rind of 1 lemon
FRUIT LOAF
100 g/4 oz blanched almonds,
chopped
200 g/7 oz candied lemon peel,
chopped
300 g/11 oz sultanas
1 tablespoon rum
50 g/2 oz butter, melted
50 g/2 oz sugar
PLAITED WREATH
1 egg yolk, beaten to glaze
50 g/2 oz nibbed almonds
50 g/2 oz sugar
2 tablespoons rum

Sift the flour into a bowl and make a well in the centre. Cream the yeast with a little of the milk then stir in the remaining milk. Pour into the flour, sprinkle with a little of the flour and leave to stand in a warm place for 15 minutes, until frothy. Pour the melted butter into the yeast liquid and mix with the flour, sugar, eggs, salt and lemon rind, to form a dough. Knead for 5–10 minutes until the dough is smooth and elastic. Cover and leave to rise for 1 hour in a warm place.

Mix the almonds, candied peel, sultanas and rum together and leave to stand for 30 minutes.

Divide the dough in two and knead each half lightly. Mix one half with the fruit mixture and leave for 15 minutes. Pre-heat the oven to moderately hot (190°C, 375°F, Gas Mark 5).

Form the fruit dough into a loaf, place on a greased baking tray and leave to stand in a warm place for a further 30 minutes. Cut a cross on the top of the loaf and bake for 30–40 minutes. While still hot, brush the loaf with the melted butter and sprinkle with sugar.

Divide the remaining dough into three equal pieces and form into long strips. Plait these together, form into a wreath and brush with beaten egg yolk. Mix the almonds, sugar and rum and spread over the wreath. Bake as for the fruit loaf.

Easter Specialities

Bremer Fruit Loaf

750 g/1½ lb plain flour
45 g/1½ oz fresh yeast
250 ml/8 fl oz lukewarm milk
100 g/4 oz castor sugar
400 g/12 oz butter
1 tablespoon vanilla sugar
1 teaspoon each salt and ground
   cardamom
150 g/5 oz blanched almonds,
   chopped
125 g/4 oz candied lemon peel,
   chopped
grated rind and juice of 1 lemon
500 g/1 lb raisins

You can bake the Bremer Fruit Loaf either in a loaf tin or on a baking tray. The following recipe uses both ways. Grease a long 1-kg/2-lb loaf tin and a baking tray.

Sift the flour into a bowl and make a well in the centre. Cream the yeast with a little of the milk then add the sugar and the remaining milk. Pour into the flour, cover and leave in a warm place for 15 minutes, until frothy.

Melt the butter, cool slightly and beat with the vanilla sugar, salt and cardamom. Beat the butter mixture into the yeast liquid and flour to obtain a dough. Knead in the almonds, chopped peel, lemon rind and juice and the raisins, until the dough is smooth. Cover and leave to stand in a warm place for a further 40 minutes.

Lightly knead the dough and then halve it. Place one half in the greased loaf tin and leave to stand in a warm place for

30 minutes. Preheat the oven to moderately hot (190°C, 375°F, Gas Mark 5). When the loaf is well risen, place in the oven and bake for 45–50 minutes. Before removing from the oven, test with a skewer. Turn out on a wire rack and leave to cool.

Shape the second half of the dough into a long loaf, place on the greased baking tray and leave to stand in a warm place for 30 minutes. Bake for 45–50 minutes then cool on a wire rack.

Cook's Tip

You can also bake fruit rolls from this dough. When the dough is ready, weigh portions of 40–50 g/1½–2 oz and roll into balls. Place on a greased baking tray, flatten slightly, cover and leave to stand in a warm place for 15 minutes. Before baking brush with beaten egg yolk. Sprinkle with sugar and bake for 20–30 minutes in a moderately hot oven (190°C, 375°F, Gas Mark 5).

Russian Mazurka

5 eggs, separated
175 g/6 oz castor sugar
2 small lemons
250 g/9 oz hazelnuts, toasted
    and ground to a powder
TOPPING
250 ml/8 fl oz double cream
2 tablespoons icing sugar
2 tablespoons rum
coloured sugar Easter eggs

Grease a 20-cm/8-inch cake
tin with butter or margarine.
Preheat the oven to moderate
(180°C, 350°F, Gas Mark 4).
   Beat the egg yolks with the
sugar until pale and creamy.
Grate the rind of both lemons
and squeeze the juice of one.
Add to the egg yolk mixture
and gradually fold in the
hazelnuts. Whisk the egg
whites until stiff and fold
in carefully with a metal spoon.
Place the mixture in the cake
tin, smooth the surface and

bake for 40 minutes. As
soon as the sides of the cake
begin to come away from the
tin, turn off the oven and
leave the cake to stand for
15 minutes in the warm oven.
Turn out to cool on a wire
rack.
   Whip the cream with the
sifted icing sugar and rum.
When stiff enough to stand in
peaks, spread thickly over the
top of the cake and decorate
with Easter eggs.

Country Rice Flan

PASTRY
300 g/10 oz plain flour
200 g/7 oz butter, cut into flakes
100 g/3½ oz castor sugar
1 egg
FILLING
50 g/2 oz short-grain rice
900 ml/1½ pints milk
175 g/6 oz sugar
25 g/1 oz butter
4 eggs
100 g/4 oz cream cheese
75 g/3 oz candied lemon peel,
    chopped
¼ teaspoon ground cinnamon
grated rind of 1 lemon
grated rind of 1 large orange
icing sugar mixed with ground
    cinnamon to sprinkle

Sift the flour into a bowl and
mix in the butter, sugar and
egg to form a dough. Chill in
the refrigerator for 2 hours.

Wash and drain the rice.
Bring the milk to the boil with
the sugar and butter, stir in
the rice and simmer gently,
stirring occasionally, for 1
hour, until thick and creamy.
Remove from the heat. Beat
the eggs with the cream cheese,
chopped peel, cinnamon and
fruit rinds. Gradually stir in
the rice and cool. Preheat the
oven to moderately hot
(200°C, 400°F, Gas Mark 6).
   Roll out two-thirds of the
pastry to line a 20-cm/8-inch
sandwich tin. Prick the base
all over with a fork then fill
with the cooled rice mixture.
Roll out the rest of the pastry,
cut into strips with a pastry
wheel and place on top of the
tart in a lattice pattern. Bake
for 50 minutes, covering with
foil if the top gets too brown.
   Leave in the tin until the
rice is set. Turn out and invert
to serve the lattice on top. Sift
over the sugar and cinnamon.

Coffee Cream Tart

PASTRY
100 g/4 oz butter
50 g/2 oz castor sugar
1 egg
1 tablespoon water
100 g/4 oz ground hazelnuts
150 g/6 oz plain flour
FILLING AND TOPPING
1 tablespoon instant coffee
  powder
250 ml/8 fl oz hot water
25 g/1 oz powdered gelatine
2 eggs, separated
125 g/4½ oz castor sugar
1 tablespoon vanilla sugar
2 tablespoons brandy
450 ml/¾ pint double cream
2 teaspoons chopped pistachio
  nuts
12 sugar Easter eggs

Knead together the butter, sugar, egg, water, hazelnuts and sifted flour to form a dough. Wrap in foil or cling film and leave for 2 hours in the refrigerator.

Preheat the oven to moderately hot (200°C, 400°F, Gas Mark 6). Roll out the pastry and use to line the base and sides of a 23-cm/9-inch flan tin. Bake blind for 25–30 minutes. Leave the flan case to cool.

Dissolve the coffee in the hot water. Dissolve the gelatine in the hot coffee over a gentle heat. Beat the egg yolks with the sugar and vanilla sugar until pale and creamy. Stir in the cooled coffee and the brandy. Whisk the egg whites and separately whip the cream until stiff. Fold the egg whites and two-thirds of the cream into the coffee mixture. Fill the tart case with this coffee cream. When set, decorate with the rest of the cream, piped in rosettes, the pistachios and Easter eggs.

Polish Easter Ring

500 g/1 lb plain flour
30 g/1 oz fresh yeast
250 ml/8 fl oz lukewarm milk
120 g/4 oz castor sugar
375 g/12 oz butter
½ teaspoon salt
grated rind of ½ orange
grated rind of ½ lemon
5 eggs
150 g/5 oz raisins
ICING
250 g/9 oz icing sugar
1 tablespoon lemon juice
3 tablespoons hot water
6 glacé cherries

Grease two 1·75-litre/3-pint savarin moulds and sprinkle with flour.

Sift the flour into a bowl and form a well in the centre. Cream the yeast with a little of the milk and a little sugar. Add the remaining milk and pour into the flour. Sprinkle a little of the flour over the yeast liquid and leave in a warm place for 15 minutes.

Melt the butter, mix with the remaining sugar, the salt, grated fruit rinds and eggs, and beat into the yeast liquid and flour to obtain a smooth batter. Leave to stand in a warm place for 30 minutes. Beat the raisins into the batter. Divide the batter between the tins and leave to rise in a warm place until approximately 2·5 cm/1 inch from the top of the tins. Preheat the oven to moderately hot (200°C, 400°F, Gas Mark 6).

Bake the cakes for 50 minutes, covering with a little foil if they become too brown. Leave to cool in the tins for 20 minutes, then turn out to cool completely on a wire rack. Blend the sifted icing sugar with the lemon juice and water, pour over the cakes and decorate with halved cherries.

147

Lombardy Easter Loaf

500 g / 1 lb plain flour
30 g / 1 oz fresh yeast
250 ml / 8 fl oz lukewarm milk
2 eggs
70 g / 2½ oz castor sugar
¼ teaspoon salt
generous pinch each of grated
*   nutmeg and ground allspice*
grated rind of ½ lemon
120 g / 4 oz butter, melted
50 g / 2 oz candied lemon peel,
*   finely chopped*
1 egg yolk, beaten to glaze

Grease a 23-cm/9-inch cake tin.

Sift the flour into a bowl and make a well in the centre. Cream the yeast with a little of the milk then add the remaining milk. Pour into the flour. Sprinkle a little of the flour over, cover and leave in a warm place for 15 minutes.

Beat the eggs with the sugar, salt, nutmeg, allspice and lemon rind. Add to the yeast liquid together with the butter and chopped peel. Mix to form a dough and knead until smooth and elastic. Leave to stand in a warm place for a further 30 minutes then knead lightly and divide into four equal portions. Roll each piece into a ball and place the balls in a ring in the prepared tin. Leave to stand in a warm place for a further 30 minutes. Pre-heat the oven to moderately hot (200°C, 400°F, Gas Mark 6).

Brush the loaf with beaten egg yolk and bake for 30–40 minutes. Leave to cool and serve with pats of butter.

Greek Easter Bread

60 g / 2 oz fresh yeast
200 ml / 7 fl oz lukewarm milk
50 g / 2 oz castor sugar
1 kg / 2 lb plain flour
pinch of salt
grated rind of 1 orange
250 ml / 8 fl oz lukewarm water
50 g / 2 oz sesame seeds
5 eggs, hard-boiled
red food colouring
1 egg yolk, beaten to glaze

Cream the yeast with a little of the milk and the sugar, add the remaining milk and leave to stand in a warm place for 15 minutes, until frothy. Sift in 125 g / 4 oz flour, stir, cover and leave to stand overnight in a warm place.

Sift the rest of the flour into a bowl, form a well and add the prepared yeast liquid, salt and orange rind. Gradually stir in the water and mix to form a dough. Knead for at least 10 minutes, until the dough is smooth and elastic. Shape two-thirds of the dough into a long, smooth loaf, 5 cm/2 inches in height. Place on an oiled baking tray. From the rest of the dough make two thin rolls the length of the loaf, roll in the sesame seeds, twist and place round the loaf. Brush the eggs with red food colouring, leave to dry then press perpendicularly into the loaf. Brush the loaf with beaten egg yolk, sprinkle with sesame seeds, cover and leave to stand in a warm place for 1 hour. Preheat the oven to moderately hot (190°C, 375°F, Gas Mark 5).

Bake for 40–50 minutes then cool the loaf on a wire rack.

Easter Specialities

Easter Nests

500 g / 1 lb plain flour
30 g / 1 oz fresh yeast
250 ml / 8 fl oz lukewarm milk
50 g / 2 oz butter
1 egg
pinch of salt
50 g / 2 oz castor sugar
1 egg yolk, beaten to glaze
18 eggs (boiled for 5 minutes)

Sift the flour into a bowl and
form a well in the centre.
Cream the yeast with a little
of the milk then add the rest
of the milk. Pour into the well
and sprinkle over a little of the
flour. Cover and leave to stand
in a warm place for 15
minutes, until frothy.

Melt the butter, beat with
the egg, salt and sugar and
work into the flour and yeast
mixture to obtain a dry dough.
Knead well then leave to rise
for 1 hour. Divide the dough
into 50-g/2-oz pieces and with

floured hands form into balls.
Roll the balls into 50-cm/20-
inch lengths, twist to form
spirals, form into a circle and
knot the ends (see illustration
above). Place the nests on a
greased baking tray, brush with
beaten egg yolk and place one
egg (still in its shell) in the
centre of each. Leave to stand
for 10 minutes.

Preheat the oven to moderately hot (200°C, 400°F, Gas
Mark 6) and bake the Easter
Nests for 15–20 minutes. After
baking, decorate the eggs using
water colours, coloured
pencils, or felt-tip pens.

Easter Ducklings

500 g / 1 lb plain flour
30 g / 1 oz fresh yeast
60 g / 2 oz castor sugar
250 ml / 8 fl oz lukewarm milk
60 g / 2 oz butter, melted
1 egg
pinch of salt
1 egg yolk, beaten to glaze
225 g / 8 oz strawberry jam
DECORATION
2 tablespoons icing sugar
1 teaspoon lemon juice
currants
crystallised flowers (optional)

Sift the flour into a bowl and
form a well in the centre.
Cream the yeast with a little
of the sugar and the milk.
Pour into the well and sprinkle
with a little of the flour. Leave
to stand for 15 minutes. Add
the rest of the sugar, the
melted butter, egg and salt and
mix to a dough. Knead well
then leave to rise for 1 hour.

Roll out to 5 mm/¼ inch
thick. From two-thirds of the
dough cut out circles 7·5 cm/
3 inches in diameter. Brush
the edges of the circles with
beaten egg yolk, spoon a little
jam in the centre and place two
circles together until all are
used. From the rest of the
dough cut out smaller rounds
for the heads and ovals for the
beaks. Attach the heads to the
body and the beaks to the head
with a little beaten egg yolk.
Place on a greased baking tray
and leave in a warm place for
15 minutes.

Preheat the oven to hot
(220°C, 425°F, Gas Mark 7).
Brush the ducklings with egg
yolk and bake for 15 minutes.
Blend the sifted icing sugar
with the lemon juice. Stick the
currants on to blobs of icing
to form eyes and decorate the
ducklings with crystallised
flowers, if liked.

Casanova Slices

SPONGE MIXTURE
*4 eggs, separated, plus 2 egg
  yolks
100 g/4 oz castor sugar
80 g/3 oz plain flour
20 g/1 oz cornflour
100 g/4 oz ground hazelnuts*
FILLING AND TOPPING
*25 g/1 oz cornflour
300 ml/½ pint milk
50 g/2 oz castor sugar
250 g/9 oz butter
2 tablespoons brandy
225 g/8 oz redcurrant jelly
2 tablespoons demerara sugar
12 glacé cherries*

Line a 28 × 18-cm/11 × 7-
inch Swiss roll tin with greased
greaseproof paper. Preheat the
oven to hot (220°C, 425°F,
Gas Mark 7).
   Beat all the egg yolks with
half the sugar until pale and
creamy. Whisk the egg whites
until stiff and fold in the
remaining sugar. Carefully
fold the whites into the yolks.
Sift over the flour and cornflour and fold in with the
hazelnuts. Spread over the
Swiss roll tin and bake for
10–12 minutes. Turn out the
cake on to clean greaseproof
paper and remove the lining
paper. Leave for 2 hours then
cut into three strips lengthways.
   Blend the cornflour with a
little of the milk and the sugar.
Heat the remaining milk and
pour over the cornflour mixture. Return to the heat and
bring to the boil, stirring until
thickened. Allow to cool. Beat
the butter until pale and
gradually mix in the cooled
sauce and brandy. Sandwich
the cake layers together with
redcurrant jelly and butter
cream. Cover the top and
edges of the cake thinly with
butter cream and sprinkle with
demerara sugar. Cut into 12
slices and decorate with piped
butter cream and cherries.

Chocolate Cake Napoleon

*6 large eggs, separated
200 g/7 oz castor sugar
100 g/4 oz plain flour
50 g/2 oz cornflour
50 g/2 oz cocoa powder
80 g/3 oz almonds, chopped
½ teaspoon ground cinnamon
¼ teaspoon ground cloves
pinch of salt
2 tablespoons brandy
25 g/1 oz butter*
ICING
*100 g/4 oz plain chocolate
1 tablespoon chopped pistachio
  nuts*

Grease a 30-cm/12-inch long
Balmoral cake tin or 1-kg/2-lb
loaf tin and sprinkle with fine
breadcrumbs. Preheat the oven
to moderate (180°C, 350°F,
Gas Mark 4).
   Beat the egg yolks with half
the sugar until pale and
creamy. Whisk the egg whites
until stiff and fold in the remaining sugar. Carefully fold
the egg whites into the egg
yolks. Sift the flour with the
cornflour and cocoa powder,
and mix with the almonds,
cinnamon, cloves and salt.
Carefully fold into the egg
mixture with the brandy. Melt
the butter and fold into the
mixture while warm.
   Turn into the prepared tin,
smooth the surface and bake
for 50–60 minutes. Leave to
cool on a wire rack. Melt the
chocolate in a basin over a
pan of hot water and use to
ice the cake. Sprinkle the
pistachios on to the icing
before it sets.

Gâteau Madame Pompadour

SPONGE MIXTURE
4 eggs, separated, plus 2 egg
 yolks
1 tablespoon hot water
120 g/4 oz castor sugar
150 g/5 oz ground almonds
50 g/2 oz plain flour
pinch of salt
FILLING AND TOPPING
25 g/1 oz cornflour
300 ml/½ pint milk
100 g/4 oz castor sugar
1 tablespoon vanilla sugar
¼ teaspoon vanilla essence
250 g/9 oz butter
50 g/2 oz toasted flaked
 almonds

Grease a 23-cm/9-inch cake
tin and sprinkle with flour.
Preheat the oven to moderate
(180°C, 350°F, Gas Mark 4).
 Beat all the egg yolks with
the water and 90 g/3 oz sugar
until pale and creamy. Fold in
the ground almonds and sifted
flour. Whisk the egg whites
with the salt until stiff and fold
in the remaining sugar. Fold
the egg whites into the egg
yolk mixture. Turn into the
prepared tin and bake for 40
minutes, then cool on a wire
rack. Leave to stand for 2 hours
then cut into three layers.
 Blend the cornflour with a
little of the milk, the sugar,
vanilla sugar and vanilla
essence. Heat the remaining
milk and pour over the blended
cornflour. Return to the boil,
stirring continuously until
thickened, then cool. Beat the
butter until creamy then gradually beat in the cooled sauce.
 Use half this butter cream to
cover two layers of cake and
place the layers one upon the
other. Cover the top and sides
of the cake with the rest of the
cream and sprinkle with
almond flakes. Leave to stand
in a cool place before serving.

Kaiser Franz-Joseph's Cake

100 g/4 oz butter
250 g/9 oz castor sugar
4 eggs, separated, plus 2 egg
 yolks
pinch of salt
1 teaspoon ground cinnamon
1 tablespoon Maraschino
50 g/2 oz fresh white
 breadcrumbs
250 g/9 oz ground almonds
50 g/2 oz candied lemon peel,
 finely chopped
80 g/3 oz self-raising flour
ICING
100 g/4 oz redcurrant jelly
200 g/7 oz icing sugar
1 tablespoon lemon juice
1 tablespoon Maraschino

Grease a 23-cm/9-inch cake
tin. Preheat the oven to
moderately hot (190°C, 375°F,
Gas Mark 5).
 Beat the butter with half the
sugar until pale and creamy,
then add the egg yolks one
after another. Mix in the salt,
cinnamon, Maraschino,
breadcrumbs, almonds and
lemon peel. Sift the flour and
fold into the mixture. Whisk
the egg whites until stiff then
whisk in the remaining sugar
until smooth and glossy. Fold
the egg whites into the creamed
mixture, turn into the tin and
bake for 1 hour.
 Turn the cake on to a wire
rack to cool. Spread the top
and sides with redcurrant
jelly. Sift the icing sugar and
add the lemon juice and
liqueur. Beat the icing until
smooth, pour on to the cake
and allow to run thickly over
the sides. Smooth the surface
with a palette knife.

Sesame Seed Biscuits

125 g/4½ oz soft margarine
250 g/9 oz castor sugar
1 egg
100 g/4 oz cracked wheat
100 g/3½ oz raisins
120 g/4 oz sesame seeds
2 tablespoons milk
225 g/8 oz plain wholemeal flour
¼ teaspoon grated nutmeg

Grease a baking tray with oil. Preheat the oven to moderately hot (190°C, 375°F, Gas Mark 5).

Beat the margarine with the sugar until pale and creamy. Stir in the egg. Mix the cracked wheat with the raisins, sesame seeds and milk and gradually stir into the mixture. Add the wholemeal flour and nutmeg and stir all the ingredients well together.

Using a teaspoon, place small amounts on the prepared baking tray and flatten slightly. Bake for 10–15 minutes. Remove from the baking tray with a palette knife and leave to cool on a wire rack.

Wholemeal Honey Hearts

450 g/1 lb plain wholemeal flour
¼ teaspoon baking powder
1 teaspoon ground ginger
50 g/2 oz cracked wheat
100 g/4 oz thick honey
150 g/5 oz syrup
150 g/5 oz margarine

Grease a baking tray with margarine.

Sift the flour with the baking powder into a bowl and mix with the ginger and cracked wheat. Warm the honey with the syrup and margarine over a low heat, stirring occasionally until the margarine is completely melted and combined with the honey and syrup. Leave to cool and when luke-warm stir into the flour mixture with a spoon. Knead well, wrap in foil or cling film and leave for 1 hour in the refrigerator.

Preheat the oven to moderate (180°C, 350°F, Gas Mark 4). Roll out the dough on a floured board to 5 mm/¼ inch thick. Cut out heart shapes and place on the prepared baking tray. Bake in the centre of the oven for 12–15 minutes. Remove with a palette knife and leave to cool on a wire rack.

Cook's Tip

Immediately after cooking, the Honey Hearts will be quite hard. If kept for 1–2 days in an airtight tin they will become softer.

Crumble-Based Fruit Tart

*18 digestive or wholemeal
  biscuits*
25 g/1 oz castor sugar
½ teaspoon ground cinnamon
*75 g/3 oz butter or margarine,
  melted*
FILLING AND TOPPING
25 g/1 oz cornflour
25 g/1 oz castor sugar
½ teaspoon vanilla essence
450 ml/¾ pint milk
*1 (298-g/10½-oz) can goose-
  berries*
*1 (213-g/7½-oz) can peach
  slices*
*1 small packet quick-setting
  jel mix (lemon)*

Grease a 23-cm/9-inch flan tin
with butter or margarine.
Place the biscuits in a polythene bag and crush finely with
a rolling pin. Mix the biscuit
crumbs with the sugar, cinnamon and melted butter or
margarine. Place the mixture
in the tin and press down
slightly with the back of a
spoon. Chill well.

Mix the cornflour with the
sugar, vanilla essence and a
little of the milk. Heat the
remaining milk and pour on to
the cornflour mixture. Return
to the heat and bring to the
boil, stirring continuously.
Leave to cool, stirring occasionally to prevent a skin
forming.

Drain the gooseberries,
reserving the juice, and also
drain the peaches. Spread the
vanilla sauce over the biscuit
base and top with the fruit as
illustrated. Prepare the glaze
using the gooseberry juice,
according to the directions on
the packet, cool slightly and
pour over the tart.

Date Crumble Cake

350 g/12 oz fresh dates
*175 g/6 oz plain wholemeal
  flour*
¼ teaspoon salt
100 g/4 oz soft margarine
100 g/4 oz castor sugar
¼ teaspoon vanilla essence
100 g/4 oz medium oatmeal

Grease a 23-cm/9-inch springform cake tin with margarine.
Preheat the oven to moderate
(180°C, 350°F, Gas Mark 4).

Stone the dates and dice
finely. Mix the flour with the
salt. Beat the margarine with
the sugar and vanilla essence
until pale and creamy.
Gradually add the flour and
oatmeal and mix with the
fingertips until crumbly.

Spread half the mixture over
the base of the cake tin, press
down over the base, raising the
sides slightly. Spread the dates
over this base and crumble the
rest of the mixture over the top.
Bake for 45–50 minutes. Leave
to cool slightly in the tin and
serve preferably warm.

Walnut and Banana Bread

150 g/5 oz soft margarine
160 g/5½ oz castor sugar
3 eggs
3 bananas
¼ teaspoon vanilla essence
275 g/10 oz plain wholemeal
  flour
2 teaspoons baking powder
¼ teaspoon salt
100 g/4 oz walnuts, chopped
2 tablespoons milk

Grease a 1-kg/2-lb loaf tin
with margarine. Preheat the
oven to moderate (180°C,
350°F, Gas Mark 4).
  Beat the margarine with the
sugar until pale and creamy
then beat in the eggs. Peel the
bananas and mash with a fork,
or press through a nylon sieve.
Stir the banana purée and
vanilla essence into the
creamed mixture. Mix the
flour and baking powder with
the salt and walnuts. Fold into
the creamed mixture together
with the milk. Turn into the
prepared loaf tin, smooth the
surface and bake for 1¼ hours.
Test with a skewer to make
sure the loaf is cooked through.
  Turn out on to a wire rack
and leave to cool.

Wheatgerm Loaf

60 g/2 oz fresh yeast
750 ml/1¼ pints lukewarm water
2 teaspoons salt
5 tablespoons thick honey
2 tablespoons oil or melted
  margarine
900 g/2 lb wholemeal flour (or
  450 g/1 lb wheatmeal and
  450 g/1 lb wholemeal flour)
150 g/5 oz wheatgerm

Cream the yeast with a little of
the water, add the salt, honey
and oil or melted margarine.
Stir in half the flour. Beat well,
cover and leave to stand in a
warm place for 30 minutes.
Stir in the remaining flour and
the wheatgerm then knead well
to give a smooth elastic dough.
Add a little more flour if the
dough is too wet. Cover and
leave to stand in a warm place
until doubled in size, about 30
minutes.
  Knead the dough thoroughly
again and form into two
loaves. Place on greased
baking trays and leave loosely
covered in a warm place for a
further 15 minutes. Preheat
the oven to moderately hot
(200°C, 400°F, Gas Mark 6).
  Using a sharp knife, lightly
cut a cross on the top of each
loaf and brush with water.
Sprinkle with a little flour and
bake for 50 minutes. Leave the
baked bread to cool on a wire
rack.

Wholemeal Breakfast Rolls

500 g / 1 lb plain wholemeal flour
30 g / 1 oz fresh yeast
1 teaspoon sugar
250 ml / 8 fl oz lukewarm water
½ teaspoon salt
2 tablespoons oil

Lightly grease a baking tray with margarine.

Tip the flour into a bowl and form a well in the centre. Cream the yeast with the sugar and a little of the water. Stir in the remaining water and pour into the flour. Sprinkle a little of the flour over this liquid, cover and leave in a warm place for 15 minutes, until frothy.

Sprinkle the salt around the edges of the flour, add the oil to the yeast mixture and knead all the ingredients together to make a smooth elastic dough. Cover again and leave to stand in a warm place for 30 minutes. Knead lightly with floured hands and divide the dough into 16 equal pieces. Roll each into a ball, sprinkle with a little flour and place on the baking tray. Leave the rolls to stand in a warm place for a further 15 minutes. Preheat the oven to hot (230°C, 450°F, Gas Mark 8) and bake for 15–20 minutes.

Wholemeal Bread

400 g / 14 oz strong plain white flour
400 g / 14 oz plain wholemeal flour
40 g / 1½ oz fresh yeast
500 ml / 17 fl oz lukewarm milk
1 teaspoon salt
7 tablespoons oil

Sift the white flour into a bowl and mix with the wholemeal flour. Form a well in the centre. Cream the yeast with a little of the milk. Add the remaining milk and pour into the flour. Sprinkle with a little of the flour, cover and leave in a warm place for 15 minutes, until frothy. Add the salt and oil and mix all the ingredients to a dough. Knead for 5–10 minutes, until smooth and elastic. Cover and leave to rise for 30 minutes in a warm place.

Knead lightly on a floured board and form into a loaf. Sprinkle a baking tray with flour, place the loaf on it, cover and leave to stand in a warm place for a further 30 minutes. Preheat the oven to moderately hot (190°C, 375°F, Gas Mark 5). Sprinkle the loaf with flour and bake for 50–60 minutes.

Rum and Raisin Loaf

100 g/4 oz raisins
2 tablespoons rum
500 g/1 lb plain flour
30 g/1 oz fresh yeast
40 g/1½ oz castor sugar
250 ml/8 fl oz lukewarm milk
80 g/3 oz butter, melted
2 eggs
1 teaspoon salt
grated rind of 1 lemon
1 egg yolk, beaten to glaze

Grease a 1-kg/2-lb loaf tin
with butter. Mix the raisins
with the rum and steep.

Sift the flour into a bowl
and make a well in the centre.
Cream the yeast with a little of
the sugar and milk. Add the
remaining milk and pour into
the flour. Sprinkle over a little
of the flour, cover and leave
to stand in a warm place for
15 minutes, until frothy.

Add the rest of the sugar,
the melted butter, eggs, salt
and lemon rind. Mix to form
a soft dough and knead for
5–10 minutes until smooth and
elastic. Leave to stand in a
warm place until doubled in
size, about 30 minutes. Knead
in the raisins, place in the loaf
tin and leave in a warm place
for 30 minutes. Preheat
the oven to moderately hot
(190°C, 375°F, Gas Mark 5).

Brush with beaten egg yolk
and bake for 40–50 minutes.

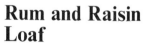

Cook's Tip

Instead of the raisins
soaked in rum, knead
100 g/4 oz chopped
blanched almonds into
the dough and bake as
above.

Savoury Bacon Baps

1 kg/2 lb light rye flour
20 g/¾ oz fresh yeast
about 900 ml/1½ pints lukewarm
  water
double quantity starter dough
  (see page 162)
200 g/7 oz bacon
2 teaspoons salt
2 teaspoons caraway seeds
2 teaspoons each caraway seeds
  and sea salt to sprinkle

Place half the flour in a mixing
bowl. Cream the yeast with a
little of the water, add the
remaining water and mix
thoroughly into the flour
together with the starter dough.
Knead until smooth, cover and
leave to stand overnight at
room temperature.

Preheat the oven to
moderately hot (200°C, 400°F,
Gas Mark 6). Lightly grill the
bacon and chop very finely.
Drain on absorbent paper and
allow to cool. Mix the salt,
caraway seeds, chopped bacon
and the rest of the flour into
the dough. Knead until
smooth.

Divide the dough into six
equal pieces and roll out thinly
into flat cakes about 25–30 cm/
10–12 inches in diameter.
Brush the tops with water,
cut with criss-cross markings
and sprinkle with the caraway
seeds and sea salt. Place on
floured baking trays and bake
for 30 minutes.

Country Loaves

Flowerpot Loaves

500 g / 1 lb plain flour
30 g / 1 oz fresh yeast
pinch of sugar
175 ml / 6 fl oz lukewarm milk
2 onions
1 clove garlic
50 g / 2 oz butter, melted
2 large eggs, beaten
¼ teaspoon salt
pinch of grated nutmeg
1 teaspoon ground aniseed
¼ teaspoon dried fennel
2 tablespoons dried dill
¼ teaspoon dried rosemary
ground aniseed to sprinkle

Grease two new 10-cm/4-inch earthenware flower pots.

Sift the flour into a bowl and form a well in the centre. Cream the yeast with the sugar and a little of the milk. Stir in the remaining milk and pour into the flour. Sprinkle over a little of the flour, cover and leave in a warm place for 15 minutes, until frothy.

Peel the onions and garlic. Finely chop the onions and crush the garlic. Mix the melted butter with the beaten eggs, salt, nutmeg, aniseed, fennel and dill. Pound the rosemary in a mortar, add to the yeast liquid with the butter mixture, onion and garlic and mix all the ingredients well together. Knead the dough until smooth and elastic. Cover and leave to stand in a warm place until doubled in size, about 30 minutes.

Knead the dough lightly and put half in each of the flowerpots. Leave to stand in a warm place for a further 20 minutes. Preheat the oven to moderately hot (200°C, 400°F, Gas Mark 6).

Brush the surface of the loaves with water and sprinkle lightly with aniseed. Bake for 35–40 minutes.

French Bread

1 kg / 2 lb strong plain flour
40 g / 1½ oz fresh yeast
600 ml / 1 pint lukewarm water
4 teaspoons salt

Sprinkle a large baking tray with flour.

Sift the flour into a bowl and make a well in the centre. Cream the yeast with a little of the water then add the remaining water and pour into the flour. Sprinkle a little of the flour over the liquid, cover and leave to stand in a warm place for 15 minutes. Sprinkle the salt on to the flour and mix all the ingredients to a dough. Knead the dough until smooth and elastic, about 5–10 minutes. Sprinkle well with flour so that the surface does not form a crust, cover and leave to stand for 2–3 hours at room temperature.

Quickly knead the dough again on a floured board and divide into four pieces. Form each piece into a long roll and place on the floured baking tray. Cover and leave to stand in a warm place for a further 30 minutes. Preheat the oven to hot (220°C, 425°F, Gas Mark 7).

Slash the loaves diagonally several times with a fine sharp knife and brush with lukewarm water. Bake for 15 minutes then reduce the oven temperature to moderate (180°C, 350°F, Gas Mark 4) and bake for a further 15–20 minutes.

Country Loaves

Northern Wheel

1 kg/2 lb light rye flour
20 g/¾ oz fresh yeast
about 900 ml/1½ pints lukewarm
water
double quantity starter dough
(see page 162)
2 teaspoons salt
2 teaspoons each caraway seeds,
dried fennel and ground
aniseed
milk to glaze

Place half the flour in a mixing
bowl. Cream the yeast with a
little of the water, add the
remaining water and mix
thoroughly into the flour
together with the starter dough.
Knead until smooth, cover and
leave to stand overnight in a
warm place.
   Preheat the oven to very hot
(230°C, 450°F, Gas Mark 8).
Mix the salt, half the spices
and the rest of the flour into
the dough until smooth. Form

one-third of the dough into a
long roll, roll up to resemble a
snail's shell and place in the
middle of a large floured
baking tray. Form the remaining dough into eight rolls,
20 cm/8 inches in length, place
around the central coil and
slightly roll the end of each
piece, as illustrated. Brush the
surface of the bread with milk
and sprinkle with the rest of
the spices. Bake for 25 minutes
until golden brown.

Fresh Herb Bread

400 g/14 oz strong plain flour
25 g/1 oz fresh yeast
350 ml/12 fl oz lukewarm milk
1 teaspoon salt
1 tablespoon chopped mixed
herbs, (dill, chives, thyme,
parsley)
1 teaspoon coarsely ground
black pepper
milk to glaze

Grease a 1-kg/2-lb loaf tin and
sprinkle with a little flour.
   Sift the flour into a bowl and
make a well in the centre.
Cream the yeast with a little
of the milk then add the
remaining milk and pour into
the flour. Sprinkle over a little
of the flour, cover and leave in
a warm place for 15 minutes,
until frothy. Mix in the salt
and the rest of the flour to
obtain a soft dough. Cover and

leave to stand in a warm place
for a further 1 hour.
   Knead the herbs and pepper
into the dough. Place in the
loaf tin and cut the surface
diagonally with a sharp knife.
Cover and leave the bread to
rise in a warm place for a
further 30 minutes. Preheat
the oven to hot (220°C, 425°F,
Gas Mark 7).
   Brush the loaf with milk and
bake for 35–40 minutes. Cover
with foil if becoming too
brown on top.

Aniseed Marble Bread

PLAIN DOUGH
350 g/12 oz plain flour
20 g/¾ oz fresh yeast
6 tablespoons lukewarm milk
pinch of sugar
50 g/2 oz butter
2 eggs
¼ teaspoon salt
RYE DOUGH
350 g/12 oz rye flour
20 g/¾ fresh yeast
6 tablespoons lukewarm milk
pinch of sugar
50 g/2 oz butter
2 eggs
½ teaspoon salt
¼ teaspoon ground aniseed
1 tablespoon aniseed to sprinkle

First make the plain dough.
Sift the flour into a bowl and
form a well in the centre.
Cream the yeast with a little of
the milk, add the remaining
milk and pour into the flour.
Add the sugar and sprinkle a
little of the flour over the
surface. Cover and leave to
stand in a warm place for 15
minutes, until frothy. Melt the
butter, stir in the eggs and salt,
add to the yeast liquid and
mix in the flour to make a
dough. Knead the dough until
smooth and elastic. Cover again
and leave in a warm place to
rise for 1 hour.

Make the rye dough in the
same way, using the rye flour.
Incorporate the ground aniseed
into this dough when adding
the butter. Finally leave the
rye dough in a warm place for
1 hour, as above.

Divide both the plain and
rye dough into two pieces.
Lightly knead a piece of each
dough together and shape into
a loaf. Repeat with the remaining two pieces. Place the two
loaves on a floured baking
tray, cover and leave in a warm
place for a further 30 minutes.
Preheat the oven to hot (220°C,
425°F, Gas Mark 7).

Brush the loaves with water,
sprinkle with aniseed and bake
for 30–40 minutes.

Country Loaves

Hearty Peasant Bread

1 kg/2 lb rye flour
20 g/¾ fresh yeast
about 900 ml/1½ pints lukewarm
  water
double quantity starter dough
  (see page 162)
200 g/7 oz streaky bacon
2 teaspoons salt
200 g/7 oz Emmenthal cheese,
  grated
100 g/3½ oz blanched almonds,
  chopped
2 tablespoons chopped parsley

Place half the flour in a mixing bowl. Cream the yeast with a little of the water, add the remaining water and pour into the flour. Mix in well, together with the starter dough, and knead until smooth. Cover and leave to stand overnight at room temperature.

Lightly grill the bacon and chop very finely. Drain on absorbent paper and allow to cool. Preheat the oven to hot (220°C, 425°F, Gas Mark 7).

Mix the diced bacon, salt, cheese, almonds, parsley and the rest of the flour into the dough and knead until smooth. Form into two round loaves. Place the loaves on a floured baking tray, brush the surface with water, sprinkle with flour and mark a criss-cross pattern on the top. Bake for 20–30 minutes.

French Onion Loaves

1 kg/2 lb rye flour
20 g/¾ oz fresh yeast
about 900 ml/1½ pints lukewarm
  water
double quantity starter dough
  (see page 162)
2 teaspoons salt
¼ teaspoon freshly ground black
  pepper
generous pinch of ground
  cardamom
4 medium onions
25 g/1 oz butter or margarine

Place half the flour in a mixing bowl. Cream the yeast with a little of the water, add the remaining water and mix thoroughly into the flour with the starter dough. Knead until smooth, cover and leave to stand overnight in a warm place.

Mix the salt and pepper, cardamom and the rest of the flour into the dough and knead thoroughly until smooth.

Peel and finely chop the onions. Brown half the onions in the butter or margarine, drain well and knead into the dough with the raw onion. Form into three loaves about 35 cm/14 inches in length and place on a floured baking tray. Cover and leave to stand in a warm place for a further 15 minutes. Preheat the oven to hot (230°C, 450°F, Gas Mark 8).

Brush the loaves with water, sprinkle with a little flour and with a fine sharp knife cut the surface diagonally several times. Bake for 30 minutes.

Country Loaves

Spiced Flat Cakes

375 g/13 oz rye flour
375 g/13 oz plain wholemeal
flour
25 g/1 oz fresh yeast
250 ml/8 fl oz lukewarm water
125 ml/4 fl oz lukewarm milk
1 teaspoon salt
2 teaspoons caraway seeds
2 teaspoons crushed coriander
seeds

Grease a baking tray with oil.
Combine the flours in a bowl
and form a well in the centre.
Cream the yeast with a little of
the water. Add the remaining
water and the milk then pour
into the flour. Sprinkle a little
of the flour over the liquid,
cover and leave in a warm
place for 15 minutes, until
frothy.
Mix in all the flour, the salt,
caraway and coriander, to
make a dough. Knead the
dough until smooth, cover and
leave to stand in a warm place
until doubled in size, about 30
minutes.
Divide the dough into four
equal pieces. Roll out each
piece to give a large round
flat cake. Place on the baking
tray, sprinkle with flour and
leave to stand in a warm
place for 30 minutes. Preheat
the oven to hot (230°C, 450°F,
Gas Mark 8), and bake for
15–20 minutes, until crisp and
golden.

Herb Ring Loaf

50 g/2 oz butter
250 ml/8 fl oz lukewarm water
25 g/1 oz fresh yeast
300 g/11 oz rye flour
300 g/11 oz plain wholemeal
flour
2 teaspoons salt
1 tablespoon chopped mixed
herbs (marjoram, sage,
tarragon, basil)
3 tablespoons chopped parsley

Melt the butter and mix with
the water. Cream the yeast with
a little of this liquid, add the
remaining liquid and leave in a
warm place for 15 minutes.
Place the rye flour in a bowl
and add the wholemeal flour,
salt, mixed herbs and parsley.
Pour the yeast liquid into the
flour and mix to a dough.
Knead the dough for about 5
minutes until smooth, cover
and leave to rise in a warm
place for 30 minutes.

Form the dough into a round
flat loaf. Make a hole in the
centre of the loaf with a
wooden spoon and rotate the
spoon to make the hole larger
until you have a ring. Place
on a greased baking tray, cover
and leave in a warm place for
30 minutes.
Preheat the oven to hot
(220°C, 425°F, Gas Mark 7).
Brush the loaf with water and
sprinkle lightly with flour.
Make slight slashes in the top
of the loaf with a knife and
bake for 30 minutes.

Country Loaves

Strong Ryebread

STARTER DOUGH
1 tablespoon milk
2 tablespoons water
¼ teaspoon oil
¼ teaspoon dried yeast
1 tablespoon lukewarm water
¼ teaspoon castor sugar
1 teaspoon salt
50 g/2 oz strong plain flour
RYEBREAD DOUGH
750 ml/1¼ pints lukewarm water
750 g/1 lb 10 oz coarse rye flour
250 g/9 oz wheaten flour
2 teaspoons salt

First make the starter dough. Combine the milk, 2 tablespoons water and the oil in a saucepan and bring to the boil. Allow to cool until lukewarm. Blend the yeast with 1 tablespoon lukewarm water and the sugar and leave for 5 minutes. Add to the milk mixture with the salt. Stir this liquid into the flour until well blended then cover and leave to stand for 12–18 hours.

The following day, mix the starter dough with 500 ml/ 17 fl oz of the lukewarm water. Mix the rye flour with the wheaten flour in a large warmed bowl. Make a well in the centre of the flours and pour in the starter dough. Stir half the flour into the starter dough until a thick flowing dough is formed. Cover the bowl with a tea towel and leave to rise overnight in a warm place.

The following day add the remaining lukewarm water and the salt. Mix the rest of the flour into the dough and knead until firm and well bound together. Form the dough into a ball and place in a warmed, lightly floured bowl. Cover it with a tea towel and leave in a warm place to rise for 3 hours.

Line a large baking tray with foil. With floured hands shape the dough into a flat round loaf. Place on the baking tray and once again leave to rise at room temperature for 1½–2 hours. During this time brush the top of the loaf three or four times with lukewarm water so that no crust forms. Cut criss-cross patterns on the top of the risen loaf with a sharp knife. Preheat the oven to moderately hot (200°C, 400°F, Gas Mark 6) and bake the loaf on the bottom shelf for 2 hours.

Turn off the oven, remove the bread, brush with cold water and return to the oven for a few minutes to dry.

Cook's Tip

Rye flour can be bought in most healthfood shops. Bread made from rye flour has an agreeable taste and will keep fresh for longer than ordinary bread.

Savoury Veal Loaf

1 (283-g/10-oz) packet bread
 mix
1 tablespoon milk to glaze
FILLING
1 (675-g/1½-lb) fillet of veal
1 teaspoon salt
1 teaspoon paprika pepper
2 tablespoons oil
1 medium onion
4 tablespoons canned green
 peppercorns
2–3 tablespoons made mustard
pinch of dried rosemary
pinch of dried sage

First prepare the filling.
Season the meat with the salt
and paprika. Heat the oil in a
pan and fry the meat for 10
minutes, turning frequently.
Leave to cool.

Peel and chop the onion
finely. Drain the green peppercorns and chop finely. Preheat
the oven to moderately hot
(200°C, 400°F, Gas Mark 6).

Mix the mustard, rosemary
and sage with the chopped
onion and peppercorns, then
spread this mixture over the
meat. Prepare the bread mix
according to the instructions
on the packet and roll out to
a rectangle large enough to
cover the meat. Place the meat
on the dough and fold the
dough over carefully to
completely cover it. Press the
edges together firmly to seal.

Place the loaf on a greased
baking tray with the join of the
dough underneath. Brush with
milk and bake for 30 minutes.
Serve either warm or cold.

Savoury Chicken Loaves

YEAST DOUGH
500 g/1 lb rye flour
15 g/½ oz fresh yeast
450 ml/¾ pint lukewarm water
1 quantity starter dough (see
 page 162)
1 teaspoon salt
1 egg yolk, beaten to glaze
caraway seeds to sprinkle
FILLING
4 (175-g/6-oz) chicken breast
 portions
20 g/1 oz butter
4 shallots
50 g/2 oz button mushrooms
225 g/8 oz sausagemeat
1 tablespoon chopped herbs
1 egg yolk
1 tablespoon single cream
pinch each of salt, pepper,
 ground coriander and allspice

Place the flour in a bowl and
form a well. Cream the yeast
with a little of the water. Add
the remaining water and mix
into the flour with the starter
dough and salt. Knead until
smooth, cover and leave overnight at room temperature.

Season the chicken, cook in
the butter then cool. Preheat
the oven to moderately hot
(200°C, 400°F, Gas Mark 6).

Finely chop the shallots and
mushrooms. Mix with the
sausagemeat, herbs, egg yolk,
cream, seasoning and spices.
Spread this around each of the
chicken portions. Lightly knead
the dough and roll out to
5 mm/¼ inch thick. Cut into
four equal-sized rounds and
place a coated chicken portion
on each. Fold the dough over
the chicken and press the edges
together to seal. Place on
a floured baking tray, brush
with beaten egg yolk and
sprinkle with caraway seeds.
Bake for 30 minutes and serve
hot or cold.

Rolls and Crescents

Poppy Seed Rolls

500 g / 1 lb plain flour
1 teaspoon salt
30 g / 1 oz fresh yeast
250 ml / 8 fl oz lukewarm milk
50 g / 2 oz butter or margarine
1 egg
pinch each of pepper and grated nutmeg
GLAZE
1 egg yolk
1 tablespoon milk
2 tablespoons poppy seeds

Sift the flour and salt into a bowl and make a well in the centre. Cream the yeast with a little of the milk, add the remaining milk and pour into the flour. Sprinkle a little of the flour over the liquid, cover and leave in a warm place for 15 minutes, until frothy.

Melt the butter or margarine and mix with the egg, pepper and nutmeg. Add these ingredients to the bowl and mix

everything to a dough. Knead until smooth and elastic. Cover and leave the dough to rise until doubled in size.

Grease two baking trays. Lightly knead the dough, break off pieces of approximately 40 g / 1½ oz, and with floured hands shape these into balls. Place them on the baking trays and press to flatten slightly. Leave the rolls to rise in a warm place for a further 20 minutes. Preheat the oven to hot (230°C, 450°F, Gas Mark 8).

Beat the egg yolk with the milk. Brush the rolls with this and sprinkle with a few poppy seeds. Cut a cross in the top of each roll and bake for 15–20 minutes.

Crusty Rye Rolls

500 g / 1 lb rye flour
15 g / ½ oz fresh yeast
about 450 ml / ¾ pint lukewarm water
1 quantity starter dough (see page 162)
1 teaspoon salt

Place half the flour in a bowl. Cream the yeast with a little of the water then add the remaining water and mix thoroughly into the flour, together with the starter dough. Knead until smooth, cover the dough and leave overnight in a warm place.

Preheat the oven to hot (230°C, 450°F, Gas Mark 8). Mix the remaining flour with the salt and work into the dough. Knead thoroughly until smooth. Divide the dough into 16 pieces and form into round rolls. Arrange the rolls on greased baking trays and

brush with water. Dust with sifted flour and make a cut in each with a knife. Bake the rolls for 20–25 minutes.

Dinner Rolls

500 g/1 lb strong plain white
flour
30 g/1 oz fresh yeast
250 ml/8 fl oz lukewarm milk
pinch of sugar
1 teaspoon salt
1 egg
1 egg yolk, beaten to glaze
sesame seeds and poppy seeds to
sprinkle

Sift the flour into a bowl and
make a well in the centre.
Cream the yeast with a little of
the milk and the sugar. Add the
remaining milk and pour into
the flour. Sprinkle a little of the
flour over the liquid, cover and
leave in a warm place for 15
minutes, until frothy.

Sprinkle the salt on to the
edges of the flour, add the egg
to the yeast liquid and mix all
together to form a dough.
Knead the dough until it is
smooth and elastic, about
5–10 minutes. Cover and leave
to rise in a warm place until
doubled in size.

Divide the dough into small
portions and form into 20-cm/
8-inch long rolls, about 2·5 cm/
1 inch in diameter. From these
shape rolls as shown in the
illustration. Place the rolls
on greased baking trays, cover
and leave to rise in a warm
place for 20 minutes. Preheat
the oven to hot (230°C, 450°F,
Gas Mark 8).

Brush the rolls with beaten
egg yolk, and sprinkle some
with sesame seeds and some
with poppy seeds. Bake the
rolls for 10–15 minutes, until
golden brown.

Rolls and Crescents

Milk Crescents

500 g / 1 lb plain flour
30 g / 1 oz fresh yeast
250 ml / 8 fl oz lukewarm milk
30 g / 1 oz butter or margarine
1 teaspoon sugar
½ teaspoon salt
1 egg
1 egg yolk, beaten to glaze

Sift the flour into a bowl and make a well in the centre. Cream the yeast with a little of the milk, add the remaining milk and then pour into the flour. Sprinkle a little of the flour over the yeast liquid, cover and leave in a warm place for 15 minutes, until frothy.

Melt the butter or margarine and mix with the sugar, salt and egg. Add to the yeast liquid and flour and mix all together to give a dough. Knead until smooth and elastic then leave in a warm place until doubled in size.

Divide the dough into pieces weighing approximately 50 g/ 2 oz and shape into balls. Roll out each into a triangular shape, with sides approximately 15 cm/6 inches long. Press the point of each triangle firmly on to a baking tray and, starting at the other end, roll up with both hands. Finally seal the point of the triangle with a little beaten egg yolk. Curve each roll into a crescent shape, arrange on a baking tray and brush with beaten egg yolk. Cover and leave to rise for 15–20 minutes in a warm place. Preheat the oven to hot (230°C, 450°F, Gas Mark 8).

Bake the crescents for 10–15 minutes until golden brown and serve fresh from the oven.

Poppy Seed Plaits

500 g / 1 lb plain flour
30 g / 1 oz fresh yeast
250 ml / 8 fl oz lukewarm water
1 teaspoon salt
1 egg
poppy seeds to sprinkle

Sift the flour into a bowl and make a well in the centre. Cream the yeast with a little of the water, add the remaining water and pour into the flour. Sprinkle over a little of the flour, cover and leave in a warm place for 15 minutes, until frothy.

Sprinkle the salt on the flour, add the egg to the yeast liquid and mix the ingredients to a dough. If it is too stiff, add a little more lukewarm water. Knead until smooth and elastic. Cover and leave to rise in a warm place, until doubled in size, about 30 minutes.

Divide the mixture into 50-g/2-oz pieces. Form three long thin strands from each piece, about 15 cm/6 inches in length, and weave into small plaits. Brush these plaits with water and sprinkle with poppy seeds. Arrange on a greased baking tray, cover and leave to rise in a warm place for about 15 minutes. Preheat the oven to hot (230°C, 450°F, Gas Mark 8).

Bake the poppy seed plaits for 10–20 minutes and serve fresh from the oven.

Croissants

550 g/1 lb 2 oz plain flour
30 g/1 oz fresh yeast
250 ml/8 fl oz lukewarm milk
225 g/8 oz butter
1 egg
1 teaspoon salt
1 egg yolk, beaten to glaze

Sift 500 g/1 lb flour into a bowl and make a well. Cream the yeast with the milk, pour into the flour, cover and leave in a warm place for 15 minutes. Mix in 50 g/2 oz melted butter, the egg and salt, then knead until a smooth, elastic dough. Cover and leave in a warm place for 1 hour.

Knead lightly and roll out to a 20 × 35-cm/8 × 14-inch rectangle. Work the rest of the flour into the remaining butter and chill. Divide into thirds and mark the pastry dough into three lengthways. Dot one-third of the butter over the top two-thirds of the pastry, leaving a border. Fold the bottom third of pastry over the middle third and the top third over that. Press the edges together, give one turn in a clockwise direction and then roll out to the original size. Repeat this folding and rolling process twice more with the remaining butter, then twice without any butter. Chill for 30 minutes between each rolling.

Finally roll out the dough to a 50-cm/20-inch square. Cut into sixteen 12·5-cm/5-inch squares and roll up each, starting from one corner to the opposite corner. Place on baking trays, brush with egg yolk and leave in a warm place for 30 minutes.

Preheat the oven to hot (220°C, 425°F, Gas Mark 7). Bake the croissants for 5 minutes then reduce to 190°C, 375°F, Gas Mark 5 for a further 15 minutes.

Brioches

500 g/1 lb plain flour
30 g/1 oz fresh yeast
6 tablespoons lukewarm milk
1 teaspoon castor sugar
200 g/7 oz butter
4 eggs
½ teaspoon salt
1 egg yolk, beaten to glaze

Grease 20 small brioche or patty tins with butter.

Sift the flour into a bowl and make a well in the centre. Cream the yeast with a little of the milk, add the remaining milk and the sugar. Pour into the well in the flour, sprinkle a little of the flour over, cover and leave in a warm place for 15 minutes.

Melt the butter, cool slightly and mix with the eggs and salt. Beat into the yeast mixture with the rest of the flour, kneading to give a smooth dough. Leave covered in a warm place for 30 minutes.

Knead lightly, take three-quarters of the dough and shape into approximately 20 small balls. Place in the greased tins. Make 20 smaller pear-shaped pieces out of the remaining dough. Make a small indentation in the dough in the tins and place the smaller pieces of dough on top, with the slightly elongated end in the indentation. Brush the brioches with beaten egg yolk and leave to rise in a warm place for 15 minutes. Preheat the oven to hot (220°C, 425°F, Gas Mark 7).

Bake the brioches for about 15 minutes, until well risen and golden brown. Remove from the oven and allow to cool on a wire rack.

Crispy Fried Cakes

Saffron Plaits

4 saffron strands
250 ml/8 fl oz hot milk
500 g/1 lb plain flour
50 g/2 oz castor sugar
½ teaspoon salt
grated rind of ½ lemon
30 g/1 oz fresh yeast
120 g/4 oz margarine
2 eggs
100 g/4 oz castor sugar to
    sprinkle
oil to deep fry

Steep the saffron in the hot
milk overnight.

Sift the flour into a bowl
then add the sugar, salt and
lemon rind. Mix these dry
ingredients together and make
a well in the centre. Strain the
milk and reheat to lukewarm.
Cream the yeast with a little of
this lukewarm milk, add the
remaining milk and pour it
into the well in the flour.
Sprinkle a little of the flour

over the yeast liquid, cover
and leave in a warm place for
15 minutes.

Melt the margarine and mix
with the eggs. Add this to the
yeast liquid and beat in the dry
ingredients to form a soft
dough. Knead on a well-
floured board for 5–10 minutes,
until smooth and elastic. Cover
and leave in a warm place for
30 minutes.

Knead the dough lightly and
divide into four pieces. Divide
each of these pieces into four
and roll out into 15–20-cm/
6–8-inch strips. Plait these
four strips together, cover and
leave to rise in a warm place
for 15–20 minutes.

Heat the oil for frying to
149°C/300°F and fry the
plaits, turning over at least
once, for 10 minutes, until
golden brown and cooked
through. Drain on absorbent
paper and coat one side with
sugar while still hot.

Sugared Knots

125 g/4½ oz soft margarine
125 g/4½ oz castor sugar
pinch of salt
3 eggs
1 tablespoon rum
450 g/1 lb plain flour
2 teaspoons baking powder
COATING
100 g/4 oz castor sugar
25 g/1 oz vanilla sugar
oil or fat to deep fry

Beat the margarine, sugar, salt
and eggs together thoroughly,
until smooth. Mix in the rum.
Sift the flour and baking
powder together over the
mixture and fold in thoroughly.
Knead well, wrap in foil or
cling film and leave in the
refrigerator for 30 minutes.
Heat the oil for frying to
182°C/360°F.

Roll out the dough on a
floured surface to 5 mm/¼ inch
thick and cut into 20 × 1·5-cm/

8 × ¾-inch strips. Knot each
strip tightly. Fry four at a
time in the deep oil for 5
minutes, turning once with a
draining spoon. Drain on
absorbent paper.

Mix the sugar and vanilla
sugar together and use to coat
the warm knots.

Tunisian Honey Rings

3 eggs
3 tablespoons oil
3 tablespoons orange juice
grated rind of 1 large orange
50 g/2 oz castor sugar
300 g/11 oz plain flour
1 teaspoon baking powder
SYRUP
300 ml/½ pint cold water
2 tablespoons lemon juice
275 g/10 oz granulated sugar
100 g/4 oz thick honey
oil to deep fry

Whisk the eggs with the oil,
orange juice, 1 teaspoon
orange rind and the sugar until
frothy. Sift the flour with the
baking powder and add a
spoonful at a time to the
whisked mixture. Beat well,
cover and leave to stand for 45
minutes.

Heat the water and lemon
juice with the sugar, stirring
continuously until the sugar
has dissolved. Bring to the
boil and simmer for 5 minutes.
Add the honey and remaining
orange rind and simmer the
syrup gently for a further 5
minutes. Keep warm while
cooking the doughnut rings.

Heat the oil for frying to
182°C/360°F. Divide the
dough into 12 pieces. Using
floured hands, form each
piece into a circle 7·5 cm/3
inches in diameter. Make a
hole in the centre, and enlarge
it using a wooden spoon until
about 3·5 cm/1½ inches in
diameter. Fry three rings at a
time in the hot oil for 5
minutes until golden brown,
turning once. Drain the rings
on absorbent paper.

Pick up each ring on a fork
while still warm and dip into
the syrup for a few minutes,
allowing the syrup to soak in.
Serve immediately.

Jam Rosettes

150 g/6 oz soft margarine
100 g/4 oz castor sugar
2 eggs
50 g/2 oz ground almonds
1 teaspoon ground cinnamon
125 ml/4 fl oz soured cream
500 g/1 lb plain flour
1 egg white, beaten
icing sugar to sprinkle
200 g/7 oz redcurrant jelly
oil or fat to deep fry

Mix the margarine with the
sugar and eggs until light. Stir
in the ground almonds, cinnamon, soured cream and a little
of the sifted flour, until well
mixed. Finally add the remaining flour. Wrap the mixture in
foil or cling film and leave in
the refrigerator for 1 hour.

Heat the oil for frying to
182°C/360°F. Roll out the
dough thinly on a floured
board, and cut out fluted
circles measuring 6 cm/2½

inches in diameter. Cut notches
into the edge of these as
illustrated. Brush them in the
centre with beaten egg white,
and lay three rounds one on
top of the other. Using the
handle of a wooden spoon,
shape a small well in the centre.
During cooking, each layer
rises to make a rosette shape.

Place two or three rosettes
in the hot oil and fry for
4–5 minutes, until golden
brown, turning once. Drain
them well on absorbent paper
and sprinkle with sifted icing
sugar. Fill the centres of the
rosettes with redcurrant jelly.

Country Plum Strudel

PASTRY
15 g/½ oz lard
6 tablespoons lukewarm water
1 egg
pinch of salt
250 g/9 oz plain flour
FILLING
1 kg/2 lb plums
140 g/5 oz butter
100 g/4 oz fresh white
  breadcrumbs
75 g/3 oz castor sugar
icing sugar to sprinkle

Melt the fat and beat with the water, egg and salt. Sift the flour on top and mix everything together to a smooth dough. Roll the dough into a ball, return to the bowl, cover and leave to stand for 1 hour.

Roll out the pastry as thinly as possible on a large floured cloth. Finally stretch the pastry with your hands, working from the middle outwards until it is paper thin. If the pastry tears join it together immediately. Put the pastry back on the cloth. Preheat the oven to moderately hot (200°C, 400°F, Gas Mark 6).

Wash the plums and quarter them, removing the stones. Melt the butter and put 2 tablespoons of it to one side. Mix the rest with the breadcrumbs and spread this over two-thirds of the pastry, leaving the bottom third uncovered. Arrange the plums over the top of the bread-crumbs and sprinkle with the castor sugar. Spread a little butter on the uncovered third of the pastry and, lifting the cloth, roll the pastry up, starting from the covered side. Place the strudel on a greased baking tray and brush with the remaining butter. Bake for 40 minutes and dust with icing sugar before serving warm with cream.

Cook's Tip

To make Apple Strudel, as illustrated left, substitute 675 g/1½ lb cooking apples, peeled, cored and sliced, and 50 g/2 oz raisins, for the plums.

Nut Strudel

1 (368-g/13-oz) packet frozen
 puff pastry
FILLING
2 egg yolks
80 g/3 oz castor sugar
50 g/2 oz butter
200 g/7 oz walnuts, finely
 chopped or ground
75 g/3 oz biscuit crumbs
½ teaspoon ground cinnamon
grated rind of ½ lemon
1 tablespoon rum
50 g/2 oz raisins
1–2 tablespoons milk
1 egg yolk, beaten to glaze

Allow the pastry to thaw at
room temperature for 1 hour.

To make the filling, whisk
the egg yolks with the sugar
until thick and creamy. Melt
the butter and mix it with the
walnuts, biscuit crumbs,
cinnamon, lemon rind, rum
and raisins. Stir into the
whisked eggs, adding just

enough milk to make a thick
mixture.

Roll out three-quarters of
the pastry thinly to a 25 × 30-
cm/10 × 12-inch rectangle.
Place the filling down the
centre of the pastry. Brush the
edges with beaten egg yolk
and fold the pastry over the
filling, sealing the edges
together. Place on a dampened
baking tray with the join
underneath. Brush with egg
yolk. Roll out the remaining
pastry and cut into strips with
a pastry cutter. Arrange in a
lattice pattern on top of the
pastry and brush with egg yolk.
Leave the strudel to stand for
15 minutes.

Preheat the oven to hot
(220°C, 425°F, Gas Mark 7).
Bake the strudel for 35–45
minutes, covering the top with
foil if it becomes too brown.

Apple Fritters

75 g/3 oz castor sugar
¾ teaspoon ground cinnamon
2 tablespoons rum
4 large ripe apples
oil or fat to deep fry
BATTER
125 g/5 oz plain flour
¼ teaspoon baking powder
pinch of salt
2 eggs, separated
1 tablespoon olive oil
9 tablespoons light ale
TO SPRINKLE
100 g/4 oz castor sugar
1 teaspoon ground cinnamon

Mix the sugar and cinnamon
with the rum in a shallow dish.
Peel the apples, remove the
cores and cut into 1-cm/½-inch
thick slices. Toss the apple
slices in the sugar mixture.
Cover and leave for 30
minutes, turning once or twice
to allow the flavour to be
absorbed.

Sift the flour and baking
powder together and mix with
the salt, egg yolks and oil,
beating until smooth. Stir in
the beer. Whisk the egg whites
until stiff and fold into the
batter.

Heat the oil or fat for frying
to 182°C/360°F. Coat the
apple slices in the batter and
fry in the hot oil for 8–10
minutes, turning them once
during the cooking time, until
golden brown. Drain on
absorbent paper and sprinkle
with the mixed sugar and
cinnamon while still hot. Serve
warm.

Sweet Plum Rounds

YEAST DOUGH
500 g/1 lb plain flour
30 g/1 oz fresh yeast
80 g/3 oz castor sugar
250 ml/8 fl oz lukewarm milk
50 g/2 oz butter, melted
grated rind of ½ lemon
1 egg, beaten
pinch of salt
1 egg yolk, beaten to glaze
FILLING
500 g/1 lb curd or cream cheese
50 g/2 oz butter, softened
200 g/7 oz castor sugar
2 eggs, separated
1 tablespoon cornflour
1 tablespoon rum
250 g/9 oz ground poppy seeds
80 g/3 oz sugar
1 tablespoon fresh white
  breadcrumbs
250 ml/8 fl oz milk
250 g/9 oz stewed plums, puréed

Make up the dough following the method for Dresden Slices (see page 178), and adding the lemon rind with the melted butter.

Mix the cheese, butter, castor sugar, egg yolks, cornflour and rum together. Whisk the egg whites until stiff and fold into this mixture.

Stir the poppy seeds, sugar, breadcrumbs and milk together and bring to the boil. Leave to cool.

Divide the yeast into 50-g/2-oz pieces. Shape into rounds, pinching up the edges to form a side, and brush with beaten egg yolk. Put 4 small spoonfuls of the cheese mixture and 4 small spoonfuls of the poppy mixture alternately into each round, and a spoonful of puréed plum in the centre. Cover and leave to rise for 10 minutes. Preheat the oven to moderately hot (200°C, 400°F, Gas Mark 6) and bake the rounds for 20–25 minutes.

Creamy Raisin Squares

YEAST DOUGH
350 g/12 oz plain flour
20 g/¾ oz fresh yeast
50 g/2 oz castor sugar
6 tablespoons lukewarm milk
50 g/2 oz margarine, melted
2 eggs
pinch of salt
TOPPING
300 ml/½ pint double cream
3 eggs, separated
50 g/2 oz castor sugar
1 tablespoon semolina
75 g/3 oz raisins

Sift the flour into a bowl and make a well in the centre. Cream the yeast with a little of the sugar and the milk. Pour into the well in the flour and sprinkle over a little of the flour. Cover and leave in a warm place for 15 minutes, until frothy.

Add the remaining sugar, the melted margarine, eggs and salt to the mixture, and beat all the ingredients to a dough. Knead until smooth and elastic on a lightly floured board. Cover and leave the dough to rise for 1 hour. Knead lightly again then roll out the dough to fit a greased 23 × 33-cm/9 × 13-inch Swiss roll tin. Preheat the oven to moderately hot (200°C, 400°F, Gas Mark 6).

Mix the cream, egg yolks, sugar and semolina together. Whisk the egg whites until stiff and fold in the raisins. Fold the egg whites into the cream mixture and spread this over the dough.

Bake for 20–25 minutes. Cut into squares and eat preferably warm.

Sugar Buns

500 g/1 lb plain flour
30 g/1 oz fresh yeast
50 g/2 oz castor sugar
250 ml/8 fl oz lukewarm milk
40 g/1½ oz butter, melted
2 eggs
1 teaspoon salt
grated rind of ½ lemon
FILLING AND GLAZE
200 g/7 oz butter, melted
100 g/4 oz castor sugar
75 g/3 oz raisins
2 tablespoons granulated sugar

Sift the flour into a bowl and make a well in the centre. Cream the yeast with a little of the sugar and the milk. Pour into the well in the flour and sprinkle over a little of the flour. Cover and leave for 15 minutes in a warm place, until frothy.

Add the butter to the bowl with the remaining sugar, the eggs, salt and lemon rind. Mix everything to a dough and knead on a lightly floured board until smooth and elastic. Leave to rise until doubled in size, about 30 minutes. Divide the dough into 50-g/2-oz pieces and roll these out into 20 × 7·5-cm/ 8 × 3-inch strips. Brush with a quarter of the melted butter and sprinkle with the castor sugar and raisins. Fold over lengthways and roll up, starting from the short side.

Pour 4 tablespoons of the remaining butter into a 23-cm/ 9-inch round cake tin. Place the buns in the tin with the rolled sides uppermost. Cover and leave to rise in a warm place for 15 minutes. Preheat the oven to hot (220°C, 425°F, Gas Mark 7).

Brush the rolls with the remaining melted butter and sprinkle with granulated sugar. Bake for 40–45 minutes then pull apart and serve warm.

Batch Buns

These buns are made using the same dough, omitting the filling. Form 50-g/2-oz pieces of the dough into round bun shapes and place in the butter in the cake tin. Leave to rise then brush with 50 g/2 oz melted butter and bake in a hot oven (220°C, 425°F, Gas Mark 7) for 35 minutes.

Old-Fashioned Treats

Buttermilk Waffles

125 g/4½ oz butter, softened
50 g/2 oz castor sugar
25 g/1 oz vanilla sugar
pinch of salt
4 eggs
250 g/9 oz plain flour
1 teaspoon baking powder
200–250 ml/7–8 fl oz buttermilk

Mix together the butter, sugar, vanilla sugar, salt and eggs, until creamy. Sift the flour with the baking powder and stir in alternately with the buttermilk. Add enough buttermilk to make a smooth batter.

Heat the waffle iron, brushing the inside well with oil. Pour a little of the mixture carefully into the iron, taking care not to overfill it, and bake the waffles for 4–6 minutes, until golden brown.

Cook's Tip

Waffles taste best when eaten almost immediately, having cooled just a little. They are good served topped with a spoonful of whipped cream.

Cream-Filled Waffles

375 g/13 oz plain flour
25 g/1 oz fresh yeast
50 g/2 oz castor sugar
500 ml/17 fl oz lukewarm milk
4 eggs
125 g/4½ oz butter, melted
pinch of salt
grated rind of ½ lemon
icing sugar to sprinkle
FILLING
300 ml/½ pint double cream
25 g/1 oz icing sugar

Sift the flour into a bowl and make a well in the centre. Cream the yeast with 1 teaspoon of the sugar and 6 tablespoons of the milk. Pour into the well and sprinkle the surface with a little of the flour. Cover and leave for 15 minutes, until frothy.

Add the remaining sugar and milk, the eggs, melted butter, salt and lemon rind, and beat all the ingredients until well mixed and the dough begins to bubble. Cover and leave in a warm place for 25 minutes.

Heat the waffle iron, brushing the inside well with oil. Put a little of the mixture into the iron for each waffle, and cook until golden brown. This will take 5–7 minutes, depending on the temperature of the iron. Break up the waffles into sections and leave to cool on a wire rack.

Whip the cream with the sifted icing sugar until it reaches a piping consistency. Sandwich the waffles together with the piped cream and sprinkle with sifted icing sugar.

Apricot Pastry Pretzels

1 (368-g/13-oz) packet frozen
  puff pastry
300 g/11 oz plain flour
1 egg yolk
100 g/4 oz castor sugar
200 g/7 oz butter, cut into flakes
1 egg yolk, beaten to glaze
175 g/6 oz apricot jam

Allow the puff pastry to thaw 1 hour at room temperature.

Sift the flour and mix with the egg yolk, sugar and butter, to form a dough. Wrap the dough in foil and leave in the refrigerator for 2 hours.

Roll out the puff pastry on a lightly floured surface to measure 50 × 35 cm/20 × 14 inches. Roll out the shortcrust pastry to the same size. Brush the shortcrust pastry with the beaten egg yolk and lay the puff pastry on top, pressing

well together. Cut into 1·5-cm/¾-inch wide strips and twist them into spirals, so that the puff pastry is on the outside. Press the ends together well and form into pretzel shapes, as illustrated.

Arrange on a baking tray and leave for 15 minutes. Pre-heat the oven to hot (220°C, 425°F, Gas Mark 7) and bake for 15 minutes. Warm the jam, sieve and brush the pretzels while still warm.

Cook's Tip

The pretzels may be frozen, but in this case do not brush them with jam. Pack them while warm and freeze at once.

The pretzels can also be glazed with a little glacé icing, as illustrated.

Featherlight Cream Sponges

4 eggs, separated, plus 1 egg
  yolk
80 g/3 oz castor sugar
45 g/1½ oz plain flour
40 g/1½ oz cornflour
pinch of salt
40 g/1½ oz butter, melted
icing sugar to sprinkle
FILLING
300 ml/½ pint double cream
225 g/8 oz fruit (raspberries,
  strawberries, redcurrants)

Line two baking trays with greased greaseproof paper or non-stick baking parchment. Draw twelve 13-cm/5-inch diameter circles on the paper with a pencil. Preheat the oven to hot (220°C, 425°F, Gas Mark 7).

Whisk the egg whites until stiff then fold in half the sugar. Whisk the egg yolks with the

remaining sugar in a basin over hot water until thick and creamy. Sift the flour and cornflour together, mix with the salt and fold into the egg yolk mixture with the melted butter. Finally fold in the whisked egg whites. Put this mixture in a piping bag fitted with a plain nozzle and pipe it on to the circles in a spiral pattern, smoothing over the surface. Bake the sponges in the centre of the oven for 10–12 minutes.

Turn the sponge rounds out on to a cloth, dampen the lining paper with cold water and peel if off carefully. Fold the sponges carefully in half and leave them to cool under the cloth. Whip the cream until stiff, and use with the fruit to fill the sponges, piping the cream for a more decorative effect. Finally sprinkle with sifted icing sugar.

Cream Cheese Crumble Cake

YEAST DOUGH
350 g/12 oz plain flour
20 g/¾ oz fresh yeast
6 tablespoons lukewarm milk
50 g/2 oz butter, melted
50 g/2 oz castor sugar
2 eggs
pinch of salt
FILLING
180 g/6 oz butter, softened
180 g/6 oz castor sugar
3 eggs
*575 g/1¼ lb curd or cream
    cheese*
25 g/1 oz cornflour
grated rind of 1 lemon
100 g/4 oz raisins (optional)
TOPPING
180 g/6 oz plain flour
50 g/2 oz sugar
pinch of salt
¼ teaspoon ground cinnamon
75 g/3 oz butter

Sift the flour into a mixing bowl and make a well in the centre. Cream the yeast with the lukewarm milk and pour into the well. Sprinkle the surface with a little of the flour. Cover and leave in a warm place for 15 minutes, until frothy. Pour the melted butter into the flour together with the sugar, eggs and salt. Work all the ingredients together to make a dough. Knead lightly, cover and leave to rise in a warm place for 1 hour.

Beat the butter and sugar until light and creamy. Add the eggs, cheese, cornflour, lemon rind and raisins, if used.

Knead the dough and roll out to line the base of a greased 23 × 33-cm/9 × 13-inch Swiss roll tin. Spread the cheese mixture on top.

To make the crumble topping, mix together the flour, sugar, salt and cinnamon. Melt the butter and gradually add to the flour, rubbing it in with the fingertips. Sprinkle over the cheese filling and leave to stand for 15 minutes.

Preheat the oven to moderately hot (200°C, 400°F, Gas Mark 6) and bake the cake for 30–40 minutes.

Country Butter Cake

450 g/1 lb plain flour
40 g/1½ oz fresh yeast
250 ml/8 fl oz lukewarm milk
225 g/8 oz castor sugar
225 g/8 oz butter
pinch of salt
1 egg, beaten
1 teaspoon ground cinnamon

Grease two baking trays with butter or margarine.

Sift the flour into a bowl and make a well in the centre. Cream the yeast with a little of the milk and 1 teaspoon sugar and pour into the well. Sprinkle over a little of the flour, cover and leave in a warm place for 15 minutes, until frothy.

Melt half the butter and place the remaining butter in the refrigerator. Add 50 g/2 oz sugar, the salt, egg, melted butter and remaining milk to the yeast mixture and beat with the flour to form a dough. Knead on a floured surface until smooth and elastic. Leave to rise for 1 hour in a warm place.

Preheat the oven to hot (220°C, 425°F, Gas Mark 7). Roll out the dough to fit two 25 × 30-cm/10 × 12-inch baking trays. Make small wells in the surface of the dough and into these put the remaining butter, cut into flakes. Mix the rest of the sugar with the cinnamon and sprinkle over the cakes. Bake for 25 minutes, leave the cakes to cool and then cut into slices.

Butter Cream Sandwich Fingers

BISCUIT MIXTURE
500 g/1 lb plain flour
15 g/½ oz fresh yeast
175 g/6 oz castor sugar
250 ml/8 fl oz lukewarm milk
90 g/3½ oz butter
1 egg
¼ teaspoon grated lemon rind
100 g/4 oz almonds, chopped
1 tablespoon cold milk
BUTTER CREAM
75 g/3 oz unsalted butter
175 g/6 oz icing sugar
¼ teaspoon vanilla essence

Sift the flour into a bowl and make a well in the centre. Cream the yeast with 1 tablespoon of sugar and 2 tablespoons of the milk. Pour into the well in the flour, sprinkle with a little of the flour and leave in a warm place for 15 minutes, until frothy.

Melt 50 g/2 oz butter in the remaining warm milk and add to the bowl with the egg, 50 g/2 oz sugar and the lemon rind. Form into a dough and knead. Spread out on a greased baking tray and leave to rise for 1–1½ hours.

Preheat the oven to moderately hot (200°C, 400°F, Gas Mark 6).

Melt the remaining butter, and stir in the remaining sugar and the almonds. Mix in the tablespoon of milk, cool, then spread over the dough. Bake for 40 minutes, cool and cut into fingers.

Split each finger in half horizontally through the centre. Cream the butter with the sifted icing sugar and vanilla essence until light and fluffy. Sandwich together the fingers with this butter cream.

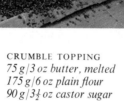

Marbled Crumble Cake

YEAST DOUGH
350 g/12 oz plain flour
20 g/¾ oz fresh yeast
50 g/2 oz castor sugar
125 ml/4 fl oz lukewarm milk
50 g/2 oz margarine, melted
2 eggs
pinch of salt
FILLINGS
250 ml/8 fl oz milk
20 g/¾ oz margarine
grated rind of ¼ lemon
30 g/1 oz semolina
100 g/4 oz ground poppy seeds
50 g/2 oz sugar
1 egg
1 tablespoon rum
¼ teaspoon ground cinnamon
250 g/9 oz curd or cream cheese
3 tablespoons milk
1 egg, separated
100 g/4 oz castor sugar
250 g/9 oz cherry jam
1 tablespoon rum

CRUMBLE TOPPING
75 g/3 oz butter, melted
175 g/6 oz plain flour
90 g/3½ oz castor sugar

Make the dough as for Dresden Slices (see right) and line a greased 23 × 33-cm/9 × 13-inch Swiss roll tin.

Bring the 250 ml/8 fl oz milk to the boil with the margarine, lemon rind and semolina, and leave for 5 minutes. Mix in the poppy seeds, sugar, egg, rum and cinnamon.

Mix together the cheese, milk, egg yolk and sugar. Whisk the egg white until stiff and fold in. Mix the jam and rum together.

Rub the melted butter into the flour and sugar until crumbly. Spread spoonfuls of the poppy seed, cheese and jam mixtures over the dough, and top with the crumble. Leave for 15 minutes then bake in a hot oven (220°C, 425°F, Gas Mark 7) for 20–30 minutes.

Dresden Slices

YEAST DOUGH
225 g/8 oz plain flour
15 g/½ oz fresh yeast
25 g/1 oz castor sugar
6 tablespoons lukewarm milk
25 g/1 oz margarine, melted
1 egg, beaten
pinch of salt
FILLING
350 g/12 oz curd or cream cheese
100 g/4 oz castor sugar
1 egg
1 tablespoon plain flour
grated rind of 1 lemon
TOPPING
100 g/4 oz butter
100 g/4 oz castor sugar
1 tablespoon plain flour
2 eggs
100 g/4 oz flaked almonds

Sift the flour into a bowl and make a well in the centre. Cream the yeast with a little of the sugar and the milk. Pour into the well and sprinkle the surface with a little of the flour. Cover the bowl and leave for 15 minutes, until frothy. Add the remaining sugar, the melted margarine, egg and salt, and beat all the ingredients until a dough is formed. Knead lightly, cover and leave to rise for 1 hour.

Mix the cheese with the sugar, egg, flour and lemon rind, beating until light and fluffy.

Lightly knead the dough and roll out to line a greased 33 × 23-cm/13 × 9-inch Swiss roll tin. Spread the cheese filling over it evenly.

Preheat the oven to moderately hot (200°C, 400°F, Gas Mark 6). Beat the butter and sugar until creamy. Add the flour and the eggs, one at a time. Spread over the cheese filling and finally sprinkle with the almonds. Bake the cake for 30–40 minutes. Allow to cool slightly then cut into slices.

Cakes for Everyday

Swiss Plum Slice

YEAST DOUGH
350 g/12 oz plain flour
20 g/¾ oz fresh yeast
6 tablespoons lukewarm milk
50 g/2 oz butter
50 g/2 oz castor sugar
pinch of salt
2 eggs
TOPPING
1 kg/2 lb plums
50 g/2 oz sugar crystals
½ teaspoon ground cinnamon

Sift the flour into a bowl and make a well in the centre. Cream the yeast with the milk and pour into the well. Sprinkle the surface with a little flour, cover and leave in a warm place for 15 minutes, until frothy.

Melt the butter but do not let it get hot. Add the butter to the flour with the sugar, salt and eggs and beat everything to a dough. Knead lightly, cover and leave to rise for 1 hour.

Wash the plums, remove the stones and cut lengthways into quarters. Knead the dough lightly and roll out to fit a greased 33 × 23-cm/13 × 9-inch Swiss roll tin. Prick all over with a fork. Arrange the plums in overlapping rows on the dough and leave to rise for a further 15 minutes. Preheat the oven to moderately hot (200°C, 400°F, Gas Mark 6).

Bake for 20–30 minutes and sprinkle with the sugar and cinnamon while still warm.

Apple Crumble Cake

YEAST DOUGH
225 g/8 oz plain flour
15 g/½ oz fresh yeast
25 g/1 oz castor sugar
6 tablespoons lukewarm milk
25 g/1 oz butter, melted
1 egg
pinch of salt
grated rind of 1 lemon
TOPPING
1 kg/2 lb apples
350 g/12 oz plain flour
200 g/7 oz sugar
25 g/1 oz vanilla sugar
200 g/7 oz butter, cut into flakes
100 g/3½ oz currants

Sift the flour into a bowl and make a well in the centre. Cream the yeast with a little of the sugar and the milk. Pour into the well and sprinkle the surface with a little of the flour. Cover and leave in a warm place for 15 minutes, until frothy. Add the remaining sugar, the melted butter, egg, salt and lemon rind, and mix all the ingredients together to a dough. Knead lightly and leave for 1 hour.

Peel, core and slice the apples. Lightly knead the dough and roll out to fit a greased 23 × 33-cm/9 × 13-inch Swiss roll tin. Arrange the apple slices in overlapping rows on the dough. Preheat the oven to moderately hot (200°C, 400°F, Gas Mark 6).

Sift the flour into a bowl and add the sugar and vanilla sugar. Rub in the butter with the fingertips until crumbly. Spread the crumble over the apples, sprinkling with the currants.

Bake the cake for 25–35 minutes. Leave to cool then cut into slices.

Hazelnut Stollen

500 g/1 lb plain flour
30 g/1 oz fresh yeast
70 g/2¼ oz castor sugar
250 ml/8 fl oz lukewarm milk
100 g/3½ oz margarine, melted
1 egg
½ teaspoon salt
grated rind of ½ lemon
FILLING AND ICING
100 g/4 oz ground almonds
100 g/4 oz soft brown sugar
100 g/4 oz ground hazelnuts
2 egg whites, lightly beaten
2 tablespoons rum
¼ teaspoon ground cinnamon
1 egg yolk, beaten to glaze
120 g/4½ oz icing sugar, sifted
1–2 tablespoons lemon juice
50 g/2 oz toasted hazelnuts

Sift the flour into a bowl and
form a well. Cream the yeast
with a little of the sugar and
the milk. Pour into the well,
cover and leave for 15 minutes,
until frothy. Add the remaining
sugar, the margarine, egg, salt
and lemon rind and mix to a
dough. Knead lightly then
leave to rise for 1 hour.

Mix the almonds, sugar,
hazelnuts, egg whites, rum and
cinnamon. Knead the dough
lightly and roll out to a 45-cm/
18-inch square. Spread over the
filling. Brush the sides with egg
yolk and roll up. Place on a
greased baking tray, brush with
egg and leave for 15 minutes.
Preheat the oven to 220°C,
425°F, Gas Mark 7.

Bake the stollen for 30–40
minutes. Ice with the sugar and
lemon juice and sprinkle with
chopped hazelnuts.

Note To make the variation on
the jacket, roll the dough into
two oblongs. Spread each with
filling, roll up and twist together
into a ring. Place in a ring tin
and cook as above. Ice and
sprinkle with flaked almonds.

Bohemian Plait

500 g/1 lb plain flour
30 g/1 oz fresh yeast
60 g/2 oz castor sugar
250 ml/8 fl oz lukewarm milk
100 g/4 oz margarine
pinch of salt
50 g/2 oz raisins
1 egg yolk, beaten to glaze
2 tablespoons sugar crystals to
  sprinkle

Sift the flour into a bowl and
make a well in the centre.
Cream the yeast with a little
of the sugar and the milk and
pour into the well. Sprinkle the
surface with a little of the
flour. Cover and leave in a
warm place for 15 minutes,
until frothy.

Melt the margarine, add it
to the bowl with the remaining
sugar, the salt and raisins, and
beat all the ingredients to a
dough. Knead on a lightly
floured surface, then cover and
leave to rise for 1 hour.

Halve the dough. Divide one
half into three 35-cm/14-inch
strips and use to make a plait.
Place on a greased baking tray.
From two-thirds of the
remaining dough, make an-
other smaller plait. From the
remaining dough, make two
strips and form a twist. Brush
the larger of the plaits with
beaten egg yolk, place the
smaller one on top and brush
this. Finally place the twist
on top and brush with beaten
egg yolk. Sprinkle with the
sugar crystals and leave in a
warm place to rise for 15
minutes. Preheat the oven to
moderately hot (200°C, 400°F,
Gas Mark 6).

Bake the loaf for 25–30
minutes and allow to cool on a
wire rack.

Creamy Rice Flan

1 (212-g/7½-oz) packet frozen puff pastry
FILLING
100 g/4 oz short-grain rice
600 ml/1 pint milk
300 ml/½ pint single cream
¼ teaspoon salt
3 tablespoons castor sugar
2 eggs plus 2 egg yolks
40 g/1½ oz chopped mixed peel
50 g/2 oz red and yellow glacé cherries, chopped
25 g/1 oz almonds, chopped
50 g/2 oz raisins
icing sugar to sprinkle

Allow the pastry to thaw for 1 hour at room temperature.

Put the rice, milk, cream, salt and 2 tablespoons of the castor sugar into a saucepan and bring to the boil. Cover and simmer for 20–25 minutes, until the rice is tender and has absorbed all the liquid. Cool then beat in the eggs and 1 egg yolk.

Preheat the oven to moderately hot (200°C, 400°F, Gas Mark 6). Roll out the pastry to line a 23-cm/9-inch flan ring and bake blind for 10 minutes. Mix all the rice with the candied peel and spread half into the pastry case. Mix the remainder with the cherries, almonds and raisins, spoon over and smooth the top. Whisk the remaining egg yolk with the castor sugar and pour over the rice mixture. Bake in the oven for a further 25 minutes. Cool then sprinkle with icing sugar.

Chelsea Cake

500 g/1 lb plain flour
40 g/1½ oz fresh yeast
60 g/2 oz castor sugar
250 ml/8 fl oz lukewarm milk
100 g/3½ oz margarine, melted
FILLING
200 g/7 oz raisins
2 tablespoons rum
125 g/4½ oz butter, melted
125 g/4½ oz granulated sugar
60 g/2 oz ground almonds
2 teaspoons ground cinnamon
80 g/3 oz chopped mixed peel
GLAZE
1 egg yolk, beaten
2 tablespoons apricot jam

Sift the flour into a bowl and make a well. Cream the yeast with a little of the sugar and the milk and pour into the well. Sprinkle over a little flour, cover and leave in a warm place for 15 minutes, until frothy. Add the margarine with the remaining sugar and mix to a dough. Knead lightly then leave to rise for 1 hour.

Soak the raisins in the rum. Knead the dough again then roll out to 3 mm/⅛ inch thick and brush with the butter. Sprinkle with the sugar, almonds, cinnamon, raisins and chopped peel. Cut the dough into 5-cm/2-inch wide strips. Roll up one strip and place in the centre of a greased 25-cm/10-inch flan tin. Roll the remaining strips around it and leave in a warm place for 15 minutes. Preheat the oven to hot (220°C, 425°F, Gas Mark 7).

Brush with beaten egg yolk and bake the cake for 35 minutes. Cool then spread with the warmed jam.

Note To make individual buns, as illustrated on the jacket, roll up the strips of dough separately and place in a cake tin. Bake and glaze as above.

Arabian Honey Cake

75 g/3 oz butter
3 eggs
125 g/4½ oz castor sugar
few drops of vanilla essence
2 tablespoons double cream
150 g/5 oz plain flour
¼ teaspoon baking powder
TOPPING
100 g/4 oz butter
80 g/3 oz castor sugar
75 g/3 oz thick honey
2 tablespoons double cream
150 g/5 oz flaked almonds
¼ teaspoon ground cinnamon
grated rind of ¼ orange

Grease a 25-cm/10-inch sandwich tin. Preheat the oven to moderately hot (200°C, 400°F, Gas Mark 6).
 Melt the butter. Whisk the eggs with the sugar and vanilla essence until frothy. Stir in the cooled butter and the cream.

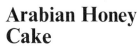

Sift the flour and baking powder into the mixture and fold in thoroughly. Turn into the prepared tin, smooth over and bake for 10–12 minutes.
 Meanwhile, make the topping. Melt the butter in a pan and add the sugar, honey, cream, almonds, cinnamon and orange rind. Stir the ingredients well to mix and bring them to the boil. Spread this mixture over the cake and return to the oven for a further 15–20 minutes. Loosen the cake from the tin and leave to cool on a wire rack.

Iced Banana Ring

225 g/8 oz margarine or butter
150 g/5 oz castor sugar
pinch of salt
5 eggs, separated
15 g/½ oz candied ginger, chopped
75 g/3 oz desiccated coconut
grated rind of 1 lemon
500 g/1 lb bananas
3 tablespoons lemon juice
1 tablespoon rum
250 g/9 oz plain flour
1 teaspoon baking powder
ICING
200 g/7 oz icing sugar
2–3 tablespoons lemon juice

Grease a fluted 23-cm/9-inch ring tin. Preheat the oven to moderately hot (200°C, 400°F, Gas Mark 6).
 Beat the margarine with the sugar and salt until light and creamy. Add the egg yolks one

at a time with the ginger, coconut and lemon rind. Mix well. Peel the bananas, dice and sprinkle with the lemon juice and rum. Fold into the egg mixture. Sift the flour with the baking powder and fold in. Whisk the egg whites until very stiff and carefully fold into the mixture. Turn into the prepared tin and bake for 1–1¼ hours. Turn out and leave to cool on a wire rack.
 Mix the sifted icing sugar with the lemon juice until smooth and use to ice the cake.

Cinnamon and Almond Flan

PASTRY
250 g/9 oz plain flour
125 g/4½ oz margarine, cut into flakes
75 g/3 oz castor sugar
1 egg
2–3 tablespoons water
pinch of salt
FILLING
3 eggs
125 ml/4 fl oz double cream
125 ml/4 fl oz milk
150 g/5 oz castor sugar
pinch of salt
1 teaspoon ground cinnamon
¼ teaspoon baking powder
200 g/7 oz ground almonds
5 plain sweet biscuits, crushed
50 g/2 oz candied lemon peel, finely chopped

Sift the flour into a mixing bowl and add the margarine, sugar, egg, water and salt. Mix to a dough, wrap in foil or cling film and leave in the refrigerator for 2 hours.

Preheat the oven to moderately hot (200°C, 400°F, Gas Mark 6). Roll out the pastry on a floured surface and use to line the base and sides of a 23-cm/10-inch flan ring or springform cake tin. Bake blind for 10 minutes.

Beat the eggs with the cream, milk, sugar, salt, cinnamon and baking powder. Add the ground almonds, biscuit crumbs and chopped peel and spread this filling into the pastry case. Bake the flan for a further 45–50 minutes, then allow to cool on a wire rack.

Mizzi's Fruit Cake

100 g/4 oz prunes, stoned
50 g/2 oz dried apricots
50 g/2 oz raisins
100 g/4 oz walnuts, chopped
225 g/8 oz soft margarine
225 g/8 oz castor sugar
pinch of salt
grated rind of 1 lemon
¼ teaspoon vanilla essence
4 eggs
350 g/12 oz plain flour
1 teaspoon baking powder
icing sugar to sprinkle

Grease a 20-cm/8-inch fluted oval or round cake tin. Preheat the oven to moderate (160°C, 325°F, Gas Mark 3).

Cut the prunes and apricots into small pieces and mix them with the raisins and walnuts.

Beat the margarine with the sugar, salt, lemon rind and vanilla, until light and creamy.

Beat in the eggs one at a time, adding a tablespoon of flour with each egg after the first. Sift the remaining flour and baking powder and fold into the cake mixture. Turn into the prepared cake tin and smooth over the surface. Bake for about 1½–1¾ hours, testing with a skewer to see if cooked.

Turn the cake out on to a wire rack, allow to cool and dust with sifted icing sugar.

Mirandola Noodle Cake

500 g/1 lb plain flour
5 eggs
1 tablespoon Maraschino
4 teaspoons lukewarm water
100 g/4 oz coconut macaroons
200 g/7 oz almonds, finely
  chopped
300 g/11 oz castor sugar
1 tablespoon vanilla sugar
6 tablespoons milk
2 eggs

Grease a 23-cm/9-inch flan tin and dust with flour.

Sift the flour into a bowl and mix with the eggs, Maraschino and water, to form a firm pastry. Halve the dough and roll out one half until almost thin enough to see your hand through it. Leave it to dry out on an oiled surface then cut into strips approximately 1·5 mm/$\frac{1}{16}$ inch wide

and 3·5 cm/1$\frac{1}{2}$ inches long.

Preheat the oven to moderately hot (200°C, 400°F, Gas Mark 6). Roll out the remaining pastry and line the prepared flan tin with it. Crumble the macaroons and mix with the almonds, sugar and vanilla sugar. Place alternate layers of the macaroon mixture and noodles into the pastry case, finally topping with a layer of noodles. Whisk the milk and eggs together and pour over the cake. Bake for 35–40 minutes and serve warm.

Date and Fig Flan

PASTRY
200 g/7 oz plain flour
100 g/3$\frac{1}{2}$ oz butter, cut into
  flakes
30 g/1 oz castor sugar
1 egg yolk
pinch of salt
2 tablespoons water
FILLING
120 g/4 oz butter
200 g/7 oz castor sugar
4 eggs, separated
grated rind of 1 lemon
1 teaspoon ground cinnamon
1 teaspoon each of ground
  nutmeg and ground cloves
$\frac{1}{2}$ teaspoon salt
100 g/4 oz ground hazelnuts
75 g/3 oz self-raising flour
75 g/3 oz walnuts, chopped
75 g/3 oz figs, finely chopped
75 g/3 oz dates, finely chopped

Sift the flour into a bowl and add the flaked butter, sugar, egg yolk, salt and water. Mix the ingredients to form a pastry dough, cover and leave in the refrigerator for 2 hours.

Preheat the oven to moderate (180°C, 350°F, Gas Mark 4). Roll out the pastry to line a 23-cm/9-inch flan tin. Beat the butter with the sugar until light and creamy. Add the egg yolks, lemon rind, spices, salt and hazelnuts. Whisk the egg whites until stiff and fold into the egg yolk mixture. Mix the sifted flour with the walnuts, figs and dates and fold carefully into the egg mixture. Spread the filling into the pastry case and bake for 55–60 minutes. Cool on a wire rack.

Plum Lattice Tart

PASTRY
300 g / 11 oz plain flour
pinch of salt
180 g / 6 oz butter, cut into flakes
1 egg yolk
120 g / 4 oz castor sugar
FILLING
1 kg / 2 lb plums
2 tablespoons cornflour
150 g / 5 oz sugar
25 g / 1 oz butter
50 g / 2 oz walnuts, chopped
icing sugar to sprinkle

Sift the flour into a mixing bowl and add the salt, flaked butter, egg yolk and sugar. Mix to a pastry dough, cover and leave in the refrigerator for 1 hour.

Wash, stone and quarter the plums and cook in a little water for 5 minutes. Mix the cornflour with 3 tablespoons cold water and stir into the plums with the sugar. Continue to cook until thickened, stirring all the time. Remove from the heat and stir in the butter and walnuts. Leave to cool.

Preheat the oven to moderately hot (200°C, 400°F, Gas Mark 6). Roll out the pastry to line a 23-cm/9-inch flan tin, reserving enough pastry to make the lattice. Spread the plum filling into the flan case. Cut the remaining pastry into thin strips and arrange in a lattice pattern over the plums.

Bake for 35–45 minutes. Sprinkle with sifted icing sugar to serve.

Grape Cream Flan

PASTRY
300 g / 10 oz plain flour
200 g / 7 oz butter, cut into flakes
100 g / 3½ oz castor sugar
1 egg
FILLING
600 ml / 1 pint milk
50 g / 2 oz cornflour
25 g / 1 oz castor sugar
2 eggs, separated
500 g / 1 lb black grapes, washed
  and pips removed
150 ml / ¼ pint double cream

Place the sifted flour in a mixing bowl with the butter, sugar and egg and mix until a dough is formed. Wrap in foil or cling film and leave in the refrigerator for 2 hours.

Preheat the oven to moderately hot (190°C, 375°F, Gas Mark 5). Roll out the pastry to line a 23-cm/9-inch flan tin and bake blind for 20 minutes, until cooked. Allow the pastry to cool.

Blend 4 tablespoons milk with the cornflour, sugar and egg yolks. Bring the remaining milk to the boil and pour on to the cornflour. Return to the heat and bring to the boil, stirring until thickened. Allow to cool, stirring frequently to prevent a skin forming. Whisk the egg whites until stiff and fold into the cooled mixture. Place half this filling in the pastry case. Reserve 12 grapes for decoration and place the remainder on top of the filling. Cover with the remaining filling, smoothing evenly. Chill in the refrigerator until set.

Decorate the flan with piped whipped cream and grapes.

Baked Vanilla Cheesecake

PASTRY
250 g/9 oz plain flour
125 g/4½ oz butter, cut into
   flakes
pinch of salt
30 g/1 oz castor sugar
1 egg
2–3 tablespoons water
FILLING
675 g/1½ lb curd or cream
   cheese
3 tablespoons oil
275 g/10 oz castor sugar
3 eggs, separated
3 tablespoons cornflour
few drops of vanilla essence
6 tablespoons milk

Sift the flour into a bowl. Add
the butter, salt, sugar, egg and
water and mix to a dough.
Wrap in foil or cling film and
leave for 2 hours in the
refrigerator.

Preheat the oven to moderate
(180°C, 350°F, Gas Mark 4).
Roll out the pastry to line the
base and sides of a 25-cm/10-
inch flan tin. Mix the cheese
with the oil, sugar, egg yolks,
cornflour, vanilla essence and
milk, until smooth. Whisk the
egg whites until stiff and fold
into the cheese mixture. Pour
into the pastry case and bake
in the centre of the oven for
50–60 minutes.

Rich Lemon Cheesecake

BISCUIT BASE
175 g/6 oz digestive biscuits
75 g/3 oz margarine, melted
FILLING
575 g/1¼ lb cream cheese
6 eggs, separated
100 g/4 oz castor sugar
1 (142-ml/5-fl oz) carton
   soured cream
grated rind of 1 lemon
1 tablespoon lemon juice
2 tablespoons cornflour
1 teaspoon baking powder

Crush the biscuits into crumbs
and mix with the melted
margarine. Press on to the base
of a greased 25-cm/10-inch
springform cake tin. Preheat
the oven to moderate
(160°C, 325°F, Gas Mark 3).
   Beat the cream cheese with
the egg yolks, sugar, soured
cream, lemon rind and juice,
cornflour and baking powder,
mixing until smooth. Whisk
the egg whites until stiff and
fold into the cheese mixture.
Pour into the prepared tin and
bake in the centre of the oven
for 1¼–1½ hours. Cover with
foil if becoming too brown.
The cheesecake should be firm
to the touch, but still slightly
springy. Loosen the sides
immediately with a knife and
allow to cool.

Classic Sand Cake

3 eggs
180 g/6 oz castor sugar
¼ teaspoon vanilla essence
grated rind of ½ lemon
pinch of salt
125 g/4 oz self-raising flour
125 g/4 oz cornflour
180 g/6 oz butter, melted
icing sugar to sprinkle

Grease a 1-kg/2-lb loaf tin and line with greased greaseproof paper. Preheat the oven to moderately hot (190°C, 375°F, Gas Mark 5).

Whisk the eggs with the sugar, vanilla, lemon rind and salt in a basin over a pan of hot water, allowing the ingredients to become lukewarm only. Remove the mixture from the heat and whisk until cooled. Sift the flour with the cornflour and fold in well.

Lastly mix in the melted butter. Turn into the prepared tin and bake for 40–45 minutes.

Cool on a wire rack and dredge the top with sifted icing sugar.

Chocolate Cherry Cake

100 g/4 oz glacé cherries, halved
200 g/7 oz butter
250 g/9 oz castor sugar
6 eggs
pinch of salt
grated rind of 1 lemon
¼ teaspoon ground cinnamon
200 g/7 oz milk chocolate, grated
100 g/3¼ oz ground hazelnuts
100 g/3¼ oz ground almonds
150 g/5 oz plain flour
1 teaspoon baking powder
DECORATION
2 tablespoons icing sugar
2 tablespoons drinking chocolate powder

Grease a 23-cm/9-inch spring-form cake tin and sprinkle with fine breadcrumbs. Preheat the oven to moderate (180°C, 350°F, Gas Mark 4).

Wash the cherries and pat dry. Cream the butter and sugar together until pale and light. Add the eggs, salt, lemon rind, cinnamon, chocolate, hazelnuts and almonds and stir well. Finally fold in the cherries with the sifted flour and baking powder. Turn the cake mixture into the tin and smooth over the surface. Bake the cake for 1–1½ hours then leave to cool on a wire rack.

Cut the centre from a paper doily, place it over the centre of the cake and sift icing sugar over the uncovered area. Remove this centre piece, place the rest of the doily over the cake and sift all over with chocolate powder.

Baking for Coffee Parties

Sweet Poppy Seed Crescents

20 g/¾ oz fresh yeast
6 tablespoons lukewarm milk
450 g/1 lb plain flour
120 g/4 oz butter, melted
pinch of salt
1 tablespoon sugar
250 ml/8 fl oz soured cream
1 egg
1 egg yolk, beaten to glaze
FILLING
175 ml/6 fl oz milk
120 g/4 oz castor sugar
1 tablespoon poppy seeds
100 g/4 oz toasted hazelnuts, finely chopped
175 g/6 oz raisins, finely chopped
175 g/6 oz honey

Grease a baking tray. Cream the yeast with the milk and leave in a warm place until frothy.

Sift the flour into a bowl.

Mix the butter, salt, sugar, soured cream, egg and yeast liquid into the flour to form a dough. Knead until smooth and elastic, then leave to rise in a warm place for 20 minutes.

Heat the milk with the sugar, stirring until the sugar dissolves. Add the poppy seeds, hazelnuts and raisins and boil until the mixture thickens. Stir in the honey and cool.

Preheat the oven to hot (220°C, 425°F, Gas Mark 7). Divide the dough in two then roll each piece out to an oblong 40 × 25 cm/16 × 10 inches. Divide into 16 oblongs, each measuring 5 × 12·5 cm/ 2 × 5 inches. Place a little of the filling down the middle of each, brush the edges with beaten egg yolk and fold the dough over to seal the filling in. Curve into crescent shapes, place on the tray and brush with egg yolk. Leave in a warm place for 10 minutes then bake for 12–15 minutes.

Fruit and Nut Pumpernickel

450 g/1 lb icing sugar
5 eggs
350 g/12 oz blanched almonds, chopped
100 g/4 oz hazelnuts, chopped
pinch of salt
1 teaspoon ground cinnamon
pinch each of ground cloves and ground cardamom
50 g/2 oz candied orange peel, finely chopped
grated rind of ½ orange
grated rind of ¼ lemon
450 g/1 lb plain flour

Whisk the sifted icing sugar with the eggs until pale and creamy. Stir in the almonds, hazelnuts, salt, cinnamon, ground cloves and cardamom. Work in the candied peel and fruit rinds with the sifted flour and knead lightly on a floured board. Preheat the oven to

moderately hot (190°C, 375°F, Gas Mark 5).

Divide the mixture in half and shape into two loaves. Place these on a greased baking tray and bake for 1 hour. Cut the hot bread into thin slices and leave to cool.

188

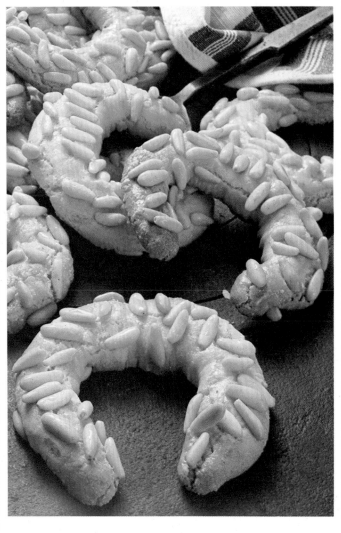

Amsterdam Squares

150 g/5 oz butter
150 g/5 oz castor sugar
1 egg
grated rind of ½ lemon
pinch of salt
pinch of baking powder
250 g/9 oz plain flour
1 egg yolk
175 g/6 oz blanched almonds,
  halved

Cream the butter with the sugar. Add the egg, lemon rind, salt, baking powder and sifted flour, mixing all the ingredients thoroughly to form a biscuit dough. Shape the mixture into a ball, wrap in foil or cling film and leave in the refrigerator for 2 hours.

Preheat the oven to moderately hot (200°C, 400°F, Gas Mark 6). Roll out the dough to 3 mm/⅛ inch thick and cut into 3·5-cm/1½-inch squares. Beat the egg yolk with a few drops of water and brush over the squares. Arrange four almond halves on each square and place the biscuits on greased baking trays, leaving sufficient room between each one to allow for spreading during cooking.

Bake for 10–15 minutes. Leave the biscuits to cool a little, then remove them from the tray with a palette knife and cool on a wire rack.

Pine Nut Crescents

250 g/9 oz ground almonds
300 g/11 oz castor sugar
4 egg whites
grated rind of 1 lemon
TOPPING
1 egg white
100 g/4 oz pine nuts or flaked
  almonds
50 g/2 oz granulated sugar
1 tablespoon water
1 tablespoon rum

Mix the almonds with the sugar, egg whites and lemon rind in a bowl over a saucepan of boiling water, stirring continuously for 15 minutes. Cool and chill thoroughly.

Preheat the oven to moderately hot (190°C, 375°F, Gas Mark 5). Form the almond dough into a roll and cut into 24 pieces. Make a small crescent shape from each piece and brush with lightly beaten egg white. Sprinkle the pine nuts or flaked almonds on to the biscuits, and press in so they do not fall off during baking. Place the biscuits on a large greased baking tray and bake for 15–20 minutes.

Mix the sugar with the water and simmer for 2 minutes. Remove from the heat and stir in the rum. Brush the biscuits with this rum glaze 5 minutes before the end of the baking time. Remove the biscuits carefully from the tray with a palette knife and leave to cool on a wire rack.

Orange Almond Cookies

250 g/9 oz butter or margarine
250 g/9 oz soft brown sugar
2 eggs
325 g/12 oz plain flour
1 teaspoon baking powder
¼ teaspoon salt
grated rind of 1 large or 2 small oranges
75 g/3 oz blanched almonds, chopped

Beat the butter with the sugar until pale and creamy. Add the eggs one at a time. Sift the flour and baking powder with the salt then stir a spoonful at a time into the creamed mixture. Finally add the orange rind and chopped almonds and mix thoroughly. Form the dough into a roll, 6 cm/2½ inches in diameter. Wrap in foil and leave in the refrigerator for 24 hours.

Preheat the oven to moderately hot (200°C, 400°F, Gas Mark 6). Cut thin slices from the roll of biscuit dough and lay on greased baking trays. Bake the cookies for 8–10 minutes. Leave to cool slightly on the tray then remove to a wire rack.

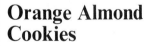

Cook's Tip

Instead of flavouring the cookies with orange, try using a mixture of lemon and orange rind and substitute desiccated coconut for the almonds.

Macaroon Bars

4 egg whites
225 g/8 oz castor sugar
225 g/8 oz flaked almonds
¼ teaspoon ground cinnamon
grated rind of 1 lemon
50 g/2 oz plain chocolate

Line a 19 × 29-cm/7½ × 11½-inch baking tray with rice paper. Preheat the oven to very cool (110°C, 325°F, Gas Mark ¼).
  Whisk the egg whites until stiff. Gradually whisk in half the sugar then fold in the remaining sugar with the flaked almonds, cinnamon and grated lemon rind. Spread the mixture over the baking tray and bake for 3–4 hours. Halfway through the cooking time cut the macaroon mixture into fingers. Cool on a wire rack when completely cooked.
  Melt the chocolate in a basin over a pan of hot water. Dip both ends of the macaroons into the chocolate and leave to set.

Cook's Tip

Place small spoonfuls of the macaroon mixture on to the rice paper. When cooked and cooled, sandwich together in pairs with a little melted chocolate.

Cream Slices

1 (368-g/13-oz) packet frozen
puff pastry
100 g/4 oz sugar crystals
FILLING
300 ml/½ pint double cream
few drops of vanilla essence
1 tablespoon castor sugar

Allow the pastry to thaw for 1
hour at room temperature.

Roll out the pastry fairly
thinly and cut out oval shapes
approximately 13 cm/5 inches
long. Rinse a baking tray with
cold water, arrange the pastry
ovals on it and sprinkle the
sugar over them. Leave to
stand in the refrigerator for 15
minutes.

Preheat the oven to hot
(230°C, 450°F, Gas Mark 8).
Bake the pastry for 10 minutes,
then leave to cool on a wire
rack. Whip the cream with the
vanilla essence and castor
sugar until stiff. Spread the

cream over half the pastry
ovals on the unsugared side,
and place a second oval on top,
sugar side up.

Lemon Ring
Biscuits

150 g/6 oz plain flour
1 teaspoon baking powder
100 g/4 oz cornflour
100 g/4 oz butter
100 g/4 oz castor sugar
2 egg yolks
grated rind of 2 lemons
ICING
125 g/5 oz icing sugar
2 tablespoons lemon juice
50 g/2 oz pistachio nuts, chopped

Sift the flour, baking powder
and cornflour into a mixing
bowl. Melt the butter and stir
into it the sugar, egg yolks and
lemon rind. Add to the flour
and mix all the ingredients
together to give a smooth
biscuit dough. Cover and chill
in the refrigerator until firm.

Preheat the oven to
moderately hot (200°C, 400°F,
Gas Mark 6). Roll out the

dough on a floured surface to
3 mm/⅛ inch thick. Using a
6-cm/2½-inch fluted cutter, cut
out circles from the dough.
Cut out the centre of each
biscuit using a 1-cm/½-inch
fluted cutter. Roll out the
centres to make more biscuits.
Place the ring biscuits on to
two greased baking trays and
bake for about 10 minutes.

Cool slightly on the trays,
then lift off with a palette
knife and cool on a wire rack.

Blend the sifted icing sugar
with the lemon juice and spread
over the biscuits. Decorate
with the chopped pistachio nuts
before the icing sets.

Florentines

100 g/4 oz butter
150 g/6 oz castor sugar
50 g/2 oz honey
4 tablespoons double cream
pinch of salt
grated rind of ½ lemon
180 g/7 oz flaked almonds
30 g/1 oz candied orange peel,
finely chopped
ICING
100 g/4 oz plain chocolate
10 glacé cherries

Grease two baking trays. Preheat the oven to moderate
(180°C, 350°F, Gas Mark 4).
  Mix the butter, sugar, honey,
cream, salt and lemon rind
together in a saucepan. Lightly
boil these ingredients for
approximately 4–5 minutes,
stirring continuously until the
mixture becomes thick and
creamy and leaves the sides of
the pan. Add the almonds and
chopped peel to the pan and

stir them well in. Remove the
pan from the heat. Place
heaped teaspoonfuls of the
mixture well apart on the
baking trays and flatten
slightly with the back of a wet
spoon. Bake the florentines for
approximately 10 minutes.
  Leave to cool on the tray for
a few minutes until they are
firm enough to be lifted on to
a wire rack. Melt the chocolate
in a basin over hot water and
spread thickly over the under-
side of the florentines, marking
into ridges with a fork. When
set, place a halved cherry on
the top of each florentine, to
decorate.

Almond Tartlets

1 (368-g/13-oz) packet frozen
puff pastry
FILLING
125 g/4¼ oz ground almonds
125 g/4¼ oz castor sugar
1 egg
3 tablespoons milk
1 tablespoon rum
grated rind of 1 lemon
12 almonds, halved

Allow the pastry to thaw for
1 hour at room temperature.
  Roll out the pastry on a
floured surface to a thickness
of 3 mm/⅛ inch. Rinse about
eight small tartlet or patty
tins in cold water. Line each
tin with pastry and prick the
pastry several times with a
fork. Leave to stand in the
refrigerator for 15 minutes.
Preheat the oven to hot (220°C,
425°F, Gas Mark 7).
  Mix the ground almonds,
sugar, egg, milk, rum and

lemon rind together. Fill the
pastry cases with this mixture.
Smooth over the surface and
put 3 almond halves on top of
each. Bake the tartlets for 20
minutes.
  Allow to cool for a few
minutes in the tins, then turn
out carefully on to a wire rack.

Baking for Coffee Parties

Swiss Choux Rings

CHOUX PASTE
60 g/2 oz butter
250 ml/8 fl oz water
pinch of salt
200 g/7 oz plain flour
4 eggs
ICING
50 g/2 oz apricot jam
100 g/4 oz plain chocolate
FILLING
40 g/1½ oz cornflour
180 g/6 oz castor sugar
4 eggs, separated
500 ml/17 fl oz milk
½ teaspoon vanilla essence

Preheat the oven to hot (220°C, 425°F, Gas Mark 7). Grease a baking tray.

Heat the butter in the water until melted, add the salt and bring to the boil. Tip in the sifted flour all at once and stir vigorously until the mixture leaves the sides of the pan and forms a smooth ball. Leave to cool slightly then add the eggs one at a time. Pipe 16 small rings on to the baking tray and bake for 20 minutes. Split the rings after cooking to allow steam to escape.

Warm the jam and spread over the top of the rings. Melt the chocolate in a basin over hot water and pour over the jam on the rings.

Blend the cornflour with the sugar, egg yolks and a little of the milk. Heat the remaining milk then pour on to the blended mixture together with the vanilla essence. Return to the pan and bring to the boil, stirring continuously. Boil for a few seconds then cool slightly. Whisk the egg whites until stiff and fold into the cornflour custard which should be just warm. Cool completely, cut the rings in half and fill with the cornflour custard.

Iced Vanilla Slices

1 (368-g/13-oz) packet frozen puff pastry
ICING
200 g/7 oz icing sugar
1 tablespoon water
1 tablespoon lemon juice
FILLING
4 eggs, separated
150 g/5 oz icing sugar
50 g/2 oz cornflour
30 g/1 oz castor sugar
½ teaspoon vanilla essence
500 ml/17 fl oz milk

Allow the pastry to thaw for 1 hour at room temperature. Preheat the oven to hot (220°C, 425°F, Gas Mark 7).

Roll out the pastry to an oblong 60 × 45 cm/24 × 18 inches. Cut it in half widthways and place on a baking tray sprinkled with cold water. Prick with a fork and leave to stand in a cool place for 15 minutes. Bake the pastry for 12–18 minutes then leave to cool on a wire rack.

Mix the sifted icing sugar with the water and lemon juice and ice one of the pastry pieces.

Prepare the filling. Whisk the egg whites with the sifted icing sugar until stiff and glossy. Blend the cornflour with the egg yolks, castor sugar, vanilla essence and a little milk. Bring the remaining milk to the boil and pour on to the cornflour mixture. Return to the heat and cook for a few minutes, stirring until thickened. Fold in the whisked egg whites and leave to cool. Spread this filling thickly over the piece of pastry without icing and put the iced pastry on top.

Leave in the refrigerator until set and then cut into slices.

Toasted Aniseed Cake

5 eggs, separated
125 g/5 oz castor sugar
3 tablespoons water
175 g/6 oz plain flour
1 tablespoon ground aniseed

Grease two 0·5-kg/1-lb loaf tins. Preheat the oven to moderate (180°C, 350°F, Gas Mark 4).

Whisk the egg yolks with the sugar and water until pale and creamy. Sift the flour and add it to the yolk mixture with the aniseed. Whisk the egg whites until stiff and fold in. Divide the cake mixture between the two tins and smooth over. Bake for 40–45 minutes.

Turn the cakes out on to wire racks to cool and leave for 2 days. Preheat the oven to moderately hot (200°C, 400°F, Gas Mark 6). Cut the cakes

into 1-cm/½-inch thick slices, and arrange on baking trays. Brown in the oven for 5 minutes on each side. Alternatively, toast the slices under a hot grill.

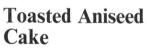

Cook's Tip

This toasted aniseed cake tastes best spread with butter and honey.

Hazelnut Buns

500 g/1 lb plain flour
30 g/1 oz fresh yeast
250 ml/8 fl oz lukewarm milk
60 g/2 oz sugar
60 g/2 oz butter, melted
1 egg
pinch of salt
grated rind of 1 lemon
1 egg yolk, beaten to glaze
FILLING
200 g/7 oz ground hazelnuts
100 g/3½ oz castor sugar
2 tablespoons rum
2 egg whites

Sift the flour into a bowl and make a well in the centre. Cream the yeast with a little of the milk, add the remaining milk and the sugar and pour into the well in the flour. Cover and leave in a warm place for 15 minutes, until frothy. Add the butter, egg, salt and lemon rind to the yeast mixture and mix thoroughly with the flour.

Knead the dough until smooth and elastic, then leave to rise in a warm place for 15 minutes.

To make the filling, mix the hazelnuts, sugar, rum and egg whites together. Roll out the dough until it is 3–5 mm/⅛-¼ inch thick, and cut out 24 rounds, each 7·5 cm/3 inches in diameter. Divide the filling between half the rounds, leaving the edges free. Brush the edges with beaten egg yolk and cover with the remaining rounds. Press the edges together well to seal and brush the buns with beaten egg yolk. Cut a cross on the top of each bun and place on greased baking trays. Leave to rise for a further 15 minutes.

Preheat the oven to hot (220°C, 425°F, Gas Mark 7) and bake the buns for 15 minutes.

Danish Buns

YEAST DOUGH
500 g/1 lb plain flour
30 g/1 oz fresh yeast
125 ml/4 fl oz lukewarm milk
100 g/4 oz castor sugar
100 g/4 oz butter
pinch of salt
grated rind of ½ lemon
pinch of ground allspice
FILLING
50 g/2 oz sultanas
50 g/2 oz currants
50 g/2 oz candied lemon peel,
  chopped
50 g/2 oz flaked almonds
30 g/1 oz butter, melted
granulated sugar to sprinkle

Grease two baking trays.

Sift the flour into a bowl and make a well in the centre. Cream the yeast with the milk. Pour into the well in the flour with the sugar and sprinkle over a little of the flour. Cover and leave to stand in a warm place for 15 minutes.

Melt the butter and add to the bowl with the salt, lemon rind and allspice. Mix the ingredients to form a dough then knead until smooth. Cover and leave in a warm place for 30 minutes.

Mix the sultanas, currants, chopped peel and almonds with the melted butter.

Roll out half the dough to a rectangle measuring 30 × 25 cm/12 × 10 inches. Cover this with half the filling. Roll up the dough from the long side and cut it into 3-cm/1¼-inch thick slices. Repeat this process using the remaining dough and filling. Put the buns on the baking trays and leave for a further 10–15 minutes to rise.

Preheat the oven to moderately hot (200°C, 400°F, Gas Mark 6). Sprinkle the buns with granulated sugar and bake for 10–15 minutes.

Danish Pastries

YEAST PASTRY DOUGH
500 g/1 lb 2 oz plain flour
30 g/1 oz fresh yeast
250 ml/8 fl oz lukewarm milk
225 g/8 oz butter
1 egg
¼ teaspoon salt
FILLING
100 g/4 oz ground almonds
1 tablespoon ground hazelnuts
1 tablespoon arrack or ouzo
1 tablespoon icing sugar
1 egg white
GLAZE
1 egg yolk
2 tablespoons icing sugar
1 tablespoon lemon juice

Make the dough as for Danish Scrolls (see page 49). Work the remaining 50 g/2 oz flour into the remaining 175 g/6 oz butter; chill then fold and roll with the yeast dough as described in the same recipe. Chill thoroughly for 15 minutes after each rolling and folding process, before rolling out again.

Finally roll out to give a rectangle measuring approximately 37·5 × 30 cm/15 × 12 inches.

Mix the ground almonds with the hazelnuts, arrack, icing sugar and egg white. Cut the dough into nine long triangles measuring 7·5 × 30 cm/3 × 12 inches. Divide the filling between these and spread it down the centre of the triangles. Roll up from the wider side to the point. Place on greased baking trays, brush with beaten egg yolk and allow to stand in a warm place for 15 minutes. Preheat the oven to hot (220°C, 435°F, Gas Mark 7) and bake for 15–20 minutes.

Mix the sifted icing sugar with the lemon juice and use to glaze the warm pastries.

Hazelnut Parcels

1 (368-g/13-oz) packet frozen
puff pastry
1 egg yolk, beaten to glaze
FILLING
100 g/4 oz ground hazelnuts
30 g/1 oz castor sugar
pinch of ground cinnamon
1 tablespoon honey
1 egg white
ICING
100 g/4 oz icing sugar
1–2 tablespoons hot water

Allow the pastry to thaw at
room temperature for 1 hour.
  On a floured surface, roll out
the pastry to make a rectangle
approximately 20 × 50 cm/
8 × 20 inches. Trim off the
edges. Halve the pastry lengthways then cut into 10-cm/4-
inch squares. Mix the hazelnuts, sugar, cinnamon, honey
and egg white together, then
divide this between the squares.
Brush the edges of the pastry

with beaten egg yolk, fold all
the corners into the middle
and press well together. Form
small pastry rounds from the
trimmings, brush with beaten
egg yolk and put on top of the
parcels, pressing to seal.
Sprinkle a baking tray with
cold water, place the hazelnut
parcels on it and leave to stand
in the refrigerator for 15
minutes.
  Preheat the oven to hot
(220°C, 425°F, Gas Mark 7)
and bake the pastries for 15–20
minutes. Transfer to a wire
cooling rack. Mix the sifted
icing sugar with the hot water
and use to ice the hazelnut
parcels.

Cherry and Almond Slices

1 (368-g/13-oz) packet frozen
puff pastry
1 egg yolk, beaten to glaze
FILLING
80 g/3 oz ground almonds
1 egg white
1 tablespoon Kirsch
50 g/2 oz castor sugar
50 g/2 oz glacé cherries, chopped
ICING
50 g/2 oz icing sugar
1 tablespoon hot water

Allow the pastry to thaw for
1 hour at room temperature.
  Roll out the pastry on a
lightly floured board into a
35-cm/14-inch square. Divide
into twenty-four 5 × 7·5-cm/
2 × 3-inch oblongs and place
on dampened baking trays.
  Mix together the ground
almonds, egg white, Kirsch,
sugar and chopped cherries.

Brush the edges of the pastry
oblongs with egg yolk and
place a teaspoon of filling in
the centre of each. Cut thin
strips from the remaining
pastry with a pastry cutter and
place crosswise over the filling.
Brush with beaten egg yolk and
leave to stand for 15 minutes.
  Preheat the oven to hot
(220°C, 425°F, Gas Mark 7)
and bake for 10–15 minutes.
Remove the slices from the
tray to a wire cooling rack.
Mix the sifted icing sugar with
the water and spread over the
slices while still warm.

Palmiers

1 (368-g/13-oz) packet frozen
puff pastry
about 100 g/4 oz castor sugar
1 egg, beaten to glaze

Allow the pastry to thaw for 1
hour at room temperature.

Roll out thinly on sugared
paper into a rectangle 30 × 35
cm/12 × 14 inches. Sprinkle
with a little sugar and roll up
the two shorter edges of the
pastry into the centre, until
they meet. Brush with a little
beaten egg and turn the roll
over. Using a sharp knife, cut
into slices 5 mm/$\frac{1}{4}$ inch thick.
Place well apart on dampened
baking trays, brush with
beaten egg yolk and leave for
15 minutes.

Preheat the oven to
moderately hot (200°C, 400°F,
Gas Mark 6) and bake the
palmiers for 8–12 minutes.

Cook's Tip

Be careful not to brush
the edges of the palmiers
with egg yolk, as this will
cause the layers to stick
together and prevent the
pastry from rising during
baking.

Orange Windmills

1 (368-g/13-oz) packet frozen
puff pastry
1 egg yolk, beaten to glaze
FILLING
25 g/1 oz ground almonds
1 tablespoon orange jelly
marmalade
1 teaspoon orange liqueur
ICING
50 g/2 oz icing sugar
1 tablespoon hot water
20 g/$\frac{3}{4}$ oz pistachio nuts, chopped

Allow the pastry to thaw for 1
hour at room temperature.

Roll out on a lightly floured
board into a 37·5-cm/15-inch
square. Divide into sixteen
8·5-cm/3$\frac{1}{2}$-inch squares,
leaving two strips of pastry
for later. Cut diagonally in
from the corner of each square
towards the centre, leaving the
pastry joined in the centre for

the filling. Mix the ground
almonds with the marmalade
and orange liqueur and place a
little in the centre of each
square. Fold the points of the
four cut corners to the centre,
to form windmills. Secure
firmly and brush with egg
yolk. Cut out 16 small rounds
from the leftover strips of
pastry and place in the centre
of each windmill. Brush with
beaten egg yolk. Place on a
dampened baking tray and
leave for 15 minutes.

Preheat the oven to hot
(220°C, 425°F, Gas Mark 7)
and bake the pastries for 10–12
minutes. Transfer to a wire
cooling rack. Blend the sifted
icing sugar with the water, use
to ice the windmills and
sprinkle with the chopped
pistachios.

Swiss Carrot Cake

5 eggs, separated, plus 2 egg
  yolks
200 g/7 oz castor sugar
pinch each of salt, ground
  cinnamon and ground cloves
1 tablespoon Kirsch
200 g/7 oz finely grated carrots
100 g/4 oz ground almonds
100 g/4 oz hazelnuts, finely
  chopped
50 g/2 oz fresh white
  breadcrumbs
50 g/2 oz plain flour
1 teaspoon baking powder
ICING AND DECORATION
200 g/7 oz icing sugar
2 tablespoons Kirsch
2 tablespoons lemon juice
2 tablespoons apricot jam
50 g/2 oz toasted flaked
  almonds
100 g/4 oz almond paste
few drops of orange food
  colouring
few pistachio nut pieces

Grease a 25-cm/10-inch
springform cake tin. Preheat
the oven to moderately hot
(190°C, 375°F, Gas Mark 5).
Whisk all the egg yolks with
the sugar, salt, cinnamon,
cloves and Kirsch, until thick
and creamy. Mix together the
carrots, ground almonds,
hazelnuts, breadcrumbs and
the flour sifted with the baking
powder; stir these ingredients
into the egg yolk mixture.
Whisk the egg whites until
stiff and fold in. Turn the cake
mixture into the prepared tin,
smooth over and bake for
45–55 minutes. Turn the cake
out on a wire rack to cool,
cover and leave it for 2 days.

Mix the sifted icing sugar
with the Kirsch and lemon
juice, and use to ice the top
of the cake. Brush the sides of
the cake with a little warmed
jam and press on the flaked
almonds. Colour the almond
paste and shape into small
carrots. Insert a couple of
pistachio nut pieces into one
end to resemble the carrot's
stalk, and arrange on top of
the cake.

Chocolate Gâteau Alice

140 g/5 oz plain chocolate
140 g/5 oz butter, softened
160 g/6 oz castor sugar
3 eggs, separated
80 g/3 oz ground almonds
80 g/3 oz rye or wheat flour
ICING
100 g/4 oz almond paste
100 g/4 oz plain chocolate
12 almonds
sugar crystals

Grease a 20-cm/8-inch spring-form cake tin and sprinkle with breadcrumbs. Preheat the oven to moderate (180°C, 350°F, Gas Mark 4).

Melt the chocolate in a basin over hot water. Cream the butter with half the sugar until light and fluffy. Stir in the melted chocolate, egg yolks and ground almonds. Whisk the egg whites until stiff and

fold in the remaining sugar. Fold into the chocolate mixture and finally fold in the flour. Turn into the prepared tin and bake for 40–45 minutes.

Roll out the almond paste thinly and use to cover the top and sides of the cake. Melt the chocolate in a basin over hot water and coat the cake thinly using a palette knife. Dip the tip of the almonds in a little melted chocolate, turn them in the sugar crystals and decorate the cake as illustrated.

Sachertorte

SPONGE MIXTURE
7 eggs, separated
200 g/7 oz castor sugar
50 g/2 oz cocoa powder
100 g/4 oz plain flour
100 g/4 oz butter, melted
50 g/2 oz biscuit crumbs
ICING
5 tablespoons apricot jam
225 g/8 oz plain chocolate
6 tablespoons double cream
350 g/12 oz icing sugar
chocolate vermicelli to sprinkle

Grease two 23-cm/9-inch sandwich tins and sprinkle with dry breadcrumbs. Preheat the oven to moderately hot (200°C, 400°F, Gas Mark 6).

Whisk the egg yolks with 100 g/4 oz castor sugar until thick and light. Fold in the sifted cocoa powder and flour with the cooled, melted butter. Whisk the egg whites until

frothy. Add the remaining castor sugar and whisk until stiff. Fold into the egg yolk mixture with the biscuit crumbs.

Spoon the mixture into the prepared tins and bake in the centre of the oven for 30 minutes. Reduce the heat to moderate (180°C, 350°F, Gas Mark 4) and bake for a further 15–20 minutes. Cool in the oven, with the door slightly open, for 15 minutes, then remove to cool completely.

Warm the jam and use to sandwich the layers and spread thinly over the top and sides of the cake. Melt the chocolate in a basin over hot water. Cool, then beat in the cream and sifted icing sugar. Spread this icing smoothly over the cake and sprinkle a little chocolate vermicelli around the base of the cake, if liked.

Viennese Chocolate Cake

CAKE MIXTURE
6 eggs, separated
1 tablespoon vanilla sugar
pinch of salt
150 g/5 oz castor sugar
100 g/3½ oz plain chocolate,
*   grated*
100 g/3½ oz biscuit crumbs
100 g/3½ oz ground hazelnuts
FILLING
3 tablespoons sherry
300 g/11 oz apricot jam
ICING
120 g/4 oz plain chocolate
1 egg
200 g/7 oz icing sugar
60 g/2 oz butter

Grease the base of a 25-cm/10-inch springform cake tin. Preheat the oven to moderate (180°C, 350°F, Gas Mark 4).

Whisk the egg yolks, vanilla sugar, salt and sugar together until pale and creamy. Stir in the grated chocolate. Whisk the egg whites until stiff and fold carefully into the yolk mixture. Mix the biscuit crumbs with the hazelnuts and fold in. Turn the mixture into the cake tin, smooth the surface and bake for 50–60 minutes. Turn the cake out on to a wire rack and leave to cool.

Cut the cake through twice to make three layers and soak each layer with sherry. Soften the jam and use to sandwich the layers together.

Melt the chocolate in a basin over a pan of hot water and allow to cool a little. Stir in the egg and sifted icing sugar. Melt the butter and add this to the chocolate, beating well until the mixture is

creamy. Cover the top and sides of the cake with this and use a palette knife to swirl the icing. Allow the icing to set before cutting the cake.

Cook's Tip

This cake may also be filled with almond paste. Knead 225 g/8 oz almond paste, divide it in half and roll out each half into a thin round the size of the cake. Sandwich the cake layers together with the almond paste and apricot jam then ice as in the recipe.

Brandy Snap Ring

CAKE MIXTURE
175 g/6 oz butter
175 g/6 oz castor sugar
¼ teaspoon salt
3 eggs
1 tablespoon rum
grated rind and juice of ½ lemon
150 g/5 oz plain flour
1 tablespoon baking powder
75 g/3 oz cornflour
ICING
175 g/6 oz butter
350 g/12 oz icing sugar
1 egg yolk
6–8 brandy snaps, crushed
150 ml/¼ pint double cream
8 glacé cherries

Grease a 23-cm/9-inch ring tin. Preheat the oven to moderate (180°C, 350°F, Gas Mark 4).
Cream the butter with the castor sugar until light and fluffy. Beat in the salt, eggs, rum, lemon rind and juice. Fold in the sifted flour, baking powder and cornflour. Pour into the ring tin and bake for 45–60 minutes. Cool slightly in the tin, then turn out on to a wire rack to cool completely. Cut into four layers.
Cream the butter with the sifted icing sugar and egg yolk. Use to sandwich together the four layers and to cover the whole cake. Press on the crushed brandy snaps to cover completely. Decorate with the cream, whipped and piped, and halved glacé cherries.

Chocolate Délice

100 g/4 oz butter
100 g/4 oz castor sugar
100 g/4 oz plain chocolate
6 eggs, separated
100 g/4 oz ground almonds
50 g/2 oz biscuit crumbs
75 g/3 oz plain flour
DECORATION AND ICING
50 g/2 oz slivered almonds
100 g/4 oz plain chocolate

Grease a 30-cm/12-inch long Balmoral cake tin or 1-kg/2-lb loaf tin and dust with flour. Preheat the oven to moderate (180°C, 350°F, Gas Mark 4).
Beat the butter and sugar together until pale and creamy. Break the chocolate into small pieces and melt in a basin over hot water. Add it to the butter mixture together with the egg yolks. Beat the mixture thoroughly until very creamy. Stir in the ground almonds, biscuit crumbs and sifted flour.

Whisk the egg whites until stiff and fold into the cake mixture. Turn into the prepared tin and bake the cake for 50–60 minutes. Turn the cake out on to a wire rack to cool and press the almonds into it as illustrated. Melt the chocolate in a basin over hot water and cover the cake thickly with this icing.

Raspberry and Lemon Cream Gâteau

*1 (20-cm/8-inch) chocolate
  cake (see page 228)*
FILLING AND TOPPING
*600 ml/1 pint double cream
100 g/4 oz icing sugar
grated rind and juice of 1 lemon
225 g/8 oz fresh or frozen
  raspberries
1 tablespoon Maraschino
25 g/1 oz macaroons, crushed
16 thin slices lemon*

Make the chocolate cake (see
page 228) and cut horizontally
into three layers.

Whip the cream with the
sifted icing sugar until stiff and
divide into three portions.
Mix one portion with the
lemon rind and juice. Reserve
16 raspberries, purée the
remainder and mix with the
second portion of cream. Put
each of the two flavoured
creams into a separate piping
bag and pipe alternate rings of
raspberry cream and lemon
cream over two of the cake
layers, until the layers are
completely covered. Sandwich
the layers together and place
the third cake layer on top.

Mix the final portion of
cream with the liqueur and
spread it over the top and
sides of the gâteau, reserving a
little for piping. Mark the top
of the gâteau into 16 slices
with a knife. Sprinkle the
centre and base of the cake
with crushed macaroons and
decorate each slice with a
rosette of cream, a slice of
lemon and a raspberry. Serve
immediately.

Cook's Tip

If the cake is not to be
served immediately,
open freeze without the
decoration. Decorate
when thawed and ready
to serve.

Charlotte Royal

SWISS ROLL MIXTURE
4 eggs, separated, plus 2 egg
  yolks
100 g/4 oz castor sugar
pinch of salt
few drops of vanilla essence
75 g/3 oz plain flour
25 g/1 oz cornflour
450 g/1 lb cherry or raspberry
  jam
FILLING
15 g/½ oz powdered gelatine
250 ml/8 fl oz white wine
100 g/4 oz sugar
1 tablespoon lemon juice
pinch of salt
350 ml/12 fl oz double cream
glacé cherries to decorate

Make the Swiss roll (see page
228), adding the salt and vanilla
essence to the whisked egg
mixture. Turn out on to
sugared paper, strip off the
lining paper and spread all
over with the jam while still
warm. Trim the edges and roll
up tightly, using the sugared
paper to help you. Leave to
cool.

Cut the Swiss roll into 18
slices. Line a 1·5-litre/2½-pint
pudding basin with 14 of the
slices, pressing well against
each other to cover the base
and sides.

Dissolve the gelatine in 4
tablespoons wine over a gentle
heat. Heat the remaining wine
with the sugar, lemon juice and
salt, then pour on to the
dissolved gelatine and stir to
mix. Allow to cool until just
on the point of setting. Whip
the cream and reserve a little
for piping. Pour the wine
mixture into the cream and
fold together carefully. Place
in the lined basin and cover
with the remaining Swiss roll
slices. Chill in the refrigerator
until set.

Turn out on to a serving
plate and decorate with rosettes
of cream and glacé cherries.

Bilberry Cream Torte

PASTRY
160 g/6 oz plain flour
80 g/3 oz butter, cut into flakes
40 g/1½ oz castor sugar
pinch of salt
1 egg yolk
1–2 tablespoons water
TOPPING
500 g/1 lb bilberries
1–2 tablespoons orange liqueur
15 g/½ oz powdered gelatine
450 ml/¾ pint double cream
50 g/2 oz icing sugar
1 small packet quick-setting
  jel mix
100 g/4 oz toasted flaked
  almonds

Place the sifted flour in a
mixing bowl and add the
butter, sugar, salt, egg yolk
and water. Mix quickly to a
dough, cover and leave in the
refrigerator for 1 hour.

Wash the bilberries, dry
them and steep in the liqueur
for 30 minutes.

Preheat the oven to hot
(220°C, 425°F, Gas Mark 7).
Roll out the pastry to cover
the base of a 20–23-cm/8–9-
inch springform cake tin. Prick
the base and bake for about
15 minutes, until cooked. Leave
to cool on a wire rack.

Dissolve the gelatine in 3
tablespoons water over a gentle
heat. Whip the cream with the
sifted icing sugar until stiff
and fold in the cooled gelatine
and three-quarters of the
bilberries. Place on top of the
cooked pastry and smooth
over evenly. Cover with the
remaining bilberries. Make up
the jel mix according to the
packet instructions, and pour
over the fruit. Leave in the
refrigerator until set.

Remove the cake from the
tin and sprinkle the sides
generously with flaked
almonds.

Black Forest Cherry Gâteau

CAKE MIXTURE
100 g/4 oz plain chocolate
100 g/4 oz butter
100 g/4 oz castor sugar
4 eggs
75 g/3 oz ground almonds
50 g/2 oz plain flour
50 g/2 oz cornflour
2 teaspoons baking powder
FILLING AND TOPPING
450 ml/¾ pint double cream
2 (425-g/15-oz) cans pitted
cherries, drained
6 tablespoons Kirsch
12 glacé cherries
chocolate caraque (see page 231)

Lightly grease three 18-cm/7-inch sandwich tins. Preheat the oven to moderate (180°C, 350°F, Gas Mark 4).

Melt the chocolate in a basin over a pan of hot water. Cool. Cream the butter and sugar

until light and fluffy. Beat in the eggs, almonds and melted chocolate. Sift the flour, cornflour and baking powder on to the creamed mixture and fold in, mixing well. Turn into the sandwich tins and bake for 20–25 minutes, until cooked. Leave to cool in the tin for a few minutes before turning out on to a wire rack.

Whip the cream until thick. Dry the cherries on absorbent paper. Sprinkle each cooled cake layer with 2 tablespoons Kirsch. Sandwich together with the cherries and cream, leaving enough cream to spread over the top and sides of the cake, and to pipe a border. Decorate with the glacé cherries and pile chocolate caraque in the centre.

Chess Board Chocolate Cake

1 (20-cm/8-inch) chocolate
cake (see page 228)
3 tablespoons orange liqueur
FILLING AND TOPPING
6 tablespoons milk
450 g/1 lb curd or cream cheese
150 g/5 oz castor sugar
grated rind and juice of 1
orange and 1 lemon
20 g/¾ oz powdered gelatine
450 ml/¾ pint double cream
DECORATION
16 small pieces orange
8 glacé cherries, halved
2 teaspoons chopped pistachio
nuts
chocolate vermicelli

Make the chocolate cake (see page 228), cool and cut horizontally into three layers. Sprinkle each layer with liqueur. Cut two layers into 2·5-cm/1-inch wide rings,

working from the outside inwards, and leave one layer whole to use as a base.

Beat the milk, cheese, sugar, fruit rinds and juice until smooth. Dissolve the gelatine in 3 tablespoons water over a gentle heat and stir into the cheese mixture. Whip the cream until stiff and fold it into the cheese mixture. Spread very thinly over the cake base. Using the first cut out layer place the largest ring (to fit the outside of the cake) on the base and then the alternate cake rings. Fill the gaps in between with the cream, smoothing evenly. Then place the remaining rings alternately on top to form the next layer. Fill these gaps with more cream. Repeat this procedure using the second cake layer, to form a chess board pattern. Finally cover the whole cake with the cream, pipe 16 rosettes on top and decorate as illustrated.

Raspberry Cream Torte

SHORTBREAD BASE
100 g/3½ oz butter or margarine
50 g/2 oz castor sugar
150 g/5 oz plain flour
SPONGE MIXTURE
4 eggs, separated, plus 2 egg yolks
100 g/4 oz castor sugar
80 g/3 oz plain flour
25 g/1 oz cornflour
35 g/1½ oz cocoa powder
FILLING
450 g/1 lb fresh or frozen raspberries
1 tablespoon raspberry liqueur or Kirsch
15 g/½ oz powdered gelatine
450 ml/¾ pint double cream
70 g/2½ oz icing sugar
DECORATION
250 ml/8 fl oz double cream
1 tablespoon icing sugar
25 g/1 oz toasted flaked almonds

Cream the butter with the sugar. Add the sifted flour and work into a dough. Wrap in foil or cling film and leave in the refrigerator for 2 hours.

If using frozen raspberries, allow to defrost at room temperature.

Grease a 23 × 33-cm/9 × 13-inch Swiss roll tin and line with greased greaseproof paper. Preheat the oven to hot (220°C, 425°F, Gas Mark 7). Whisk all the egg yolks with half the sugar until thick and creamy. Whisk the whites until stiff then whisk in the remaining sugar and fold into the egg yolk mixture. Sift the flour, cornflour and cocoa powder on to the eggs and fold in carefully using a metal spoon. Spread this mixture into the prepared tin and bake for 10–12 minutes. Turn the sponge out on to clean grease-proof paper sprinkled with sugar. Remove the lining paper from the cake, cover

with a damp cloth and leave to cool.

Reduce the oven temperature to moderately hot (190°C, 375°F, Gas Mark 5). Roll out the shortbread dough to line the base of a 20-cm/8-inch springform cake tin. Bake for 15–20 minutes and leave to cool in the tin.

Lightly crush two-thirds of the raspberries and mix with the liqueur. Reserve the remaining fruit for decoration. Dissolve the gelatine in 3 tablespoons cold water over a gentle heat. Whip the cream with the sifted icing sugar until stiff. Fold in the cooled gela-tine together with the rasp-berries. Spread the sponge evenly with the fruit and cream mixture and cut length-ways into 5·5-cm/2¼-inch strips. Roll up one of the strips and stand upright on the centre of the shortbread. Shape the other strips carefully into circles around the central roll,

until the whole base has been covered. Place the cake in the refrigerator and leave to set.

Whip the cream for decora-tion with the sifted icing sugar until stiff. Remove the cake from the tin and place on a serving plate. Spread some of the whipped cream over the top and sides of the cake, smoothing with a palette knife. Place the remainder in a piping bag and pipe an attractive design on top of the cake, as illustrated. Decorate the rosettes with the reserved raspberries and sprinkle flaked almonds over the centre.

Cherry Cream Layer Gâteau

1 (368-g/13-oz) packet frozen
   puff pastry
FILLING AND TOPPING
50 g/2 oz redcurrant jelly
100 g/4 oz icing sugar
1 tablespoon lemon juice
1 (425-g/15-oz) can red
   cherries
pinch of ground cinnamon
1 tablespoon cornflour
450 ml/¾ pint double cream
40 g/1½ oz castor sugar
12 glacé cherries

Allow the pastry to thaw for 1
hour at room temperature.
Sprinkle a baking tray with
cold water. Preheat the oven to
moderately hot (200°C, 400°F,
Gas Mark 6).

Divide the pastry into three
portions and roll out each into
a 20-cm/8-inch round. Arrange
on the baking tray and leave
for 15 minutes. Bake for 10–12
minutes, until lightly browned.

Cover the best pastry round
with the warmed redcurrant
jelly. Mix the sifted icing sugar
and lemon juice together and
spread this glaze over the jam.
Leave to cool then divide the
glazed pastry layer into 12
slices.

Drain the cherries, reserving
the juice. Heat the juice from
the cherries with the cinnamon.
Blend the cornflour with a
little cold water and add to the
cherry juice. Bring to the boil,
stirring continuously until
slightly thickened. Stir in the
stoned cherries and leave to

cool. Spread the cooled cherry
sauce over the bottom pastry
layer.

Whip the cream with the
castor sugar until stiff. Put
about 5 tablespoons of this
cream into a piping bag fitted
with a star nozzle. Spread
some of the remaining cream
over the cherries and put the
last uncovered pastry layer on
top. Spread the remaining
cream thickly over this and
around the sides of the gâteau.
Arrange the glazed pastry
slices on top and decorate
each with a rosette of cream
and glacé cherry.

Cook's Tip

It is important to cut the
glazed pastry layer into
slices before placing over
the cream filling. If you
try to cut it when serving
the gâteau, the cream
filling will spill out.

Chocolate Hazelnut Meringue

6 egg whites
200 g/7 oz castor sugar
80 g/3 oz icing sugar
1 tablespoon cornflour
80 g/3 oz ground hazelnuts
DECORATION AND FILLING
100 g/4 oz plain chocolate
300 ml/½ pint double cream
1 tablespoon icing sugar
1 teaspoon drinking chocolate powder

Line two or three baking trays with non-stick baking parchment and draw five 23-cm/9-inch circles on them in pencil. Preheat the oven to very cool (120°C, 250°F, Gas Mark ½).

Whisk the egg whites until stiff. Add the castor sugar and whisk again until stiff. Sift the icing sugar with the corn-

flour, mix with the hazelnuts and fold into the egg whites.

Spread one-fifth on each circle and dry out in the oven for 3–4 hours, leaving the oven door slightly open.

Melt the chocolate and spread thinly over waxed paper to cover an area of 24 × 30 cm/ 9 × 12 inches. Cool, then divide the largest side into ten equal strips. Cut eight of these strips equally into three, making 24 short strips of chocolate. Cut the remaining two long strips into four each, giving eight shorter strips.

Whip the cream with the sugar until stiff. Spread the meringue layers with cream and place one on top of the other. Cover the cake with the remaining cream, piping rosettes to decorate. Sift the chocolate powder over the cream, and arrange the shorter strips of chocolate on the cake, and the 24 longer strips over-lapping around the sides.

Peach Gâteau Genevieve

1 (20-cm/8-inch) chocolate cake (see page 228)
FILLING AND DECORATION
450 ml/¾ pint double cream
60 g/2 oz icing sugar, sifted
30 g/1 oz cocoa powder, sifted
1 (213-g/7½-oz) can peach slices
2 tablespoons Maraschino
1 tablespoon chopped pistachios
ICING
200 g/7 oz plain chocolate
225 g/8 oz icing sugar, sifted
15 g/½ oz butter

Make up the cake as on page 228 and cut into three layers.

Whip the cream with half the sugar until thick and divide into three. Mix one-third with the remaining sugar and the cocoa powder, and spread over the cake base. Halve the peach slices and place almost

all over the second cake layer. Mix the second portion of cream with the liqueur and spread over the peaches. Top with the third cake layer.

Melt the chocolate and mix with the icing sugar, 2 table-spoons water and the butter. Spread smoothly over the entire cake. When cooled decorate with swirls of piped cream, peach segments and pistachios.

Note To make the variation illustrated on the jacket, use two rounds of chocolate sponge cake and one of plain. Place diced peaches and strawberries over the base and sandwich the layers with sweetened whipped cream. Spread cream all over and cover with finely grated chocolate. Decorate as illustrated.

Dobostorte

6 sponge rounds (see below)
FILLING
300 ml/¼ pint milk
25 g/1 oz cornflour
50 g/2 oz castor sugar
1 egg yolk
250 g/9 oz butter
50 g/2 oz marshmallows
50 g/2 oz plain chocolate
CARAMEL GLAZE
200 g/7 oz sugar
15 g/¼ oz butter

Prepare and bake the sponge
cake layers as in the recipe for
Prince Regent Cake (see
right). When cool fill with the
following cream mixture.

Mix a little of the milk with
the cornflour. Heat the
remaining milk with the sugar
and pour on to the blended
cornflour. Return to the heat
and bring to the boil, stirring
constantly until thickened.
Add the egg yolk and cool.

Cream the butter until soft
and then beat it, a spoonful at
a time, into the cooled cornflour mixture. Melt the marshmallows and chocolate in a
basin over hot water. Beat
into the cooled mixture and
chill until firm enough to
spread.

Spread five sponge rounds
with this cream and arrange
on top of each other. Spread
the rest of the cream around
the sides of the cake.

Caramelise the sugar and
butter to a light brown colour,
stirring all the time. Spread
this over the top of the cake
immediately. While the caramel
covering is still soft, divide
the top into 12 slices with an
oiled knife. (The caramel will
certainly not cut after it has
hardened.)

Prince Regent Cake

SPONGE MIXTURE
7 eggs, separated
150 g/5 oz castor sugar
pinch of salt
150 g/5 oz self-raising flour
FILLING
300 ml/¼ pint milk
25 g/1 oz cornflour
50 g/2 oz castor sugar
1 egg yolk
250 g/9 oz butter
50 g/2 oz plain chocolate
50 g/2 oz cocoa powder
ICING
200 g/7 oz plain chocolate

Grease and flour three baking
trays. Preheat the oven to hot
(220°C, 425°F, Gas Mark 7).

Whisk the egg yolks with
half the sugar and the salt until
thick. Whisk the egg whites
until stiff, whisk in the remaining sugar and fold into the

yolks. Sift over the flour and
fold in. Spread the sponge
mixture into six 25-cm/10-inch
rounds on the baking trays and
bake in the centre of the oven
for 5–7 minutes. Cool on wire
racks.

Mix a little milk with the
cornflour. Heat the remaining
milk with the sugar and pour
on to the cornflour. Return to
the heat and bring to the boil,
stirring. Add the egg yolk and
allow to cool. Cream the butter
until soft and then beat it a
spoonful at a time into the
cooled cornflour sauce.

Melt the chocolate in a basin
over hot water and add it to
the butter cream with the
sifted cocoa powder. Spread
over the rounds, placing one
on top of the other, and use to
cover the top and sides of the
cake. Leave in the refrigerator
until the cream has set.

Melt the chocolate for the
icing and pour over the cake,
smoothing with a palette knife.

Milanese Almond Cake

SPONGE MIXTURE
4 eggs
100 g/4 oz castor sugar
grated rind of ½ lemon
50 g/2 oz plain flour
25 g/1 oz cornflour
25 g/1 oz ground almonds
25 g/1 oz butter, melted
FILLING AND TOPPING
225 g/8 oz raspberry jam
400 g/14 oz ground almonds
100 g/4 oz castor sugar
6 egg yolks
4–5 tablespoons rum
1 egg white
80 g/3 oz toasted flaked
  almonds

Grease and flour a 20-cm/8-inch springform cake tin. Preheat the oven to moderately hot (190°C, 375°F, Gas Mark 5).

Whisk the eggs and sugar with the lemon rind until thick and creamy. Sift the flour and cornflour together, mix with the ground almonds and fold into the egg mixture using a metal spoon. Lastly fold in the melted butter. Turn into the cake tin and bake for 35–45 minutes.

Leave the cake on a wire rack to cool overnight then slice through into three layers. Sandwich the layers together with some of the raspberry jam.

Mix the ground almonds with the sugar, egg yolks and rum, until soft enough to pipe. Put half this mixture into a piping bag and mix the remainder with sufficient egg white to give a spreading consistency. Spread over the top and sides of the cake and

pipe the remainder over the cake in an attractive petal design, as illustrated, to make a flower pattern.

Preheat the oven to very hot (240°C, 475°F, Gas Mark 9) and bake the cake for a few minutes until the almond icing begins to turn light brown. Warm the remaining jam, sieve it and spread a little into the flower petals. Spread the rest of the jam over the sides of the cake and press on the toasted flaked almonds.

Cook's Tip

As the sponge is already cooked, the cake need only be put in the oven for long enough to brown and slightly crispen the top. Alternatively the cake could be placed briefly under a hot grill.

Celebration Nut Cake

SPONGE MIXTURE
5 eggs, separated
100 g/4 oz castor sugar
100 g/4 oz ground hazelnuts
2 tablespoons plain flour
¼ teaspoon almond essence
FILLING
15 g/½ oz cornflour
25 g/1 oz castor sugar
150 ml/¼ pint milk
2 egg yolks, beaten
TOPPING AND DECORATION
200 g/7 oz almond paste
100 g/4 oz icing sugar
2–3 tablespoons lemon juice
walnut halves to decorate

Grease a 20-cm/8-inch spring-form cake tin. Preheat the oven to moderately hot (190°C, 375°F, Gas Mark 5).

Whisk the egg yolks and sugar until pale and creamy and fold in the hazelnuts, sifted flour and almond essence. Whisk the egg whites until stiff and fold into the mixture. Bake the cake for 40 minutes then cool overnight on a wire rack.

Cut the cake through into two layers. Mix the cornflour with the sugar, a little of the milk and the beaten egg yolks. Bring the remaining milk to the boil. Pour on to the cornflour mixture, bring back to the boil and cook for a few seconds, stirring until thickened. Leave to cool then sandwich the cake layers together with this filling.

Knead the almond paste and roll it into a round the size of the cake. Place on the cake, pressing it in lightly. Mix the sifted icing sugar with the lemon juice and ice the cake all over. Decorate with walnut halves.

Chocolate Chestnut Gâteau

1 (20-cm/8-inch) chocolate cake (see page 228)
FILLING
1 (250-g/8¾-oz) can sweetened chestnut purée
1 tablespoon lemon juice
4 tablespoons single cream
ICING
3 tablespoons apricot jam
225 g/8 oz almond paste
175 g/6 oz plain chocolate

Make the chocolate cake (see page 228), cool and cut horizontally into three layers.

Mix the chestnut purée, lemon juice and cream together to make a smooth filling. Sandwich the layers together with this filling. Warm the jam, sieve it and brush the cake all over.

Roll out the almond paste, reserving enough to make the figures for decoration. Cover the top and sides of the cake with a thin layer of almond paste and trim the edges. Shape the reserved almond paste into small figures, as illustrated.

Melt the chocolate in a basin over hot water and cover the cake completely with this icing, smoothing it evenly with a palette knife. Decorate with the marzipan figures and allow the icing to set.

Coffee Cream Cake

*1 (20-cm/8-inch) coffee sponge
  cake (see method)*
3 tablespoons cherry jam
ICING
300 ml/½ pint milk
25 g/1 oz cornflour
50 g/2 oz sugar
*2 tablespoons instant coffee
  powder*
250 g/9 oz butter
2 tablespoons icing sugar
DECORATION
16 candied coffee beans
16 almonds

Make the whisked sponge cake
(see page 228), adding 1 tablespoon dissolved coffee powder
to the eggs and sugar before
whisking. Cut the cooled cake
in half and sandwich together
with the jam.

Mix a little of the milk with
the cornflour. Heat the
remaining milk with the sugar
and pour on to the blended
cornflour. Return to the heat
and bring to the boil, stirring
constantly until thickened.
Add the coffee powder
dissolved in a little boiling
water and allow to cool. Cream
the butter until soft, then beat
it a spoonful at a time into
the cooled cornflour mixture.
Mix in the sifted icing sugar.
Spread this coffee cream over
the top and sides of the cake.
Pipe the remainder on top of
the cake, as illustrated, and
decorate with candied coffee
beans and almonds.

Strawberry Layer Gâteau

PLAIN SPONGE MIXTURE
3 eggs
75 g/3 oz castor sugar
50 g/2 oz plain flour
25 g/1 oz cornflour
CHOCOLATE SPONGE
MIXTURE
3 eggs
75 g/3 oz castor sugar
50 g/2 oz plain flour
25 g/1 oz cornflour
15 g/½ oz cocoa powder
FILLING AND DECORATION
100 g/4 oz strawberries
7 g/¼ oz powdered gelatine
600 ml/1 pint double cream
50 g/2 oz icing sugar
16 glacé cherries
*50 g/2 oz chocolate caraque
  (see page 231)*
*25 g/1 oz toasted flaked
  almonds*
icing sugar to sprinkle

Make both the plain and
chocolate sponges according
to the instructions on page 228,
and bake in two 20-cm/8-inch
greased and floured cake tins
for 30–40 minutes. Turn out
and cool on a wire rack.

Cut each cake into two
layers. Purée the strawberries.
Dissolve the gelatine in 2 tablespoons water over a gentle
heat. Cool. Whip the cream
until stiff then fold in the sifted
icing sugar. Mix a third of this
cream with the strawberries and
the cooled gelatine. Spread
some of the remaining cream
over both plain cake layers and
put a chocolate layer on top of
each. Sandwich together with
the strawberry cream and
cover the cake with plain cream.

Decorate as illustrated with
piped rosettes of cream,
cherries, chocolate caraque and
almonds. Sift with icing sugar
and chill before serving.

Honey Crunch Cake

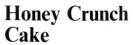

6–7 tablespoons milk
25 g/1 oz castor sugar
¼ teaspoon salt
25 g/1 oz butter
20 g/¾ oz fresh yeast
2 tablespoons lukewarm water
80 g/3 oz flaked almonds
380 g/13 oz plain flour
1 egg
2 tablespoons raisins
FILLING
25 g/1 oz butter
25 g/1 oz castor sugar
½ teaspoon ground cinnamon
TOPPING
25 g/1 oz butter
4 tablespoons honey
25 g/1 oz sugar
100 g/4 oz almonds, chopped

Grease a 23-cm/9-inch spring-form cake tin. Bring the milk to the boil and stir in the sugar, salt and butter. Leave to cool.

Cream the yeast with the lukewarm water. Mix the almonds with the flour, add the milk and yeast mixtures, the egg and raisins. Knead all the ingredients until smooth then cover and leave in a warm place for 20 minutes.

Roll out the mixture to a 30 × 35-cm/12 × 14-inch rectangle. Melt the butter and spread it over the dough, then sprinkle with the sugar and cinnamon. Roll it up from the shorter side and cut into 2·5-cm/1-inch slices.

Melt the butter for the topping with the honey, sugar and almonds, and pour into the prepared tin. Form balls from the slices of dough and arrange them over the honey mixture. Leave to rise in a warm place for 25 minutes.

Preheat the oven to moderately hot (190°C, 375°F, Gas Mark 5), and bake for 30–40 minutes. Invert on to a wire rack to cool.

Iced Rum Cake

50 g/2 oz pumpernickel
  breadcrumbs
2 teaspoons rum
8 eggs
150 g/5 oz castor sugar
120 g/4 oz ground almonds
50 g/2 oz plain chocolate,
  grated
grated rind of ¼ lemon
pinch of ground cloves
50 g/2 oz chopped mixed peel
ICING
200 g/7 oz icing sugar
1 tablespoon rum
1–2 tablespoons water
12 glacé cherries

Grease a 25-cm/10-inch springform cake tin. Preheat the oven to moderately hot (200°C, 400°F, Gas Mark 6).

Mix the breadcrumbs with the rum. Separate 6 of the eggs. Whisk the whole eggs, egg yolks and sugar together until thick and creamy. Stir in the almonds, chocolate, lemon rind, cloves and chopped peel, mixing well. Whisk the egg whites until stiff and fold into the mixture. Finally stir in the soaked breadcrumbs and transfer to the prepared tin, smoothing over the surface. Bake the cake in the centre of the oven for 45–55 minutes, covering with foil if it becomes too brown.

Turn the cake out on to a wire rack to cool. Mix the sifted icing sugar with the rum and water and spread over the cake. Decorate with the glacé cherries.

Great Traditional Cakes

Linzertorte

200 g / 7 oz butter or margarine
200 g / 7 oz castor sugar
3 eggs plus 1 egg yolk
pinch each of salt and ground
    cloves
½ teaspoon ground cinnamon
grated rind of ½ lemon
100 g / 3½ oz sweet biscuit
    crumbs
150 g / 5 oz ground almonds
1 tablespoon flour
225 g / 8 oz raspberry jam
1 egg yolk, beaten to glaze

Grease a 25-cm/10-inch
springform cake tin.

Beat the butter or margarine
with the sugar until light and
creamy. Add the eggs and egg
yolk one at a time with the
salt, cloves, cinnamon and
lemon rind. Mix the biscuit
crumbs with the ground almonds and stir into the
mixture.

Roll out two-thirds of this
pastry and place in the base of
the cake tin, shaping it so it is
about 1·5/¾ inch high around
the edges. Mix the remaining
pastry with the tablespoon of
flour, cover and leave for 30
minutes in the refrigerator.

Preheat the oven to
moderately hot (190°C, 375°F,
Gas Mark 5). Spread the jam
over the pastry base and roll
out the remaining pastry dough.
Cut this into strips, using a
pastry cutter, and arrange in a
lattice pattern over the jam.
Brush with beaten egg yolk and
bake for 35–40 minutes.

Leave to cool in the tin for a
while before turning it on to
a wire rack to cool completely.

Mandorla
Almond Cake

PASTRY
200 g / 7 oz plain flour
100 g / 3½ oz butter, cut into
    flakes
40 g / 1½ oz castor sugar
1 egg yolk
pinch of salt
grated rind of ½ lemon
2 tablespoons water
FILLING
3 tablespoons apricot jam
1 whole egg plus 2 eggs,
    separated
125 g / 4½ oz castor sugar
pinch of salt
few drops of vanilla essence
1 tablespoon plain flour
100 g / 4 oz ground almonds
60 g / 2 oz butter
MERINGUE TOPPING
2 egg whites
100 g / 4 oz castor sugar
100 g / 4 oz ground almonds

Sift the flour into a bowl and
mix in the butter, sugar, egg
yolk, salt, lemon rind and
water, until a dough is formed.
Cover and leave in the
refrigerator for 2 hours.

Roll out the pastry and use
to line the base and sides of a
23-cm/9-inch sandwich tin.
Spread the jam over the base.
Preheat the oven to moderate
(180°C, 350°F, Gas Mark 4).

Mix together the egg, egg
yolks, half the sugar, the salt,
vanilla essence, flour and
ground almonds. Whisk the
egg whites with the remaining
sugar until stiff and fold into
the mixture. Melt the butter
and fold it in. Pour the filling
on to the pastry base and
bake for 45 minutes.

Whisk the egg whites with
the sugar until stiff and fold
in the almonds. Spread over the
hot cake and bake for a further
15 minutes in a moderately hot
oven (200°C, 400°F, Gas
Mark 6).

Feather-Iced Layer Cake

*1 (20-cm/8-inch) plain
sponge cake (see page 228)*
FILLING
*70 g/2¼ oz ground almonds
30 g/1 oz icing sugar
3 tablespoons rum
150 ml/¼ pint orange juice
1 tablespoon lemon juice*
TOPPING
*200 g/7 oz orange marmalade
100 g/3½ oz almond paste
100 g/4 oz icing sugar
1–2 tablespoons hot water
1 teaspoon cocoa powder
75 g/3 oz toasted flaked
    almonds*

Make the cake (see page 228)
and cool on a wire rack. Cut
the cake horizontally into
three layers.

Mix the ground almonds
with the sifted icing sugar and
half the rum. Spread this over

the base and place the second
cake layer on top. Mix the
orange and lemon juice with
the rest of the rum and pour
this over the second layer,
allowing it to soak in. Place the
third cake layer on top.

Warm the marmalade, sieve
it and brush over the entire
cake. Roll the almond paste
out thinly to a round large
enough to cover the top of the
cake. Sift the icing sugar and
mix it to a smooth paste with
the water. Take 2 tablespoons
of the icing and mix with the
cocoa powder.

Spread the white icing over
the almond paste, smoothing
it with a palette knife. Pipe the
chocolate icing on to the cake,
in a spiral starting from the
centre. Using a knife or
skewer, draw lines outwards
from the centre of the cake.
Press the toasted flaked
almonds on to the sides of the
cake.

Malakoff Cake

*32 sponge finger biscuits
1 tablespoon sugar
3 tablespoons Marsala
1 tablespoon rum
50 g/2 oz redcurrant jelly*
BUTTER CREAM
*40 g/1½ oz cornflour
500 ml/17 fl oz milk
70 g/3 oz castor sugar
250 g/9 oz butter
2 tablespoons icing sugar
2 tablespoons rum*
DECORATION
*100 g/4 oz toasted flaked
    almonds
14 sweet biscuits, half-coated
    in melted chocolate*

First make the butter cream.
Blend the cornflour with a
little of the milk and the sugar.
Boil the remaining milk, pour
on to the cornflour and return
to the boil, stirring until
thickened. Cool. Beat the
butter with the sifted icing

sugar until creamy, then beat
gradually into the cooled
cornflour sauce with the rum.

Line the base of a 20-cm/8-
inch springform cake tin with
sponge fingers. Dissolve the
sugar in 1 tablespoon water
then add the Marsala and rum.
Spoon half this syrup over the
sponge fingers and dot with
half the warmed redcurrant
jelly. Spread over a layer of
butter cream. Repeat the
layers, ending with a layer of
butter cream and reserving
enough butter cream for the
sides and decoration of the
cake.

Leave the cake overnight in
the refrigerator to set, then
remove from the tin. Spread
butter cream over the sides of
the cake, sprinkle all over
with flaked almonds and pipe
14 butter cream rosettes on
top. Chill in the refrigerator
and, just before serving,
decorate with the biscuits.

Chocolate Cherry Layer Gâteau

SPONGE MIXTURE
4 eggs
100 g/4 oz castor sugar
pinch of salt
pinch of ground cinnamon
25 g/1 oz plain flour
30 g/1 oz cornflour
15 g/½ oz cocoa powder
25 g/1 oz ground almonds
1 tablespoon rum
FILLING AND TOPPING
25 g/1 oz cornflour
2 teaspoons cocoa powder
100 g/4 oz castor sugar
2 egg yolks
300 ml/½ pint milk
200 g/7 oz butter
2 tablespoons cherry liqueur
80 g/3 oz chocolate, finely grated
12 glacé cherries
chocolate caraque (see page 231)

Grease a 20-cm/8-inch spring-form cake tin. Preheat the oven to moderately hot (190°C, 375°F, Gas Mark 5).

Whisk the eggs with the sugar, salt and cinnamon until creamy. Sift the flour, cornflour and cocoa and fold in with the almonds and rum. Turn into the tin and bake for 35–45 minutes.

Turn on to a wire rack to cool for at least 2 hours, then cut into three layers. Blend the cornflour, cocoa powder, sugar and egg yolks together with a little of the milk. Bring the remaining milk to the boil then pour on to the blended cornflour. Return to the heat and cook, stirring continuously, until just boiling. Cool. Beat the butter until pale and soft then gradually beat in the cornflour sauce with the liqueur and chocolate. Sandwich the cake together with this cream and cover thinly all over. Pipe 12 rosettes around the cake and decorate with the cherries and chocolate caraque.

Gâteau Saint-Honoré

PASTRY BASE
80 g/3 oz butter, cut into flakes
40 g/1½ oz castor sugar
pinch of salt
1 egg yolk
160 g/6 oz plain flour
CHOUX PASTE
60 g/2 oz butter
250 ml/8 fl oz water
pinch of salt
200 g/7 oz plain flour
4 eggs
FILLING AND GLAZE
*1 quantity custard butter cream
  (see page 229)*
3 tablespoons apricot jam

Knead together the butter, sugar, salt, egg yolk and sifted flour to form a pastry dough. Cover and leave in the refrigerator for 30 minutes. Roll out the pastry to a 25-cm/10-inch round and place on a baking tray. Preheat the oven to moderately hot (200°C, 400°F, Gas Mark 6).

Prepare the choux paste. Over a low heat, melt the butter in the water with the salt. Quickly bring to the boil, remove from the heat and beat in the sifted flour all at once, stirring vigorously. Return to the heat and cook for 1 minute, stirring all the time. Allow to cool slightly. Beat the eggs separately and beat into the choux paste gradually, making sure they are thoroughly incorporated. Pipe a thick ring of the choux paste over the edge of the pastry base, and pipe 8–10 choux puffs separately on the baking tray. Bake for 25–35 minutes then cool on a wire rack.

Make up the custard butter cream (see page 229) and use to fill the choux ring. Place the choux puffs on top and brush the ring and puffs with warmed, sieved apricot jam.

215

Bacon Twists

1 (283-g/10-oz) packet bread mix
100 g/4 oz streaky bacon
1 egg, beaten to glaze

Preheat the oven to moderately hot (200°C, 400°F, Gas Mark 6).

Make up the dough according to the instructions on the packet. Divide into 10 pieces and roll into 20-cm/8-inch strips. Cut the bacon rashers into strips, stretching them with a knife, and twist a strip of bacon with a strip of dough. Brush the twists all over with beaten egg.

Arrange the twists on a baking tray and bake for 15 minutes until crispy brown.

Cook's Tip
You can make these twists with ham instead of bacon. Cut strips of ham and twist with the strips of dough as above. Brush with beaten egg and bake as described. The twists make a very good snack to serve with drinks.

Alsace Cheese Bakes

1 (283-g/10-oz) packet bread mix
TOPPING
1 large or 2 small onions
25 g/1 oz butter
100 g/4 oz streaky bacon
1 egg, beaten
225 g/8 oz cream cheese
1 tablespoon chopped parsley

Preheat the oven to moderately hot (200°C, 400°F, Gas Mark 6).

Make up the dough according to the instructions on the packet. Peel the onion, slice and separate the slices into rings. Fry these lightly in the butter. Chop the bacon into small pieces and fry briefly with the onion.

Divide the dough into six portions and roll out each to give a 12·5 cm/5-inch round.

Brush the rounds with beaten egg. Cut the cream cheese into flakes and scatter over the rounds. Arrange the onion rings and bacon pieces over the cheese and place on a baking tray. Bake in the centre of the oven for about 20 minutes, until crispy brown.

Sprinkle the rounds with parsley and serve hot.

Sausage Crescents

1 (283-g/10-oz) packet bread mix
350 g/12 oz chipolata sausages
1 egg yolk, beaten to glaze

Preheat the oven to moderately hot (200°C, 400°F, Gas Mark 6).

Make up the dough according to the instructions on the packet. Roll out to a 25 × 37·5-cm/10 × 15-inch rectangle. Cut into six 12·5-cm/5-inch squares then cut these in half diagonally to give 12 triangles.

Place a sausage on each triangle and roll up from the wide end. Place on baking trays and brush with beaten egg yolk. Bake for 20–25 minutes, until golden and crispy.

Cook's Tip

These crescents are also delicious made with puff pastry. Roll out thinly, cut triangles as above and roll up with the sausages inside. Glaze and place on a baking tray which has been sprinkled with cold water. Bake as above.

Flat Breads

1 (283-g/10-oz) packet bread mix
flour to sprinkle

Preheat the oven to moderately hot (200°C, 400°F, Gas Mark 6).

Make up the dough according to the instructions on the packet. Divide into 10 pieces then flatten each to give a thin round. Place on baking trays and leave in a warm place for 15 minutes.

Score the top of each round in a criss-cross pattern with a sharp knife. Brush with water, dust lightly with flour and bake for 15–20 minutes.

Cook's Tip

These flat breads taste best when eaten freshly baked. Accompany them with smoked salmon and cream cheese sprinkled with freshly ground black pepper.

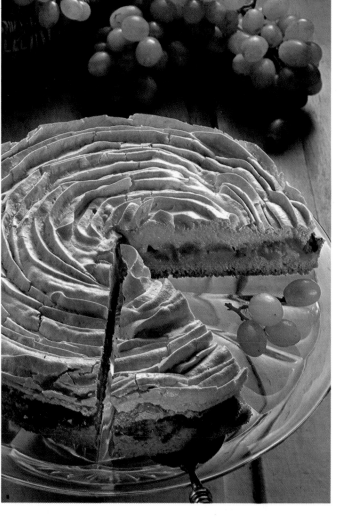

New-Style Pear Cake

*1 (326-g/11½-oz) packet plain
    sponge cake mix
½ teaspoon ground cinnamon*
TOPPING
*4–5 ripe pears
2 tablespoons lemon juice
2 tablespoons slivered almonds*

Grease a 25-cm/10-inch
springform cake tin. Preheat
the oven to moderately hot
(200°C, 400°F, Gas Mark 6).

Make up the cake mix
according to the instructions
on the packet, adding the
ground cinnamon to the dry
ingredients. Turn into the tin
and smooth over the top.

Peel the pears, remove the
cores and cut into quarters.
Keeping the quarters together,
cut them into slices and dip in
lemon juice so they do not
discolour. Arrange the sliced

quarters over the cake in a
pattern as illustrated. Press well
in so the cake mixture rises
up between the pears. Sprinkle
with almonds and bake for
25–30 minutes. Cool on a wire
rack.

Cook's Tip

If you want to sprinkle
a large quantity of fruit
with lemon juice, to
prevent discoloration,
dilute the lemon juice
with water to make it go
further.

Meringue Surprise Cake

*1 (326-g/11½-oz) packet plain
    sponge cake mix
1 kg/2 lb green grapes*
MERINGUE TOPPING
*4 egg whites
150 g/5 oz castor sugar*

Grease a 25-cm/10-inch deep
cake tin. Remove the stalks
from the grapes. Wash and
halve the grapes, remove their
pips and arrange them over
the base of the tin. Preheat
the oven to moderately hot
(200°C, 400°F, Gas Mark 6).
Make up the cake mix according to the instructions on the
packet. Turn into the tin on
top of the grapes and smooth
over. Bake for 30–40 minutes
then carefully invert and turn
out on to a lightly greased
baking tray. Reduce the oven
temperature to moderate

(180°C, 350°F, Gas Mark 4).
Whisk the egg whites until
stiff, fold in the sugar and put
this meringue mixture into a
piping bag. Pipe over the
grapes in a spiral pattern and
bake for a further 30–35
minutes.

Allow the cake to cool
completely before cutting.

Cook's Tip

The cake can also be
made with canned pears
which have been well
drained and sliced.

Lemon Apple Cake

*1 (329-g/11·6-oz) packet lemon
  sponge cake mix*
3–4 dessert apples
juice of 1 lemon
ICING
225 g/8 oz icing sugar
2 tablespoons lemon juice
*75 g/3 oz pistachio nuts,
  chopped*

Grease a 25-cm/10-inch
springform cake tin. Preheat
the oven to moderately hot
(200°C, 400°F, Gas Mark 6).
  Make up the cake mix
according to the instructions
on the packet and turn into
the prepared cake tin. Peel,
core and slice the apples and
sprinkle with lemon juice.
Press the apple slices well into
the cake mixture. Bake for
20–25 minutes then turn out
and cool on a wire rack.

  Mix the sifted icing sugar
with the lemon juice and beat
until smooth. Pour over the
cake, allowing it to run down
the sides, and decorate with
the chopped pistachios.

Apple Cake with Raisins

*1 (326-g/11¼-oz) packet plain
  sponge cake mix*
TOPPING
4–5 dessert apples
juice of 1 lemon
2 tablespoons raisins
*3 tablespoons apple jelly or
  apricot jam*

Grease a 25-cm/10-inch
springform cake tin. Preheat
the oven to moderately hot
(200°C, 400°F, Gas Mark 6).
  Make up the cake mix
according to the instructions
on the packet and turn into the
tin. Spread the top smoothly.
  Peel the apples, quarter
them and remove the cores.
Cut in*o thin slices. Dip the
apple slices in the lemon juice.
Sprinkle half the raisins over
the cake and arrange the apple
slices thickly in a rosette shape

on top. Sprinkle with the rest
of the raisins and bake for
25–30 minutes.
  Warm the apple jelly or
apricot jam, stirring all the
time, and brush over the apples
while they are still hot.

Cook's Tip

When using apricot jam
as a glaze, warm it first
then sieve it before
brushing over fruit or
filled flans.

Variations from a Packet

Cherry Slice

1 (425-g/15-oz) can red or
  black cherries
1 (322-g/11·4-oz) packet
  hazelnut cake mix
⅛ teaspoon ground cinnamon
icing sugar to sprinkle

Grease a 28 × 18-cm/11 × 7-
inch cake tin. Preheat the oven
to moderately hot (190°C,
375°F, Gas Mark 5). Drain the
cherries, reserving the juice,
and remove the cherry stones.

Make up the cake mix
according to the instructions
on the packet, using half
cherry juice and half water
instead of all water. Fold in
the cherries and ground
cinnamon and turn the
mixture into the prepared tin.

Bake in the centre of the
oven for 20–25 minutes.
Remove from the oven and
allow to stand in the tin for
5 minutes before turning out

to cool on a wire rack.

When cold, cut into slices
and sprinkle with sifted icing
sugar. If liked, serve with
whipped cream that has been
sweetened with the packet
filling mix.

Nut Cake with Cinnamon Icing

1 (322-g/11·4-oz) packet
  hazelnut cake mix
50 g/2 oz candied orange peel,
  finely chopped
50 g/2 oz plain chocolate,
  grated
ICING
½–1 teaspoon ground cinnamon
2–3 teaspoons hot water
2 slices candied orange and
  angelica to decorate

Grease a 1-kg/2-lb loaf tin. Preheat the oven to moderately hot
(190°C, 375°F, Gas Mark 5).

Make up the cake mix
according to the instructions
on the packet. Fold in the
chopped peel and grated
chocolate. Pour into the tin
and bake immediately for
45–55 minutes, until firm to
the touch. Allow to cool in the
tin for 10 minutes before

turning on to a wire rack.

Empty the packet filling mix
into a small bowl. Add the
cinnamon and mix to a
spreading consistency with the
hot water. Spread over the top
of the cake and decorate with
the candied orange and
angelica.

Mocha Ring Cake

*1 (322-g/11·4-oz) packet coffee
  cake mix
100 g/4 oz plain chocolate,
  grated or finely chopped
225 g/8 oz icing sugar
2 tablespoons hot water
generous pinch of ground
  cinnamon*

Grease and flour a 20-cm/8-
inch fluted ring tin. Preheat the
oven to moderately hot (200°C,
400°F, Gas Mark 6).

Make up the cake mix
according to the instructions
on the packet. Fold in half the
grated chocolate and turn into
the prepared tin. Bake for
30–35 minutes and allow to
cool in the tin for 5 minutes
before turning out on to a wire
rack.

Mix the sifted icing sugar
with the water and cinnamon
and beat until smooth. Pour
over the cake and decorate
around the bottom edge with
the remaining grated chocolate.

This cake is delicious served
with a bowl of spiced whipped
cream.

Whisky-Iced Loaf Cake

*1 (326-g/11½-oz) packet plain
  sponge cake mix
225 g/8 oz chopped mixed peel
50 g/2 oz glacé cherries,
  quartered
50 g/2 oz crystallised ginger,
  chopped
50 g/2 oz walnuts, chopped
½ teaspoon ground cinnamon
½ teaspoon ground cloves*
ICING
*200 g/7 oz icing sugar
2 tablespoons whisky
glacé cherries, candied fruits
  and angelica to decorate*

Grease and line a 1-kg/2-lb
loaf tin. Preheat the oven to
moderate (180°C, 350°F, Gas
Mark 4). Make up the cake
mix according to the instructions on the packet. Mix
together the chopped peel,
cherries, ginger, walnuts,
cinnamon and cloves. Stir
into the cake mixture, turn
into the prepared tin and bake
for 55–60 minutes. Test the
cake with a skewer before
cooling on a wire rack.

Sift the icing sugar and mix
with the whisky. Spread this
over the cake and decorate as
illustrated with the cherries,
fruit and angelica.

Variations from a Packet

Festive Savarins

*1 (326-g/11½-oz) packet plain
  sponge cake mix*
6 tablespoons orange juice
2 tablespoons orange liqueur
DECORATION
*mandarin segments, cherries,
  gooseberries, peach slices,
  chopped pistachio nuts,
  toasted flaked almonds*

Grease nine 10-cm/4-inch
savarin moulds. Preheat the
oven to moderately hot (200°C,
400°F, Gas Mark 6).

Make up the sponge mix
according to the instructions
on the packet. Divide between
the savarin moulds, place
them on a baking tray and
bake for 15–18 minutes.

Remove the savarins care-
fully from their moulds and
allow to cool slightly. Mix
together the orange juice and
liqueur and pour over the
savarins, allowing it to soak in.

Make up the filling mix for
the cake, put into a piping bag
and pipe into and around the
savarins. Alternatively use
250 ml/8 fl oz double cream,
stiffly whipped. Decorate with
fruit, pistachios and almonds
as illustrated.

Chocolate Cream
Gâteau

*1 (322-g/11·4-oz) packet
  hazelnut cake mix*
FILLING AND TOPPING
200 g/7 oz icing sugar
15 g/½ oz cocoa powder
*25 g/1 oz drinking chocolate
  powder*
150 g/5 oz butter, softened
2 teaspoons Kirsch
*candied coffee beans to
  decorate*

Grease two 18-cm/7-inch
sandwich tins. Preheat the
oven to moderately hot (200°C,
400°F, Gas Mark 6). Make up
the cake mix according to the
instructions on the packet.
Pour into the tins and bake
immediately for 15 minutes.
Turn out on to a wire rack to
cool.

Sift the icing sugar, cocoa
and chocolate powder with the

packet filling mix. Cream the
butter in a mixing bowl until
light then beat in the sifted
ingredients with the Kirsch.
Place a quarter of this butter
cream in a piping bag fitted
with a large star nozzle.
Spread a third of the remaining
butter cream over one of the
cakes and sandwich the two
together. Use the remaining
cream to cover the top and
sides of the cake.

Decorate the top with swirls
of piped butter cream and top
each swirl with a candied
coffee bean.

Chocolate Raisin Slice

1 (326-g/11¼-oz) packet
  chocolate sandwich cake mix
100 g/4 oz raisins
ICING
175 g/6 oz icing sugar
1 tablespoon rum
1 tablespoon warm water
1 tablespoon chocolate caraque
  (see page 231)

Line a 33 × 23-cm/13 × 9-inch Swiss roll tin with greased greaseproof paper. Preheat the oven to moderately hot (200°C, 400°F, Gas Mark 6).

Make up the cake according to the instructions on the packet. Stir in the raisins. Spread the mixture over the Swiss roll tin and bake for 15–20 minutes.

Turn the cake out on to a wire rack to cool. Remove the greaseproof paper and cut into two strips lengthways.

Make up the filling mix according to the instructions on the packet. Pipe a little of the filling over half the cake and place the other half on top. Mix the sifted icing sugar with the rum and water until smooth, spread over the top of the cake and decorate with the remaining butter cream and the chocolate caraque.

Cook's Tip

Alternatively make a chocolate butter cream by creaming 100 g/4 oz butter with 125 g/5 oz sifted icing sugar, until soft and creamy. Blend 2 tablespoons cocoa powder with a little boiling water and beat into the creamed mixture.

Alicante Gâteau

1 (329-g/11·6-oz) packet
  orange cake mix
2 teaspoons hot water
DECORATION
6 candied orange slices
16 glacé cherries
angelica strips

Grease a petal-patterned or springform cake tin. Preheat the oven to moderately hot (190°C, 375°F, Gas Mark 5).

Make up the cake mix according to the instructions on the packet. Turn into the tin and bake for 35–40 minutes. When cooked, allow the cake to cool in the tin for 10 minutes before turning out on to a wire cooling rack.

Prepare the packet filling by mixing it with 2 teaspoons hot water. Use to ice the top of the warm cake and decorate with the orange slices, halved glacé cherries and angelica.

Cook's Tip

For a stronger orange flavour, add finely grated orange rind to the cake mixture, and make up the filling with fresh orange juice instead of water.

The Art of Baking

Baking is an art – but one which everyone can master with patience, a pride in working precisely and a certain amount of basic knowledge. By reading the following pages carefully, you will be able to acquire at least the beginning of this art.

Baking Hints

- Before you begin baking always remember to get out all the necessary equipment. Do not forget the small things such as spoons, knives, pastry brush, wooden spoon, pastry scraper, grater and absorbent paper, so that they are all easily available when you need them.
- Baking is an exact art! Therefore weigh or measure all necessary ingredients exactly. Unless specified otherwise, the recipes in this book have been tested using a size 3 egg: if you use smaller or larger eggs you may need to adjust the recipe accordingly.
- In our recipes we always use sifted flours. If you sift your flour you can be sure that no lumps will spoil the baking results.
- If the recipe indicates that the dough should be kneaded on a floured board, or rolled or worked in some other way, sprinkle the board with only a very little flour; dough absorbs flour readily and too much would alter the recipe proportions.
- Lemons or oranges whose rind is to be grated must be washed thoroughly beforehand.
- If the tin or baking tray is to be greased, sprinkled with breadcrumbs or flour, or lined with greaseproof paper, do this first. Then when the mixture is ready there will be no delay before baking. This is especially important with cake mixtures.
- Remember to always preheat the oven sufficient time in advance; an electric oven must be preheated 20 minutes in advance, a gas oven about 15 minutes. Place the oven shelves in the correct position before switching the oven on. As a general rule, yeast mixtures and pastry dishes should be cooked towards the top of the oven, cakes and biscuits should always be placed in the centre of the oven, while meringues should be cooked as low down in the oven as possible to prevent browning during the slow cooking time. This does not apply in fan-assisted ovens where there is constant all-round heat.
- Always place cake tins directly on to the oven shelf, never on to a baking tray, unless stipulated in the recipe.
- If the cakes are browning too quickly during baking, cover the tops with greaseproof paper or foil.
- Never open the oven door during the early cooking stage. You can look at small biscuits or cookies after 5 minutes, but generally the door should not be opened during the first 15–20 minutes.
- Test cakes with a skewer at the end of the given baking time, to see if cooked throughout. Insert a warmed metal skewer into the centre: if it comes out with no uncooked mixture clinging to it the cake is ready.

Cook's Tips

- Apples, pears and bananas quickly turn brown when peeled and cut. Always use a stainless steel knife to cut and immediately sprinkle with lemon juice or lemon juice and water.
- If pastry dough is difficult to roll place between two floured sheets of greaseproof paper, or wrap in cling film and leave to chill in the refrigerator for 30 minutes before rolling.
- If you have made up pastry that you do not wish to bake immediately, wrap it firmly in foil or cling film and place in the refrigerator. It can remain there for up to a week and then be rolled, shaped and baked.
- Fruit cake with a high dried fruit content will stay fresh and moist after cutting if you keep it well wrapped in an airtight container.
- Ground spices will not keep their flavour for much longer than a year and then only if stored in airtight and light-proof containers. It is best to buy spices unground and to mark the purchase date on the container.
- Non-stick baking parchment saves time and effort. For all kinds of biscuits line the baking tray with this paper, then the baking tray need not be greased and will remain clean. When cool it is easy to remove the biscuits from the paper with a palette knife and they will be less likely to break. The paper can be used again several times.
- It is easier to turn a cake out of the tin on to a wire cooling rack if you place the rack on the tin, hold the tin and rack with a cloth and turn both together.
- Cheesecakes and cream cheese cakes should be left to cool in the oven after baking. Turn off the oven and leave the door open until the temperature inside the oven is the same as that outside. This will prevent the cheesecake from sinking.
- You can collect egg whites for meringues. When you need an egg yolk alone for a cake or glaze, lightly whisk the white and place it in a small screw-topped jar or freezing container and then freeze it. When thawed it can be used like fresh egg white.
- When cutting out shortcrust pastry or biscuit dough with small cutters, dip the cutter into flour to make it easier.
- When baking biscuits it is a good idea to bake one or two trial biscuits to see how much they spread during baking. You can then optimise the use of the space on the baking tray.
- If you notice too late that you have no icing sugar to sift over a cake, grind granulated sugar in a coffee grinder or blender and use this instead.
- Above all familiarise yourself with the basic recipes that follow. There all the stages of work are clearly explained and much useful advice is given.

The Art of Baking

Yeast Cookery

Handling Yeast Correctly

Yeast is a living matter composed of tiny cells which, when combined with a liquid and possibly sugar at a suitable temperature, will divide continually. This produces carbon dioxide which forms bubbles in the dough, causing it to rise and give the bread its structure. Fresh yeast must be really fresh and not dried out; it should be pliable and soft to the touch, creamy in colour and crumbly when broken. Old yeast is hard, cracked and discoloured in places; in this condition it will have lost most of its effectiveness. To keep yeast fresh, store in a container with a tight-fitting lid, or wrap in cling film. It will keep for 4–5 days in a cool larder or 1–2 weeks in the refrigerator. You can also freeze fresh yeast and store it for up to 6 months in the freezer. It is advisable to divide the yeast into workable quantities e.g. $15\,g/\frac{1}{2}\,oz$ pieces, and then wrap individually in foil or freezer film.

Active dried baking yeast is composed of granules similar in colour to fresh yeast. When using dried yeast remember it is more concentrated than fresh and therefore you will need only half the stated amount of fresh yeast. Always read the instructions on the package before beginning.

Yeast works most effectively in a warm temperature and should always be allowed to reach room temperature before use. Make sure all baking ingredients are at room temperature in advance; ingredients such as milk or fat which has to be melted before adding to the dough, should never exceed 38–43°C/100–110°F. Many recipes state 'leave the dough to rise in a warm place'; the room temperature of most modern kitchens is warm enough for the yeast to act. However, the dough should always be covered with a damp cloth or cling film, to protect it from possible draughts which could prevent its rising, and also to prevent a skin forming.

Basic Yeast Dough

The following method is basically valid for all types of yeast dough. Sometimes a little sugar is added as well.

500 g/1 lb plain flour	*50 g/2 oz butter, melted*
30 g/1 oz fresh yeast	*½ teaspoon salt*
250 ml/8 fl oz lukewarm liquid	*1 egg*
(milk or water)	*1 egg yolk, beaten to glaze*

Make sure all the ingredients are at room temperature before beginning. Prepare all the necessary ingredients and equipment. Weigh solid ingredients exactly. Measure liquids precisely and bring them to the correct temperature. Grease a 1-kg/2-lb loaf tin or two 0.5-kg/1-lb loaf tins.

Sift the flour into a mixing bowl and make a well in the centre. Cream the yeast with a little of the lukewarm liquid, then add the remaining liquid. Pour into the well in the centre of the flour and sprinkle a little of the flour over the top. Cover the bowl with a damp cloth so that the warmth can circulate beneath it, and leave the mixture in a draught-free place for about 15 minutes, until the layer of flour which covers the yeast shows deep crevices and bubbles appear. It is better to rely on your eyes rather than the clock when judging whether the yeast has stood for long enough.

When ready, beat the yeast mixture into the remaining flour with the melted butter (not too hot), salt and beaten egg. For this it is best to use a large, strong wooden spoon, beating until a dough is formed. Knead the dough on a lightly floured surface until smooth and elastic, 5–10 minutes. If the dough remains too moist and sticks to the fingers, it must be vigorously beaten again. If necessary you can gradually work in a little extra flour.

When the dough has been kneaded sufficiently, sprinkle with flour, cover with a damp cloth and leave to rise in a warm place until double in size. This is called the first rising. When well risen, knead lightly again and shape the dough to fit the prepared loaf tin, or form into individual bread rolls and place on a greased baking tray.

Before baking, the shaped dough must be risen again or proved. The tin or baking tray containing the dough should be put inside a large oiled polythene bag. The proving time depends on the temperature at which it takes place but is usually shorter than the first rising period. When placing the dough in a tin or mould, fill only halfway up with the dough and leave until it rises to the top of the tin. While the dough is proving preheat the oven to hot (230°C, 450°F, Gas Mark 8).

When proving the dough, fill the tin or mould only half-full, and then leave until the dough rises to the top of the tin.

Brush the bread with beaten egg yolk and finally place in the oven. Bake the large loaf for 35–45 minutes, the smaller loaves for 25–35 minutes, and the individual rolls for 15–20 minutes. The cooked loaf should be slightly shrunken from the sides of the tin and when turned out it should sound hollow when tapped on the bottom.

Pastries

Puff Pastry

Cook's Tips

- Allow frozen puff pastry to thaw out at room temperature for approximately 1 hour.
- Roll out puff pastry on a board which is only lightly floured. During rolling it is important to remember never to roll this type of pastry in one direction only, but in two directions, that is from top to bottom and from left to right. If rolled in one direction only it will not rise evenly during baking.
- Cut puff pastry with a very sharp knife, to prevent the edges sticking together. If using pastry cutters it is advisable to dip them in cold water before cutting out the pastry.
- When brushing puff pastry with egg yolk avoid the cut edges, or it will cause them to stick together and thus prevent the pastry layers from rising during baking.
- Puff pastry leftovers can be laid one upon the other, pressed firmly together and rolled out again. Small pieces and strips are suitable for decoration.
- Always place puff pastry on a baking tray or in a tin which has been lightly sprinkled with cold water, and leave to stand for 15 minutes before baking.

Shortcrust Pastry

If you follow the basic rules for making this pastry you can be sure of success. Shortcrust pastry is easy and quick to prepare, but extra time must be allowed for it to rest in the refrigerator before rolling out. If a sweet pastry is required sugar is added to the basic ingredients. Sugar adds to the crispness of the pastry and eggs can also be added to give a richer dough. The higher the fat content in relation to the flour the shorter will be the pastry. Following are basic recipes and methods for both sweet and savoury shortcrust pastries.

Sweet Shortcrust Pastry

300 g/10 oz plain flour
100 g/3¼ oz castor sugar or icing sugar

200 g/7 oz butter or margarine, cut into flakes
1 egg

Prepare and weigh exactly all the necessary ingredients. The fat for the pastry can be used straight from the refrigerator if it is cut into small flakes. Sift the flour to remove any lumps. Since the pastry contains enough fat of its own it is not necessary to grease the tin or baking tray.

Sift the flour into a mixing bowl. Work the sugar and butter or margarine into the flour with the egg, and as quickly as possible knead all the ingredients together with the fingertips to obtain a smooth dough. Keep your fingers as cool as possible and on no account overwork the dough or it will become crumbly and tough. Form the prepared dough into a ball, wrap in foil or cling film and leave to stand for 2 hours in the refrigerator. (It is essential to wrap the dough to prevent it from drying out.) The higher the fat content in relation to the other ingredients, the longer the pastry should stand in the refrigerator.

Preheat the oven to moderately hot (200°C, 400°F, Gas Mark 6), and place the oven shelf in the correct position.

After removing the dough from the refrigerator, knead it gently. Sprinkle the board and rolling pin lightly with flour and roll out the pastry. Take care that too much flour is not incorporated into the dough when rolling or shaping it as this would alter the proportions and texture of the pastry. If the dough does become too soft you can return it to the refrigerator for 30 minutes, to firm up again.

Flan and tartlet cases are sometimes baked 'blind'. For this they should be pricked at close intervals with a fork before baking, to prevent the pastry rising or bubbles forming. The flan case is then lined with foil or greaseproof paper and filled with dried beans. The pastry is baked blind for 10–15 minutes and the beans are then removed. At this stage the pastry case can either be returned to the oven to finish cooking for a further 10–15 minutes, or a filling is added and then cooking is continued.

Freshly baked pastry breaks easily. It should therefore always be left to cool for a few minutes before being carefully turned out of the tin or lifted from the baking tray with a palette knife. On no account leave pastry in the baking tin or on the baking tray until completely cool, or the fat from the pastry will set and make it difficult to remove.

Shortcrust pastry can also be made by another method: sift the flour on to a pastry board, form a well in the centre and pour in the egg and sugar. Spread the flaked butter around the flour border and with hands as cool as possible work all the ingredients quickly to obtain a smooth dough. This method requires a certain amount of skill.

Savoury Shortcrust Pastry

200 g/7 oz plain flour
100 g/3¼ oz butter or margarine, cut into flakes

1 small egg (size 4)
pinch of salt
2 tablespoons water

Sift the flour into a mixing bowl and form a well in the centre. Place the flaked butter or margarine, egg and salt in the well. Work all the ingredients quickly together with the fingertips, gradually adding the water to form a pastry dough. Form the dough into a ball, wrap in cling film or foil and leave to chill for 1–2 hours in the refrigerator.

Preheat the oven to moderately hot (200°C, 400°F, Gas Mark 6). Knead the pastry lightly and roll out on a lightly floured board. Line tartlet, flan or patty tins with it, adding any filling and covering with lids if required. Seal the edges with a little beaten egg. Prick the lid several times with a fork or make a small hole, to allow steam to escape during baking. Brush the top with beaten egg yolk or milk and bake for the required time to cook the pastry and filling. The pastry case can also be baked blind, as for Sweet Shortcrust Pastry (above).

Choux Pastry

Choux pastry is prepared by a completely different method from other pastries. It is extremely important to measure all the ingredients accurately. Since choux pastry is unsweetened it is very versatile and can be used for both sweet and savoury dishes.

Basic Choux Paste

190 g/7 oz plain flour
60 g/2 oz butter
250 ml/8 fl oz water

pinch of salt
4 eggs

Prepare and weigh the ingredients. Sift the flour on to a folded sheet of greaseproof paper. Grease a large baking tray and preheat the oven to hot (220°C, 425°F, Gas Mark 7).

Over a low heat, melt the butter in the water with the salt. Quickly bring to the boil, turn off or remove from the heat and beat the sifted flour into the boiling liquid all at once, stirring vigorously with a wooden spoon. Return to the heat and cook for 1 minute, stirring all the time until the dough comes away from the sides of the pan. Remove from the heat and allow to cool.

Turn off the heat and pour the sifted flour all at once into the boiling liquid.

Beat vigorously with a wooden spoon until the dough forms a ball which comes away from the sides of the pan.

Beat the eggs in a bowl and beat gradually into the choux paste, making sure each addition is thoroughly incorporated before the next one. This can be done using an electric mixer or beating by hand with a wooden spoon. When the egg is completely incorporated the choux pastry should be soft, glistening and golden, and will fall in a thick stream from a spoon.

Place the choux pastry into a piping bag fitted with a plain or star nozzle. For cream puffs pipe small round shapes on to the baking tray, for éclairs pipe in 7·5-cm/3-inch lengths, and for tart bases pipe in circles. If you have no piping bag the choux pastry can be spooned on to the baking tray. Bake for 20 minutes then cool on a wire rack.

Cook's Tips

● When initially melting the butter in the water, make sure the butter has melted completely before bringing quickly to the boil. Remove from or turn off the heat immediately to prevent evaporation of the liquid and add the flour all at once.

The Art of Baking

- Choux pastry tends to 'grow' during cooking, so leave sufficient space on the baking tray to allow for this.
- Immediately after baking, make a small hole in the choux buns or éclairs to allow the steam to escape.
- Use on the day of making as choux pastry tends to go soft very quickly.
- Choux pastry freezes well cooked or uncooked. Allow 1 hour to thaw, then crisp in a hot oven for a few minutes, or bake according to the recipe.

Cake Making

A sandwich cake is fat creamed with sugar, whereas a sponge is usually fatless and the eggs are whisked with the sugar before folding in the flour.

Basic Sandwich Cake

100 g/4 oz butter or margarine	*2 eggs*
100 g/4 oz castor sugar	*100 g/4 oz self-raising flour*

Prepare and weigh all the ingredients. Grease a 20-cm/8-inch cake tin or two 18-cm/7-inch sandwich tins and line with greased greaseproof paper. Preheat the oven to moderate (160°C, 325°F, Gas Mark 3).

Place the softened fat and sugar in a mixing bowl and cream with a wooden spoon until light and fluffy. Beat in the whole eggs one at a time, adding a little of the flour with the second egg. If the eggs are added all at once or if they are too cold, the fat and sugar mixture can curdle.

If the recipe necessitates flavourings such as vanilla essence, grated lemon rind, etc., then mix in before the flour is added.

Finally fold in the sifted flour using a metal spoon. Spread into the prepared cake tin and bake for 35–40 minutes, or 25–30 minutes if baking two smaller cakes. If the surface of the cake is browning too quickly, cover with foil or greaseproof paper.

Allow to cool in the tin for about 10 minutes before turning out on to a wire cooling rack.

Cook's Tips

- Sift the flour before using to remove any lumps. If using any other dry ingredients such as cornflour or baking powder, sift these with the flour, so that all the ingredients are thoroughly and evenly incorporated.
- Butter or margarine, eggs and milk must be taken out of the refrigerator in advance so that they reach room temperature before you begin baking.
- If the butter or margarine is very hard, soften before using. Soft margarine in tubs is very good for cake making.
- If the quantity of flour in the cake is high in proportion to the amount of fat and sugar, corresponding to about the weight of the combined fat and sugar, baking powder is sometimes added to the mixture to act as a raising agent.
- Do not over-mix at the folding in stage as essential air can be knocked out.

Variations

- In some recipes the eggs are separated and added separately. The yolks are added to the creamed fat and sugar, then the egg whites are whisked and folded into this mixture.
- Some cake mixtures contain dried fruit. The fruit must be tossed well in the flour before folding into the cake mixture as this will prevent it from sinking to the bottom of the cake.
- If you are making a marble cake, add sifted cocoa powder to half the cake mixture with a little extra sugar. Place alternate spoonfuls of the plain and chocolate mixtures in the tin and swirl with a skewer to give a marbled effect.

Whisked Sponge Cake

This method of cake making is used for gâteaux, bases for fruit flans, layered cakes and various small cakes. Whisked sponge cakes freeze well.

The eggs and sugar are whisked together until light and fluffy. The flour is then very carefully folded in together with cornflour if used. To add richness to the cake sometimes a little melted butter is added at the end. Another method of making this type of cake is to separate the eggs and whisk the yolks with the sugar, and then to fold in the whisked egg whites.

4 eggs	*25 g/1 oz cornflour*
100 g/4 oz castor sugar	*15 g/½ oz ground almonds*
50 g/2 oz plain flour	*25 g/1 oz butter, melted (optional)*

Prepare all the ingredients and equipment. Weigh solid ingredients exactly. Grease a 20-cm/8-inch springform cake tin with butter or margarine and sprinkle with flour or fine breadcrumbs. Preheat the oven to moderately hot (190°C, 375°F, Gas Mark 5).

Whisk the eggs with the sugar until thick and creamy and the whisk leaves a trail. Sift the flour with the cornflour and mix with the ground almonds. Using a metal spoon, fold into the egg mixture with the melted butter, if used.

Turn the mixture into the prepared tin, smooth the surface and bake for 35–45 minutes. Do not open the oven door during the first few minutes, or the cake will sink. Test with a skewer to check if the cake is cooked.

Remove the cake from the oven and leave to cool in the tin for a few minutes, then turn on to a wire rack to cool completely.

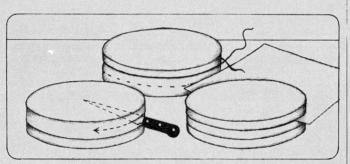

To cut a sponge cake into layers, either pierce to the centre with a sharp pointed knife and turn the cake around until one layer is cut off, or cut through the layers with a strong thread. It is best to lift off the layers with thick paper or thin cardboard.

Chocolate Cake

4 eggs	*25 g/1 oz cornflour*
100 g/4 oz castor sugar	*15 g/½ oz cocoa powder*
50 g/2 oz plain flour	

Follow the method given for Whisked Sponge Cake, sifting the cornflour and cocoa powder with the flour, and omitting the melted butter.

Swiss Roll

4 eggs, separated, plus	*80 g/3 oz plain flour*
* 2 egg yolks*	*25 g/1 oz cornflour*
100 g/4 oz castor sugar	

Line a 33-cm × 23-cm/13 × 9-inch Swiss roll tin with greaseproof paper and grease well. Preheat the oven to hot (220°C, 425°F, Gas Mark 7).

Whisk the egg yolks with half the sugar until frothy. Whisk the egg whites until frothy, slowly sprinkle in the rest of the sugar and continue to whisk until very stiff. Pour the egg whites on to the egg yolks.

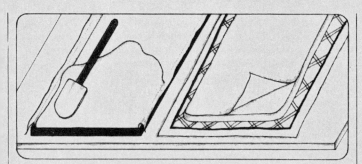

Spread the mixture evenly over the lined Swiss roll tin. After baking turn on to clean greaseproof paper placed over a damp tea towel and strip off the lining paper.

Sift the flour with the cornflour on to the egg whites and fold all into the yolk mixture, blending carefully with a metal spoon. Place in the prepared Swiss roll tin and smooth over. Bake in the preheated oven for 10–12 minutes.

Turn the cake out on to greaseproof paper sprinkled with castor sugar and placed over a damp tea towel. Strip off the greaseproof lining paper, trim the edges, fill and roll up. If the Swiss roll is to be filled when cold, place a sheet of clean greaseproof on top and carefully roll up with the paper inside. Leave until cold then carefully unroll, fill as required and roll up again.

Cook's Tips

- A delicate mixture of egg yolks, sugar and egg whites must be made quickly. The whisked egg whites should never be beaten into the yolks, for this would break down the air incorporated into the whites and the lightness of the cake would be lost. The sifted flour too, mixed with cornflour, cocoa or baking powder as the case may be, must be carefully folded in using a metal spoon.
- Do not allow the mixture to stand for long once it is mixed, but place in a preheated oven and bake immediately. If left to stand, the mixture can fall and lose its lightness.

Meringues

A meringue mixture consists of egg white and sugar. This light structure, as the name suggests, is of French origin.

6 egg whites　　　　　　*75 g/3 oz icing sugar*
225 g/8 oz castor sugar　*25 g/1 oz cornflour*

Whisk the egg whites until stiff, preferably using an electric whisk, and slowly sprinkle in the castor sugar, whisking continuously. Sift the icing sugar and cornflour on to the egg whites and fold in with a metal spoon. (On no account use a whisk.)

Fill a piping bag fitted with a plain or star nozzle with the mixture and pipe the shapes indicated in the recipe. The baking tray must be lined with non-stick baking parchment or rice paper

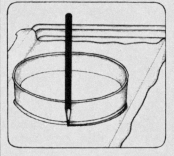
To make a meringue base, draw a circle on the paper round a cake tin.

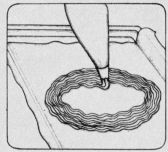
Place the mixture in a piping bag and fill the previously drawn circle.

for meringues. It is easiest to mark out the required shapes on the paper with a pencil, then to use this as a guide.

Meringues should be baked at a very low temperature, overnight if possible, with the oven door propped open slightly with the handle of a wooden spoon. Alternatively, bake the meringues in a cool oven (140°C, 275°F, Gas Mark 1) for 3–4 hours.

Cook's Tips

- When whisking egg whites make sure that the bowl and whisk are spotlessly clean, and there is not a trace of egg yolk, otherwise the egg whites will not whisk properly.
- Make sure that the whites are thoroughly whisked before adding the sugar. An electric whisk is an invaluable piece of equipment when making meringues.

Fillings and Icings

If you have baked a light sponge, for example, or a rich fruit cake, a well-risen Kugelhopf or a tray of biscuits, now the next stage can begin: completing your *pièce de résistance* with a filling, an icing or a decoration of some kind. To assure your success, the following section gives you all the basics, as well as suggesting many new and unusual ideas to put the finishing touches to your masterpiece.

Elaborate Fillings

There are several types of cream filling. Whether the filling is based on eggs or cream, cream or curd cheese, or butter, any number of varied combinations will give the desired taste and colour. Simply remember to follow the recommended quantity for the ingredients and to use the correct method.

Whipped Cream

Use lightly whipped cream to fill cream slices, choux pastry puffs, sandwich and sponge cakes and meringues, and to decorate fruit flans and gâteaux.

Keep the cream in the refrigerator until ready for use and whip with a balloon whisk until it reaches the correct consistency. Beating by hand produces more volume than using an electric whisk.

Butter Cream

We give two recipes for butter cream: a very light butter cream, prepared with custard, and the French butter cream which is heavier but has a delightful flavour. Both creams can be used to fill and cover flans, tartlets, slices and gâteaux.

Custard Butter Cream

225 g/8 oz butter　　　*25 g/1 oz custard powder*
140 g/5 oz icing sugar　*2 egg yolks*
350 ml/12 fl oz milk

Beat the softened butter with the sifted icing sugar until light and fluffy.

Blend 4 tablespoons milk with the custard powder and egg yolks. Bring the rest of the milk to the boil. Pour on to the custard powder, stirring, then return to the pan and bring to the boil again, stirring constantly. Remove the custard from the heat and leave to cool, stirring repeatedly to prevent a skin forming. (Alternatively, place a sheet of dampened greaseproof paper over the custard.)

When the custard has cooled to the temperature of the butter mixture, beat it gradually into the butter with a wooden spoon.

The Art of Baking

French Butter Cream

250 g/9 oz butter
4 eggs
generous pinch of salt

160 g/6 oz castor sugar
few drops of vanilla essence

Beat the butter until light and fluffy.

Beat the eggs with the salt and sugar in a basin over a pan of hot water until quite warm. Then remove from the heat and beat until cool. Gradually beat the cooled egg mixture into the butter, using a wooden spoon, and flavour with vanilla.

Variations
● To make a chocolate butter cream, stir 40 g/1½ oz sifted cocoa powder and 20 g/¾ oz icing sugar into the French butter cream.
● Butter cream can also be enriched with ground almonds or nuts, melted marshmallows, liqueurs, grated rind and juice of citrus fruits, or puréed fruit. Be careful to incorporate fruit, fruit juices and liqueurs slowly into the butter cream, to prevent curdling.

Icings

Icing gives a festive appearance to every kind of cake, and also helps to prevent cakes from drying out too quickly. When making an icing always add the liquid gradually until you finally obtain the required consistency. If you require a shiny icing, spread the cake first with apricot jam; sieve the apricot jam and bring it to the boil with a little water, stirring continuously, then spread over the still warm cake. Leave the jam to dry for a short time before icing. Spread the icing over the flat surface of cakes with a palette knife which has been dipped into hot water.

Brush a cake while still warm with heated and sieved apricot jam, and then ice when dry.

To decorate cake portions individually, divide into equal portions in advance with a spatula or long knife.

Glacé Icing

250 g/9 oz icing sugar   2-3 tablespoons hot water

Sift the icing sugar and gradually beat in the water, which should preferably be hot, until the icing reaches the correct consistency.

Variations
● Instead of water you can also mix the icing with milk, fruit juice, wine or spirits, according to the type of cake. You can colour the icing with a few drops of food colouring, and flavour it by adding flavourings such as almond essence, rose water or vanilla essence.

Royal Icing

2 egg whites   1 teaspoon glycerine
450 g/1 lb icing sugar

Very lightly whisk the egg whites until frothy. Gradually beat in the sifted icing sugar until the correct consistency is obtained, then finally add the glycerine.

Variations
● Like glacé icing, royal icing can be altered in both colour and flavour by adding food colourings and flavourings. If you add extra liquid then compensate for this by adding a little more icing sugar, until the right consistency is reached.

Chocolate Icing

125 g/5 oz plain chocolate   1 tablespoon water
150 g/6 oz icing sugar   15 g/½ oz butter

Melt the chocolate in a basin over a pan of hot water, stirring continuously. Add the sifted icing sugar, water and butter and stir until the ingredients are thoroughly mixed. Remove from the heat and continue stirring until the icing reaches the correct consistency.

Tart Glaze

Tart glaze (quick-setting jel mix) can be bought in red, orange and yellow colours. It is a jelly powder which when mixed with liquid produces a suitable glaze for fruit flans and tarts. It is poured over the flan while still liquid and then sets to a jelly over the fruit.

Always prepare and use the glaze exactly as instructed on the packet, making it up with fruit juice or wine, instead of water, if suitable. Almond flakes, crystallised sugar or grated chocolate are suitable to decorate the sides of the glazed flan or cake. Do not decorate the top of the flan with whipped cream until the glaze has set.

Cake Decorations

The illustrations which accompany the recipes in this book offer many ideas on how to decorate cakes, tarts, biscuits and buns. Most are highly effective, yet trouble-free – you need only to learn the right techniques.

Sifting and Sprinkling

Icing sugar, drinking chocolate and cocoa powder are suitable for sifting. Always place only a small quantity into a small hair or nylon sieve and sprinkle the cake by evenly moving the sieve to and fro.

Use doilies to form a decorative pattern over a cake or tart. When removing doilies you must be especially careful not to smudge the pattern. With a little skill you can make your own paper patterns, stars, for example, or a fir tree for Christmas, small birds, flowers or even letters.

For sprinkling you can use crystallised sugar, chocolate vermicelli, flaked or nibbed almonds, desiccated coconut, other

Whether you buy doilies or make patterns yourself for sifting, this is a quick and effective way to decorate gâteaux, cakes and tarts for every occasion.

nuts or finely chopped glacé fruit. In many recipes you will find the instruction 'sprinkle the edges of the cake with . . .'. Do not take this literally but rather press the chosen decoration on to the sides with a plastic pastry scraper or palette knife. You can even roll the cake in the chopped nuts, etc., to coat the sides evenly.

Piped Rosettes and Garlands

You can pipe rosettes or garlands with whipped cream or butter cream. For this you will need a piping bag fitted with a star or plain nozzle. Both star and plain nozzles come in various sizes; the smaller the nozzle the more delicate will be the decoration.

If you wish to avoid the bother of boiling a fabric piping bag after using it each time, then use greaseproof paper bags. Fill the piping bag no more than half full with cream so that the open end is easy to hold. If you are inexperienced at using a piping bag, pipe the planned design once on to foil. (This does not waste the cream; you can remove it from the foil with a knife and return it to the piping bag.)

To pipe rosettes, squeeze equal peaks from a piping bag with a star nozzle. A large rosette can be topped with a glacé cherry, candied coffee bean or segment of fruit. If you pipe several small peaks in a circle with a larger rosette in the centre, this will give a flower pattern. Garlands piped with a star nozzle can be made to radiate from the centre to the edge of each slice of gâteau or tart, ending in a rosette. Garlands can also be piped to form a border around the edge of the cake, into a heart shape or any other chosen shape which suits the occasion for which the cake has been baked.

You can pipe your favourite variations of rosettes and garlands using a piping bag fitted with a star nozzle. Rosettes are often topped with small segments of fruit.

Sweet Writing and Figures

For more delicate icing, such as writing or figures, you will need to use royal icing (see page 230).

Praline

Praline is often used to sprinkle on to cakes and gâteaux. It can be made in advance, crushed and stored in an airtight jar.

175 g/6 oz granulated sugar   *75 g/3 oz almonds, roughly chopped*

Heat the sugar with the almonds in a saucepan over a gentle heat. When the sugar has dissolved, boil slowly until golden. Pour on to an oiled baking tray and leave until set. When cold crush the praline with a rolling pin and use as required.

Chocolate Caraque

To make chocolate caraque, spread melted plain chocolate on to a large melamine chopping board. Leave until just set. Using a

sharp knife, scrape the chocolate, allowing it to peel off into long curls. For a quicker method, simply scrape a vegetable peeler along the flat side of a bar of chocolate, shaving it off into curls. Alternatively, grate coarsely.

Nougat

Nougat is sometimes melted to use in cake fillings and icings. If you are unable to obtain a very good quality nougat, substitute marshmallows, as these will give excellent results.

Preparing the Piping Bag

Fold a large square piece of greaseproof paper diagonally and cut down the fold to give two triangles which can be used for different coloured icings. Roll the triangles to make cone shapes. Fold over the top edge of the seam side twice so that the cone keeps its shape. With scissors cut off the point. It is important to cut it straight for only in this way will you obtain an even 'thread'. The higher you cut the point, the thicker the thread will be.

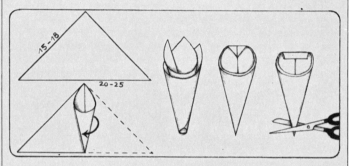

To make a piping bag, cut a triangle out of greaseproof paper, roll into a cone and fold the edge over twice at the seam. Cut straight across the point to the size of 'thread' required.

It is advisable to practise piping on to greaseproof paper or foil first. Take care not to hold the tube too near the icing surface. The icing must flow freely as only in this way will you have enough elbow room to control the resulting shapes. It is a great help if you first mark out the desired shapes – letters, figures or numbers – on to the writing surface using a pin. You can then ice over the shapes with ease.

Deep Frying

When frying foods coated in a batter or pastry, the fat or oil must be at the correct temperature i.e. 176–182°C/350–360°F. For frying use a fat which contains absolutely no water and which will not smoke or burn at high temperatures, or choose a good-quality oil. A generous amount of fat or oil is necessary so that the food can float in it, but never fill the pan more than two-thirds full or when the food is added the fat or oil may come over the top.

An electric deep-fat fryer can be set at any temperature. The red light comes on when the fat has reached the required temperature. If frying in an ordinary saucepan or chip pan the fat must be heated on top of the stove. The temperature can be controlled best with a frying thermometer but if you do not have one then try the wooden spoon test; dip the handle of a wooden spoon into the hot fat – if bubbles immediately form round the handle the temperature is correct.

Fry small quantities at a time, allowing the fat to reach the correct temperature between each addition of food. Drain all fried food on absorbent paper. Immediately after draining toss in salt, spices or sprinkle with sugar, as required.

The Art of Baking

Dip the handle of a wooden spoon into the hot fat – if bubbles immediately form around it, the temperature is correct for frying.

It is best to fry small items in a frying basket. It is easier to remove them from the fat and they can drain well in the basket over the pan.

Cook's Tips

- For small items to be fried in batter always use a frying basket.
- As well as small pieces of fruit dipped in batter, some yeast doughs and choux pastries are also delicious deep fried.
- The cooled fat should be strained well through filter paper or muslin and poured back into the bottle or other container until needed again.

Useful Kitchen Aids

Aluminium foil The extra-strong type is ideal for wrapping cakes, tarts and doughs for freezing. The thinner gauge foil is suitable to cover cakes during baking to prevent the top burning.

Greaseproof paper This is used to line cake tins and baking trays, to cover cakes during baking to prevent the top burning, and to make piping bags for icing.

Non-stick baking parchment This is used to line the tray when baking biscuits, meringues and delicate cakes. It makes removal of the baked items much easier and it can be re-used several times.

Absorbent paper Very useful for draining food and for keeping the work top continually clean.

Electric mixer The electric mixer saves a lot of work, time and energy. Electric whisks and food mixers operate basically on the same principle. A hand whisk will only cope with small quantities of mixture, whereas a free-standing food mixer can handle larger quantities. The beaters are used to whisk sponge mixtures, biscuit mixtures, egg whites, cream and custards. The dough hook is used in the preparation of yeast doughs. When using an electric mixer remember to begin mixing or kneading at a slow speed and then gradually increase it. Be careful not to over-mix the mixture.

Food processor The food processor is becoming increasingly popular as an invaluable kitchen aid, and is a great help for making bread, cakes and biscuits.

Preparation of Baking Tins

For this it is best to follow the instructions in the recipe. The decision whether to grease a tin or baking tray, whether to sprinkle it with flour or breadcrumbs, or to line it with grease-proof paper or foil, does not always depend only on the type of pastry, but also on the tin that you are using; several of the modern non-stick baking tins need no preparation before the mixture is added. Use butter or margarine for greasing.

To line the tin, fold the greaseproof paper and measure around the outside of the tin. Cut off any projecting edges and the corners and fold the paper into the required shape. For those types of mixture which require a greased tin, also grease the greaseproof lining paper or foil.

Baking trays, cake tins and tartlet tins should be treated as below for the following types of mixture:

Sponge cake mixture Grease the cake tin and sprinkle with flour. If necessary line with greased greaseproof paper.

Sandwich cake mixture Grease the tins. If necessary line with greaseproof paper and grease this too.

Swiss roll mixture Grease the inside of the tin and line with greased greaseproof paper.

Meringue mixture Line the baking tray with non-stick baking parchment or rice paper.

Macaroon mixture Line the baking tray with non-stick baking parchment or rice paper.

Shortcrust pastry Do not grease the baking tray or tins, except for a pastry containing little fat.

Puff pastry Sprinkle the baking tray with a little cold water.

Choux pastry Grease the tins.

Yeast dough Grease the tins or baking tray. Brioches and croissants are the only exception; tins for these do not need greasing as the dough already contains sufficient fat.

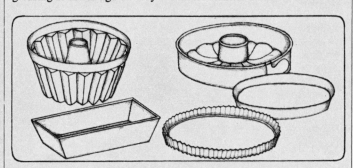

A selection of tins for baking. Above: a loaf tin for breads and loaf cakes, a Kugelhopf mould for yeast doughs, a springform cake tin with savarin funnel and border pattern, and plain and fluted flan tins for tarts and flans. Below: a Balmoral cake tin for long rounded loaf-shaped cakes, a ring tin or savarin mould, a plain springform cake tin and a petal-patterned cake tin.

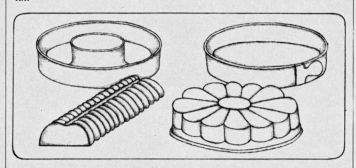

Glossary of Baking Ingredients from A to Z

Many of the ingredients required for the recipes are everyday basics to be found in any kitchen. Nevertheless these ingredients are sometimes used in a different way for baking and for this reason several of them are included in the following list.

Almonds Sold blanched or unblanched, whole, chopped, ground or in flakes. To blanch almonds yourself, pour over boiling water, leave for a short time and then simply squeeze the nuts out of their brown skins. Chopped or flaked almonds have their own special aroma when lightly roasted.

Almond Paste see Marzipan.

Angelica Dried and candied stem of the angelica plant with a slightly bitter aromatic flavour. Used mainly to decorate cakes and gâteaux.

Aniseed Spice from the fruit of Mediterranean plant. This wonderful baking spice is rich in natural oils. You can buy aniseed whole, crushed or ground. It is best to grind whole aniseeds yourself as you need them.

Arrack Rice brandy. Arrack is a prized flavouring for baking, but it should be used sparingly. Icing with arrack stirred into it tastes delicious.

Baking powder A raising agent, mainly consisting of sodium bicarbonate, sold in small quantities. Always use the exact amounts given in the recipes in this book. Store in a cool, dry place and sift baking powder with other dry ingredients before use.

Bitter chocolate Chocolate containing at least 60% pure cocoa.

Butter This is the ideal fat for all good baking. Instead of butter you can use margarine.

Buttermilk This is the milk which is left after churning butter.

Candied coffee beans Coffee-flavoured chocolate shaped into coffee beans, used to decorate cakes and gâteaux.

Candied fruit Fruits soaked in a thick sugar syrup and finally dried, used mainly to decorate cakes: chopped finely they can also be mixed into cake mixtures or form part of a filling.

Candied orange or lemon peel The candied rind of oranges or lemons which is used finely chopped for cakes, yeast doughs and biscuits. It is also sold in large pieces which can be cut up and used for decoration.

Caraway seed Spice from the fruit of the caraway plant. Savoury flans, breads and rolls are often sprinkled with caraway seeds, and they are also used in some cakes and biscuits.

Cardamom Sharply flavoured spice used in some yeast and biscuit doughs.

Cinnamon Spice from the dried bark of the cinnamon tree. Ground cinnamon is light brown in colour and has a mildly aromatic smell. It should be stored in airtight containers for it easily loses its aroma. Cinnamon sticks are mostly infused in milk for fillings and flavourings.

Cloves Spice from the dried buds of the clove tree, gathered before they flower. Cloves are sold as whole buds or ground. They taste nice in apple and plum tarts but should be used sparingly.

Cocoa The raw material for all cocoa products is the cocoa bean. Cocoa butter is obtained from it, an aromatic and easily melted ingredient of chocolate, and cocoa powder. If cocoa powder is used for chocolate cakes you should add a little extra sugar, to avoid a bitter taste. Larger quantities of cocoa should be sifted so that no lumps can form.

Colourings Food colourings are available in a wide range of colours: blue, yellow, green, orange, red and black. Use sparingly.

Cooking chocolate Plain, inexpensive chocolate in thick blocks, with an exceptionally high cocoa content. Used grated or melted as an ingredient for various mixtures.

Coriander Spice from the dried fruit of the coriander, sold whole or ground.

Cornflour Used in cake and biscuit mixtures – mostly mixed with flour – but also for thickening mixtures. If cornflour is used for thickening or binding, it must be blended with a little cold water or milk before adding to the hot liquid, and then brought to the boil, stirring continuously until thickened.

Cream Cream must be stored in a cool place away from any food that might taint it. Always add icing sugar for sweetened whipped cream at the beginning of the process. When whipping cream the whisk and bowl should be really cold.

Currants Small, dried and stoneless dark-coloured grapes, mainly from Greece. Currants should be washed and dried before use.

Demerara sugar A brown, slightly caramelised sugar.

Desiccated coconut Finely grated flesh of the coconut, sold packed in airtight bags. Once the packet is opened it should be used quickly. Fresh coconut which you have grated yourself tastes even better.

Dried fruit Dried ripe fruit includes apricots, apples, bananas, pears, dates, figs, plums, peaches and of course raisins, currants and sultanas. Dried fruit is used often in baking, for fruit bread and cakes.

Evaporated milk This can be used in baking as a substitute for fresh milk, but should be diluted with water according to the instructions on the can. It is not recommended for use in creams or custards.

Fat Butter and margarine are the ideal baking fats. Pure vegetable fat is recommended for some types of cooking, frying for example.

Flavourings and essences Oil extracts of basic substances used to flavour baking, often prepared from artificial flavours and fragrances. You can buy vanilla, almond, rum and lemon essence, among others.

Flour Flour is the finely ground meal of wheat and other cereals, including rye, buckwheat, rice, oatmeal and corn. Wheat flour is best for breadmaking because of its gluten content; choose a strong plain flour. Wholemeal flour or coarsely ground flour for some cakes and bread can be obtained from a specialist shop, as can rye and maize flour.

Fondant Basically a sugar icing made with lump sugar, water and glucose.

Frying oil For frying, a pure vegetable oil such as corn, sunflower or safflower oil, is suitable. The frying temperature should be somewhere between 176–182°C/350–360°F, according to the type of food you are cooking.

Gelatine A setting agent which can be bought in leaf or powder form. Soften gelatine leaves in a little cold water for up to 1 hour then drain well and dissolve in hot but not boiling water. If a particular recipe contains no hot fluid it is best to melt the gelatine by standing it in a bowl over a saucepan of hot water. Dissolve powdered gelatine in a little water in a bowl over a saucepan of hot water, stirring continuously over a gentle heat.

Ginger Spice from the dried root of the ginger plant, sold whole or ground, or preserved in syrup as stem ginger. Ginger is very strong in flavour and should be used sparingly. Crystallised ginger is used as a decoration or can be chopped and added to cake mixtures.

Glacé cherries See Candied fruit. Glacé cherries are sold in yellow, green and red colours.

Hazelnuts For cake and biscuit mixtures, hazelnuts are often nicer left unpeeled, as their skins are full of flavour. Hazelnuts are also sold ground.

Instant coffee Powdered coffee which dissolves immediately in boiling water and is very rich in flavour. Follow the quantities given for powdered coffee in the recipes exactly, as too much will spoil the flavour of the cake.

Mace Dried shell of the nutmeg which is sometimes sold ground for particular types of baking.

Margarine Can be used instead of butter in all baking recipes. Soft margarine in tubs is especially useful for all cake making, whereas a firmer margarine is more suitable for pastry making.

Marshmallows A confection made of egg whites and sugar that can be successfully used in place of nougat for cake icings.

Marzipan or Almond paste Marzipan is sold ready-made in 225 g/8 oz and 500 g/1 lb blocks, but you can make your own from ground almonds. It is used for filling and decorating cakes.

The Art of Baking

Kneaded with sifted icing sugar, it gives a workable paste from which figures, sweets and decorations can be prepared.

Milk Every available type of milk is suitable for baking as long as the correct quantity for the recipe is added. Instead of fresh milk you can use reconstituted powdered milk, thinned evaporated milk or thinned cream. Buttermilk or soured milk can also be used if suitable. It is important in every recipe to take note of the method of adding the milk and the temperature it should be at.

Nougat A mixture consisting of finely ground toasted hazelnuts or almonds combined with sugar and sometimes cocoa. It is usually melted and added to cake fillings or used to sandwich biscuits together.

Nutmeg Spice from the seed of the nutmeg plant. Nutmeg is sold either whole or ground and adds a subtle flavour to spiced cakes, biscuits, fruit flans and yeast doughs.

Orange flower water Made from the concentrated essence of distilled bitter orange flowers, it is a valuable flavouring and aromatic agent used in baking and desserts.

Peanuts Use unsalted peanuts in baking like other nuts; they make a cheaper substitute when you are not baking a cake which needs a particular kind of nut.

Pecan nuts In their shells pecan nuts look like large hazelnuts, but when shelled they resemble walnuts. Pecan nuts are used for all types of nut baking, in cakes or biscuits, or for decoration.

Pine nuts Nut-like seed kernel of the pine, used ground in cake mixtures instead of almonds and whole for decorating cakes.

Pistachio nuts Fruit of the pistachio tree. They are always used shelled for baking, and are a pretty light green in colour. Add finely chopped to cake mixtures or use as decoration.

Poppy seeds Seeds of the poppy plant which are used ground as an ingredient for fillings or doughs. You can grind poppy seeds yourself in a grinder or buy them ready-ground. Whole poppy seeds can be sprinkled on savoury bread rolls.

Potato flour A type of cornflour made from potatoes.

Raisins Light and dark-coloured dried grapes from Greece, Turkey, California and Australia. Wash in hot water and dry before using.

Rice paper This is used as a base for macaroons, gingerbread and sweets and is wholly edible.

Rose water Condensed liquid, by-product of rose oil. In baking it is a valuable flavouring, especially in icings, and it is also used to prepare marzipan.

Saffron Spice from the dried stamens of the saffron or cultivated crocus. This slightly bitter spice is used mainly on account of its yellow colour; use in baking wherever an intense yellow colour is required.

Sesame seeds Small, flat seed kernels of the sesame plant. They contain valuable oils and are used crushed as a cake and biscuit ingredient, or whole to sprinkle on cakes and bread.

Semi-bitter chocolate Chocolate sold in blocks with at least 50% cocoa content.

Sugar Castor sugar is most usually used in baking, while icing sugar is used to sift over cakes for decoration, and in icings.

Sultanas see Raisins.

Vanilla Vanilla can be used either in its original form, as a pod, or as an extract (vanilla essence). The dark leathery pods can be cut open lengthways and then infused in boiling milk, to obtain the full flavour.

Vanilla sugar This is a sugar flavoured with vanilla and which is especially useful for baking. The vanilla pod is placed in a jar of castor sugar to infuse its aromatic flavouring into the sugar. The jar should be sealed and left for at least a week before using.

Walnuts Walnuts are either used ground or chopped to be added to cake mixtures, and halved to use as decoration.

Yeast A biological raising agent, which should be sold as fresh as possible. Dried yeast can be stored until the date given on the container.

Baking for the Freezer

Anyone who enjoys baking and possesses a freezer can have a wide selection of food available with little extra effort. Cakes, pastries, biscuits, bread and rolls can be baked from double or treble the quantities and then frozen. Food mixers really come into their own when you are making large quantities, saving a lot of time and effort. Fuel bills are also reduced by baking large quantities at the same time. It is sometimes advisable to freeze large cakes already sliced, interleaving with greaseproof paper, so that you can thaw small quantities as required. A freezing chart at the end of this chapter is full of useful hints on how to freeze, pack and thaw cakes and pastries, together with recommended storage times.

Freezing Hints

- Baked cakes which have been frozen should not be refrozen once thawed. This will spoil their quality.
- It is best to open freeze small cakes, tarts and buns on baking trays. When frozen they should be carefully packed into rigid polythene containers, with greaseproof paper or foil between the layers.
- Wrap food to be frozen carefully, and only in packaging intended for freezer use. Secure tightly, excluding all the air.
- Place the food to be frozen in the coldest part of the freezer, or on the fast freeze shelf if your freezer has one.
- Do not bring food newly placed in the freezer into contact with food which is already frozen.
- Do not freeze too much food at any one time; always read the manufacturer's instructions for your freezer carefully.
- Open freeze foods that will be used in their frozen state e.g. fruit such as strawberries or raspberries, piped rosettes of cream and elaborate cream gâteaux.

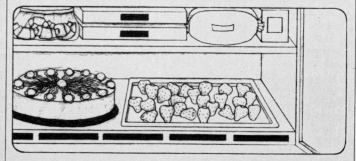

Open freeze foods that will be used in their frozen state e.g. soft fruits such as strawberries or raspberries, and elaborate cream gâteaux. Pack carefully once frozen.

Correct Packaging

The quality of frozen foods depends upon correct packaging. Use containers that are moisture-vapour proof. Many years of experience have shown that packaging material for frozen foods should have the following qualities: it must be genuine food wrapping able to resist extreme cold and heat; it should have no inherent taste, smell or aromas which could taint the food; and it must withstand fat and acidity, as both these substances are present in food. Special material for packing frozen foods can be obtained readily in supermarkets, department stores and specialist freezer shops. Be careful when you are buying it that the material is intended for freezing, as some aluminium foil, plastic bags and containers are only suitable to keep food fresh in the refrigerator.

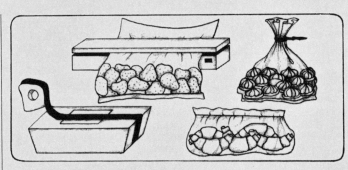

For sealing, ties or plastic clips or freezer tape which will resist frost are suitable, also the heat-sealing device for polythene bags.

Packaging Materials Available

Foil This material is particularly useful being in sheet form, as it can be moulded or shaped around the food to be frozen, making it completely airtight. It comes in two thicknesses, domestic and heavy duty, the latter being suitable for freezing purposes. Cakes which are thawed in their foil wrapping are at the same time well protected against drying out.

Foil containers These are extremely suitable for cakes, particularly uncooked cake mixtures, as they can be frozen and cooked in the same container. They are sold in various sizes and shapes; pie plates, basins, loaf tins, flan dishes and gussetted foil bags.

Polythene bags These fulfil almost all the requirements of an ideal freezer wrapper. With careful handling they can be used several times. For freezer use, polythene bags must be of thick gauge (200–250) to be moisture proof. The much thinner bags are suitable only for keeping food fresh. If using bags for freezing several times, test well before using to ensure there is no hole in the bag, no matter how small (test by filling with water). After use, wash well in detergent, rinse several times in hot water and hang up to dry. This material should be sealed with a heat-sealing device, rubber bands, plastic or metal clips, or with sealing tape.

Polythene containers These must be able to withstand sub-zero temperatures without cracking or warping. The seal must be airtight. Make sure that you buy reputable makes as cheaper containers will not last for very long.

Sheet wrapping This comes in the form of polythene sheets or cling film. Polythene sheeting requires sealing with freezer tape or a heat sealer, whereas film will cling itself automatically. Cling film comes in two thicknesses, one for short term freezing and freezer film for long term storage. Its advantage is that it is invaluable for wrapping irregular shapes, and it also makes frozen food easily recognisable.

Other packagings Yogurt, cream and butter containers can also be used for freezing when cleaned thoroughly. They are suitable for biscuit crumbs, raw cake mixture, egg whites or whipped cream. Always be careful not to fill these containers to the brim.

Sealing For this, depending on the type of packaging, rubber bands, ties or plastic clips, or freezer tape which will resist frost are all suitable, and also the heat-sealing device which gives polythene bags an airtight seal.

Labelling Every container, no matter how small, should be labelled. On the label you must note the contents, freezing date and any special characteristics such as 'halved fruit', 'whole fruit', etc. Either use the self-sticking labels which withstand cold, or sealing tape which you can write on. Write with a ball-point or felt-tip pen. There are also special marker pens which will write directly on to foil or plastic.

Whichever packaging material you choose, it is important that the air is expelled before sealing and that the material is pulled tight (with the exception of yeast dough – this expands slightly in the freezer, so the wrapping should be loosely sealed). With foil you expel the air by pressing firmly and folding the edges over double. Only use foil once for freezing, then use it for covering or keeping food fresh in the refrigerator. With each time of using the foil, small, barely visible tears are formed which, if used again, would cause the food to dry out. With bags suck out the air with a straw or a vacuum pump. Never fill boxes, beakers or jars too full as the frozen food will expand slightly; leave 2·5 cm/1 inch clear at the top. If necessary secure lids with freezer tape. Boxes without lids should be covered with foil folded double and the foil then fastened down firmly with a rubber band.

Food Freezing Chart

Food	Storage Time	Hints on Packaging	Thawing Hints
Yeast and Yeast Doughs			
Fresh yeast	Up to 6 months	Divide into 15 g/½ oz or 30 g/1 oz portions, wrap in freezer film and store in an airtight container.	Allow to thaw at room temperature for 1–2 hours and use as required.
Small yeast cakes e.g. doughnuts and croissants	Up to 4 months	Freeze cooked or uncooked. If freezing raw dough, place in an oiled polythene bag, leaving enough space for expansion.	Thaw cooked food at room temperature, wrap in foil to prevent drying out and reheat in a moderate oven. Thaw raw dough at room temperature and shape as required.
Large yeast cakes e.g. Kugelhopf	Up to 4 months	Wrap in a polythene bag or freezer film.	Thaw at room temperature, wrap in foil and reheat in a moderate oven.
Pizza	Up to 3 months	Freeze the shaped raw dough bases, with a sheet of greaseproof between each one, and pack in a polythene bag, *or* freeze baked.	Top with chosen filling whilst frozen and bake immediately in a hot oven. Thaw the baked pizza at room temperature and reheat in a moderately hot oven, wrapped in foil.
Bread rolls	Up to 3 months	Pack in polythene bags.	Wrap in aluminium foil and place still frozen in a moderately hot oven. Reheat until thawed thoroughly.

The Art of Baking

Food Freezing Chart

Food	Storage Time	Hints on Packaging	Thawing Hints
Pastries			
Puff pastry (uncooked)	3 months	Wrap in freezer film and place in a polythene bag.	Thaw in a refrigerator overnight, or at room temperature. Use as required.
Puff pastry (cooked)	4–6 months	Open freeze and store in a rigid polythene container.	Thaw at room temperature and reheat in a moderate oven.
Shortcrust pastry (uncooked)	3 months	Pack in usable quantities in freezer film and place in a polythene bag.	Thaw in a refrigerator overnight or at room temperature. Use as required.
Shortcrust pastry (cooked)	4–6 months	Open freeze and pack in rigid polythene containers. (Flan and tartlet cases are better frozen baked but unfilled.)	Thaw at room temperature.
Sweet or savoury filled and baked flans	Up to 3 months	Wrap in freezer film and place in a rigid polythene container. Individual slices can be wrapped in freezer film and frozen as above.	Allow to thaw overnight in a refrigerator and crisp up in a moderately hot oven if to be served hot.
Choux pastry	4–6 months	(*a*) Uncooked paste – pack in a rigid polythene container. (*b*) Uncooked paste – pipe on to greaseproof paper and open freeze, then pack into rigid polythene containers. (*c*) Baked, but unfilled – slightly undercook, open freeze and pack in rigid polythene containers.	Thaw in the refrigerator overnight. Thaw in the refrigerator overnight or at room temperature, then bake according to the recipe. Allow to thaw and crisp up in a moderately hot oven.
Cakes and Biscuits			
Whisked sponge cake	Up to 3 months	Interleave the sponge layers with greaseproof paper and pack in a polythene bag. Can be frozen filled and decorated; open freeze and pack in a rigid polythene container.	Thaw at room temperature, fill and decorate as liked. Thaw at room temperature.
Swiss roll	Up to 3 months	Freeze filled wrapped in freezer film or a polythene bag.	Thaw at room temperature.
Meringues (unfilled)	4–6 months	Open freeze, then pack in rigid polythene containers.	Thaw at room temperature and fill as required.
Basic sandwich cake	Up to 3 months	As for whisked sponge cake.	Thaw at room temperature.
Cheesecake	Up to 3 months	Freeze whole or in slices. Wrap individual slices in freezer film.	Thaw overnight in the refrigerator.
Biscuits (baked) **Biscuits (unbaked)**	Up to 3 months 4–6 months	Wrap in polythene bags. Wrap dough in freezer film.	Thaw 2–3 hours at room temperature. Thaw 2–3 hours at room temperature then bake.
Fillings and Icings			
Double cream, whipped	Up to 6 months	Add a little icing sugar to act as a stabiliser and store in a rigid polythene container *or* pipe on to greaseproof paper and open freeze before packing in a rigid polythene container.	Thaw overnight in the refrigerator. Use almost immediately.
Custard butter cream	Up to 3 months	Store in a rigid polythene container.	Thaw 2–3 hours at room temperature.
French butter cream	Up to 3 months	Store in a rigid polythene container.	Thaw 2–3 hours at room temperature.

Index